AUSTRALIA 55

Australia 55

A Journal of the MCC Tour

ALAN ROSS

Illustrated with photographs
by the author

faber and faber

This edition first published in 2012
by Faber and Faber Ltd
Bloomsbury House, 74–77 Great Russell Street
London WC1B 3DA

All rights reserved
© The Estate of Alan Ross, 1955

The right of Alan Ross to be identified as author of this work
has been asserted in accordance with Section 77 of the
Copyright, Designs and Patents Act 1988

This book is sold subject to the condition that it shall not, by way of
trade or otherwise, be lent, resold, hired out or otherwise circulated
without the publisher's prior consent in any form of binding or cover other than
that in which it is published and without a similar condition including this
condition being imposed on the subsequent purchaser

A CIP record for this book is available from the British Library

ISBN 978-0-571-29592-0

Contents

INTRODUCTION 9

1 THE VOYAGE OUT *11*

2 PERTH: REFLECTIONS ON THE SWAN RIVER *27*

3 NOTES IN THE NULLARBOR *43*

4 ADELAIDE: COLONEL LIGHT'S VISION *47*

5 MELBOURNE UNDER WATER *60*

6 APPROACHES TO SYDNEY *70*

7 NORTH TO BRISBANE *83*

8 THE FIRST TEST MATCH *90*

9 ROCKHAMPTON AND THE BARRIER REEF *108*

10 PROSERPINE TO MASCOT *124*

11 THE SECOND TEST MATCH *128*

12 MELBOURNE AND THE THIRD TEST MATCH *153*

13 NOTES IN TASMANIA *184*

14 ADELAIDE AND THE FOURTH TEST MATCH *192*

15 SYDNEY DAY BY DAY *207*

16 THE FIFTH TEST MATCH *219*

17 AT SEA *242*

SCOREBOOK *245*

INDEX *267*

Illustrations

PLACES I   *between 32 & 33*

THE TESTS   *between 96 & 97*

PEOPLE   *between 160 & 161*

PLACES II   *between 224 & 225*

'The words of Mercury are harsh after the songs of Apollo'.

—*Love's Labour's Lost*

Introduction

In one sense, this book needs no introduction. I have introduced it as I have gone along. In form, it is a journal, though a journal without dates. They are not important. I have written sometimes in the present tense, sometimes in the past, according to circumstance. Living out of suitcases and in hotel bedrooms is not conducive to order. I have written when I have had time, and I have preferred to sacrifice formality to immediacy.

What follows is in part a cricket book, in part an experience of Australia. I should have liked to have written two separate books, because, travelling about the country, I was torn often between duty and pleasure. I should have liked to have visited Alice Springs and the aborigine reserves of the Northern Territories. My obligations required me generally to hug the coastal cities.

But I was lucky, for my duties were the extremely pleasant ones of describing perhaps the most remarkable Test series in living memory. If I had to do without visits to Australian vineyards and the painted caves of the interior, I was rewarded by the bowling of Tyson and Statham, the batting of Cowdrey and May. Incidentally, the wines of Australia, though they lack the bouquet of European wines, were a revelation. With the oysters of Sydney, the tall coconut trees of the north-east, the pale eucalypts of the bush, and the fizzy blue seas of New South Wales, they remain among my pleasantest memories of Australia.

My accounts of the Tests I have left exactly as they were cabled to *The Observer*, as whose correspondent I went to Australia, and to the various clients of *The Observer's* foreign news service for whom I also wrote. They are examples, therefore, of daily journalism, written to a regulated length and with specific ends in view. Where it has seemed to me that extra comment was required, I have speculated afterwards. But, by and large, the discipline of writing on the spot between 1,000 and 1,500 words on a day's cricket appears to me beneficial. In retrospect, it is difficult to pick up the clues of a match and to keep clear track of its development. Too many words can obliterate the natural dramatic crises. I was tempted, at the end of the book, to comment on various subsidiary features and conditions of Australian life. I resisted the temptation, happily; for, had I once started, I should be writing still. Australia, like all countries developing at a forced rate, offers plenty of scope for both criticism and prediction. But that was not what I wanted to do in this book, which is, I hope, entirely recreational.

Travelling, one depends greatly on people. Fortunately, Australia is an immensely friendly country. No one, for instance, could have been more agreeable or helpful than those Australian cricket correspondents, with whom, necessarily, I spent a lot of time: Tom Goodman, Ray Robinson, Jack Fingleton, Lindsay Hassett, Bill O'Reilly, Keith Butler, and many others. The Press Box was a very congenial place, to whose atmosphere absorbed concentration, affectionate interest, irony, cynicism and robust farce variously contributed.

I owe many and profound debts of hospitality, too numerous to acknowledge here. I only hope I have done so privately. What must be acknowledged, however, is my indebtedness to the Editor of *The Observer* both for making my journey possible and for allowing me to use material that was originally written for that newspaper. I should like as well to thank the Editor of the *Sydney Morning Herald* for providing me with material from their files on the curious origins of surfing.

Last, but not least, I am grateful to Mr John Woodcock for permission to use seven of his photographs.

A. R.
Indian Ocean, April, 1955

1 The Voyage Out

The sky is sealed up all round as we nose our way through a tank built out of mist. An hour or two ago the sun, for the first time for a fortnight, sheltered under thin cloud, which then thickened as though being pumped up with smoke. The sea began to spill into the sky, the waves curdled, and now for twenty minutes a slow heavy rain has sweetened the air, running off the decks and gathering in the scuppers.

It has taken the rain to drive me into my cabin and to keep me there. I meant to begin this journal somewhere around Gibraltar, but the sun liquefies the conscience as it does the body, and we are past Colombo. Each day one postpones the fatal first entry, the sentence that will condition the style and tone and manner of all those that follow. Cutting cleanly through the middle seas of the world in this stately hotel, life has seemed to have no future, no past. Once the painful ties have been broken, the separation achieved, only the blueness remains real. An hour out of Gibraltar the blue began, deepening steadily as we sailed eastward, changing from the classical blue of the Italian and Greek seas to the bronze, heat-beaten blue of the Indian Ocean.

It grows impossible to pick up a pen, to open a book. Not only because the heat pours off one, leaving dog-marks of wet at the foot of chairs, but because the moving frieze of shipboard life exerts a fascination stronger than anything between the pages of a book. People move round one's gaze like fish in an aquarium. Some cling together in schools, some lie open to the sun all day like starfish, some seek out the unwary and grip them like an octopus. Each week the victim's smile grows more sickly, his self-will dwindles; in the end, so devoid of resources does he become, it is he who seeks out his noisy, unwanted familiar, his hateful gaoler.

Yet this buff and white 29,000-ton *Orsova*, commissioned this year and Australia-bound for only the second time, is big enough for numerous completely different kinds of life to be going on with virtually no overlap at all. The passenger-fish may come nosing round their glass walls with such monotonous regularity that one gradually thinks to have seen them all, only for one to find, on an unsuspecting excursion, new unknown varieties—self-absorbed beauties docile as pilot fish, forbidding lampreys on the look-out for slights.

After a bit, one recognizes the quoit-throwers, the methodical padders of the deck, the splayed sun-women and men round the swimming pool, the bar-proppers with stories to get rid of, the smooth prowlers whose *amour propre* does not allow them to be seen girl-less, the grey and volcanic bridge players, whose swelling behinds in flowered chintzes bulge like exotic fruits against the backs of the library chairs. Shipboard life has a romantic antique ritual of its own which pleases, interests and bores in turn. At moments, especially during the long hours between lunch and dinner, it seems endless and futile; then one gets a sort of second wind, an acquaintanceship blossoms and one secretly dreads the end of idleness and irresponsibility. There is, of course, consistently too much drinking and eating, and too little sleep. But there is always the generosity of the sun, the liberal blue of the sea, the magic cocktail of the dusk.

The writing of this book sets many problems, for I want to do several things at the same time and I am not at all sure how happily they will settle down together. Nor how much that may be of interest to one reader will be to another. For that reason I think the journal form will be best; everything can go in, cricket, Australia, architecture, people, places, and ideas, and they need have no more formal relationship than the idiosyncrasies of my moods. Specifically, I shall be writing about the M.C.C. tour of Australia during the next six months, about the cricket they play, the kind of life they and I lead. But I am as much interested in Australia as I am in cricket (it would indeed be a dull fellow who was not) and I intend to digress at least as often as I stick to the main theme. It may not work out that way, my interest in one may dwindle at the expense of the other, but that is my intention this October evening as we slant south-east on the tail of a trade wind. Yet already, reading through what I have written, I am conscious of a lack of balance. I have begun in mid-ocean, taking for granted the ship, its passengers and its route, and have all but omitted the reason why I am travelling at all. Stories, even of such an informal nature as this, should have a beginning, a middle and an end, and I will therefore, before I am too hopelessly behindhand, try and set out the facts in some kind of order. If we are half-way across Australia by the time I have finished the preliminaries I shall have only myself to blame. A writer's whipping-boy is always himself. It is better that way.

* * *

To go back, then, we sailed—seventeen cricketers, some twenty cricket correspondents—on September 15 from Tilbury. After the worst summer in my lifetime, the afternoon was clear and sunny, the sea a bright herring-bone pattern that softened gradually so that, as we altered course to the southward, the horizon was all blue and gold. We were due to call at Gibraltar, Naples, Port Said, Aden and Colombo, docking at Fremantle on October 7. Three weeks therefore lay ahead for meditation, exercise, sleep or contemplation of the open spaces—the latter an occupation dear to the English and second only in fascination to watching others at work. I had hoped to read and perhaps write, freed for the first time for months from the weekly labours of literary criticism. In fact, as I have already hinted, I have so far done neither—conversation is always preferable to composition, a chair in the sun to a stuffy cabin. There were other distractions, too, which, when one got tired of them, bred still more. And so it goes on.

However, before a ball is bowled in earnest, I want to sketch in roughly the background of this tour, and outline what seem to be the possibilities.

Most of the past summer has been spent in mental preparation for this M.C.C. visit to Australia, with the result that facts and figures on the cricket field have meant little. The leading English players had an exhausting winter in the West Indies immediately after the constant strain of the 1953 Tests against Australia, and these past few months have been, as far as county cricket allows, which is not much, something in the nature of a rest. In fact, the gloomy succession of cold, rain-filled skies took much of the pleasure out of cricket, and what should have been pleasant relaxation ended up, in the Tests against Pakistan, as a series of frustrating anti-climaxes.

Long before the team for Australia was picked, a hue and cry was raised in the Press about the possibility of D. S. Sheppard of Sussex being preferred to Hutton as Captain. Hutton was, when he returned from the West Indies, a man evidently sick of cricket, suffering from a mental weariness that also had physical symptoms. He played throughout the summer as though the crease had become for him the equivalent of the dentist's chair. There was a real possibility that he would not be in the mood for Test cricket by the autumn, or that, should he be well enough, he might be happier and fitter without the burdens of captaincy. In either of the latter cases, the natural alternative was Sheppard. Sheppard had captained Sussex with remarkable skill the previous summer, he was one of the best close to the wicket fieldsmen in the country, and he seemed as likely to make runs going in first as anyone else. While Hutton was at home with neuritis in June and July, Sheppard captained England against Pakistan, no great task but one which he did with style, authority and absence of fuss. He is a natural leader, and, with the important proviso that he showed himself good enough as a batsman to make his place in the side certain, he would have been an ideal choice.

In the event, of course, Hutton recovered, Sheppard never quite reached his best as a batsman, and the issue was quietly shelved. The Press had made some play of the amateur *versus* professional aspect of the business, which no one but a complete moron could have supposed had anything to do with it whatsoever. A team, however, needs positive leading and control if its performances are to add up to the full potential of its members, and that does have something to do with it.

Hutton, I must confess at this stage, has not, hitherto, seemed to me an ideal captain. He is the greatest batsman I have ever seen and I find him always a sympathetic and engaging figure on the field. Yet, curiously enough, his captaincy has lacked, to my mind, the qualities of character and determination that distinguish his batsmanship. He showed, in the 1953 Tests, an inability to establish a stranglehold on a match, he let good positions slip away too often without appearing able to do very much about it. He started out, as at Lords in the Second Test, with defensive fields, as if preferring to save a possible 4 and miss a wicket than take the right risks. His native caution showed itself again in his reluctance to use his slow bowlers, especially when Bedser and Bailey were under fire from Davidson, Archer and Lindwall. More than once 50 or 60 runs might have been saved had Lock or Laker been brought on earlier to take the wicket they did take immediately they were brought on. Nor again, had Hutton struck one as a captain greatly encouraging to his bowlers. A good captain needs, as well as an astute cricket brain, to be something like a destroyer captain, a father confessor as well as an object of fear and inspiration. A body of men as disparate in character as an M.C.C. team requires to be moulded, however unobtrusively, by the personality of its captain, if it is not to sprout a number of warring personalities of its own. Hutton's own batting, too, has seemed to have a depressing effect on those that followed him, perhaps not so much because they tried to bat like him, as because he failed to advise them how they should bat. Hutton is a law unto himself, a classical maker of strokes with unique technical gifts and powers of concentration, and he safely creates his own tempo. But players like Simpson and Graveney need to follow altogether different laws, and they have not flourished under Hutton. The fault, however, is probably in themselves.

This seems to add up to a telling indictment, and I have not meant it to be so. Rather have I meant to suggest that these seventeen players on their way to Australia—Denis Compton is to follow later, when his knee has had further treatment—will require all the resources at Hutton's command, both on the field and off, if they are to assume the stature required of them for the retention of the Ashes.

The rest of the side divides itself up quite simply into two departments: of all-rounders there is only Bailey, though had the team been chosen a few weeks later it is more than likely that Watkins of Glamorgan would have found a place. And Oakman of Sussex is the kind of player whom a winter in Australia might have brought on considerably, and who would have been invaluable in State matches.

The batsmen are Hutton, Compton, May, Edrich, Graveney, Cowdrey, Simpson and Wilson. Hutton has lain fallow all summer, not in the best of health and conserving his resources, yet he is the most priceless asset on either side. Compton was back to nearly his best against Pakistan and, if his knee holds, he should be the other English batsman without equal on the Australian side. May frequently batted in county matches like a great player and if his performances in Tests are uneven he will surely these next four months establish himself once and for all as a Test cricketer. Since his return from the West Indies he has hit with great power off the back foot and, driving as well as he does anything remotely over-pitched, he never allows the innings to grow becalmed. He is deceptively slim, a beautiful on-side player, and he has the virtues of elegance and attack one hopes of from a No. 3. Hutton's opening partner will presumably be Edrich, whose experience and courage against fast bowling make up for his limitations as a stroke player. Once Edrich drove straight and high; now he only pushes forward at the half volley, preferring to cut late and occasionally to unleash a boxer's hook. Thus he scores next to nothing between cover and mid-on, except when he has been at the wicket most of the day. Sometimes then he swings his bat and turns his wrists and the ball sails to the long-on boundary. But he gets himself solidly into the line of fire and never surrenders his wicket through indecision or lack of concentration. Simpson and Graveney, on the other hand, are graceful players, with strokes all round the wicket; yet they are both terribly fallible and prone to moral lapses when things are not easy, when hair-shirts should be on and loins girded. Australian wickets should suit both, but the Tests will put a premium on character as much as technique. Cowdrey was perhaps fortunate on 1954 form to get a place, but anyone who saw him in 1953 could hardly doubt that he is a vintage player, mature beyond his years. He is heavily built, not unlike Hammond in his follow-through to the cover drive, though with an economical, bat-brushing-pad forward defensive method modelled on Fagg, and he scores in the bountiful arc between cover and mid-wicket. Parks was the probable alternative, but Cowdrey to him is as a burgundy to a sparkling hock, and on a tour of this kind body is preferable to fizz. Wilson, a left-hander, was chosen when Compton's fitness seemed not certain. He is a fine driver of the ball, who puts the full face of the bat to fast bowling. Against spin he is something of a half-cock player, his wrists not quite loose enough to drop the turning ball dead. However, he is wonderfully strong, a close field with hands as enveloping as soap boxes. All the same, I should much have preferred Watson.

Our Test bowling is likely to be in the hands of Bedser, Statham, Bailey and Appleyard. Statham will be an altogether different proposition from what he was when the Australians last saw him. He is a genuine fast bowler, with a whippy action that gives him great pace off the pitch, and he attacks the stumps the whole time. He uses the crease shrewdly, constantly altering angle of approach and length, and shifting the batsman from one foot to the other. He swings more often in than out, and with his straight, aiming action his length and speed are misleading to the extent that batsmen playing back to him frequently hear the dreaded rattle when their bats are still aloft.

Bedser is a great bowler who may have passed his peak; but that remains to be seen. He looked wonderfully loose this summer, though moving the ball less than usual. However, his arts are not likely to have deserted him, for he has rested this last winter and, like Hutton, needs Australian opposition to draw him out. Bailey at half or full pace commands respect and, from time to time, especially when his energies have not been sapped by the need to bowl defensively, he can make inroads into the strongest-looking batting. He, too, is essentially a Test match player, preferably against Australia, and he must be judged in that context.

Appleyard, a bowler of varying method, is accurate, moves the ball off the seam a shade either way, and can bowl off-spinners. He is not yet recognizably a Test bowler, but if England are to succeed, he must become one on this tour. Lock and Laker, who won us the Fifth Test at the Oval, remain in England and, whatever the reasons, this is a pity, for they are our two best bowlers of their kind. Lock's fielding, moreover, would have been of incalculable value, for we have virtually no close wicket catchers certain to make the side.

The supporting attack consists of Tyson and Loader, to use the new ball, Wardle, slow left-arm, and McConnon, off-spin. Tyson, without much doubt the fastest bowler now playing, has yet to run through a county side and he can only be accounted a gamble. His long and necessarily tiring run is an odd mixture of lope and stutter, beauty and ugliness, but he shows his left shoulder to the batsman and he is splendidly tense at the moment of delivery. His direction, however, is far from being what it should be and, in consequence, when he is not bowling well, overs go by in tedious stagnation without bat hitting ball.

Loader, slim, wiry and hostile at medium pace, had a great summer in 1953 when more or less a reserve in the Surrey side, getting his chances only when Bedser was playing in the Tests. This past season he bowled superbly for the Players at Lord's, but otherwise has seemed not quite certain of his methods, rather in between styles. He bowls front-on, which causes jerking of the arm and means the right leg is bent forward instead of braced. All the same, Loader shoots the ball off the pitch, swings late, and has a masked slow one which is difficult to spot.

Wardle is an admirable county cricketer, steady, reliable, but no great spinner of the ball. It is hard to see him getting much bite on Australian wickets, but his all-round values are such that he is a pleasure to see in any side. McConnon, the Glamorgan off-spinner, has always bowled round the wicket for his county, as did J. C. Clay, and this has never been a successful method in Australia. He joined Glamorgan as a batsman, is an excellent gully or short leg, and must be regarded as an interesting experiment.

Evans, of course, will keep wicket; he is still the best in the world, safer with the near-impossible than the easy, largely because when he is stationary he tends to make a kangaroo-like jump in the air at the moment of catching the ball. Perhaps it would be too simple otherwise. Standing up to Bedser, with the ball darting late, or scurrying to right or left for the snick or glide when standing back, he is a marvel and a mystery. Andrew, his reserve, is a complete contrast. He gets his feet in the right position, moves his arms not at all, and his wrists a bare inch or so. His lack of fuss would, in anyone else, be greatly ostentatious; as it is, he takes Tyson's thunderbolts as a butler might accept a visiting card, with no notice at all. He would not, I think, get near some of the things Evans catches: but greatness and great competence are rarely akin.

These, then, make up the team under Hutton's command. Geoffrey Howard, the Lancashire secretary, is manager; George Duckworth, scorer, and baggage man. They are a very likeable party.

At the moment of writing this—the flying fish skidding off our bows in mid-Indian Ocean—our chances of retaining the Ashes seem even. The enemy are likely to be much as before, though without Hassett, Arthur Morris or Ian Johnson will probably be captain. England should be stronger in both batsmen and bowlers pure and simple; Australia greatly stronger in all-rounders, and vastly better in the field. I doubt whether this England side will please admirers or critics when fielding; there are insufficient close catchers, too many to hide, few quick movers. I hope I am wrong. It is undoubtedly the strongest batting side to go to Australia since the war, though that is not saying much. Less, therefore, should depend on Hutton as a batsman. I believe that if we are well-led we shall win; if not, lose. It is a matter of authority and balance.

* * *

We have crossed the equator and steam under the ceiling of the Southern Cross. An hour ago I watched the sea deepen into ink, the sunset rib the sky cinnamon, apricot, blue-green. These layers transferring themselves on to the wave-tops were not so much colours as ideas of colour—the word 'colour' implies substance and this sky of dusk is an abstraction, devoid of depth. Out of this melting-pot of the day's sweetness the evening star has hoisted itself up and shines hard and cold with a tinfoil gleam over us. We cruise at 21 knots and the wake is dead straight to the horizon—a churned pound-note greenness.

Tomorrow we shall arrive. This is my last chance to make of the voyage something I shall remember, before Australia is upon me. For three weeks, all but a few hours and two slight monsoon squalls, we have lived in sunshine and under clear skies. A gently sliding sea the first day out subsided round Finisterre and since then we have moved from Mediterranean autumn into the breathless heat of the Red Sea, which these last days has cooled down as we approach the perimeter of Australian spring.

Five hundred miles a day has been our usual progress along the invisible string held taut between Tilbury and Fremantle, and we have scarcely tilted against it. We carry stabilizing fins in any case, and at the least movement out they come, cutting a twenty-degree roll to four degrees, though with what stresses on the hull nobody yet knows. I have lain mostly in the sun all this time, book open but unread on my lap. From time to time I toy with D. H. Lawrence's *Kangaroo*, which, though I have read only a hundred pages or so, already makes the experience of Australia real to me. It is one of his best books. I have swum daily in the tepid salt water of the swimming pool, played a little deck quoits and tennis, danced an evening or two. One afternoon the cricket correspondents played the ship's officers at cricket; the wicket was matting, the ball made of rope, the bat narrower than Alfred Mynn's. A great deal was at stake one way and another, but we duly won without great difficulty. Our batting was headed by Charles Bray of the *Daily Herald*, who before the war captained Essex; John Woodcock of *The Times*, a post-war Authentic at Oxford; F. R. Brown, captain of the last M.C.C. side in Australia, now writing for the *Daily Mail;* E. W. Swanton, a lordly figure at the crease, who has played for Middlesex; and E. M. Wellings, Oxford and Surrey. The bowling end of the batting order was formidably represented by Ross, Peebles and Bowes. Umpire was Arthur Gilligan, who led England in Australia in 1924–25. Other than no-balling Jim Swanton to appease the unbridled desires of the large assembly, his performance was immaculate.

There is a good deal of luck in one's pleasures aboard ship, not a little depending on one's table companions. I have been fortunate indeed: there are eight of us, presided over at uncertain intervals by Mr Thorpe, the purser, Arthur and Penny Gilligan, Freddie Brown, Ian Peebles, Jim Swanton, John Woodcock and myself. Conversation, encouraged by the wines shipped by Peebles' firm, the quantities of whose hocks and moselles consumed at our table alone should ensure the directors a comfortable and early retirement, has been brisk and entertaining. Peebles and Swanton are excellent together, and should journalism or, in the former case, wine-broking, ever fail them, the Halls would be the gainers. I should like, from a box at the Chelsea Palace, to see Swanton in Free Forester cardigan feeding Peebles with the indulgent adroitness that brings forth in sharp return a spacious and weltering interior monologue. Peebles, who has a knowledgeable fondness for Dr Johnson, Dickens, Hornblower, Sherlock Holmes and the French comedian Jacques

Tati; is also an authority on marine engineering. He would fit decently into an early Waugh novel, quite capable of creating his own dialogue.

Arthur Gilligan is Chairman of the Sports Committee, a duty he fulfils with impressive devotion. At all hours of the day he is to be seen arbitrating at deck quoits between ageing but relentless women competitors, who, skirts hoisted and faces set, throw their rings with stern skill. The penalties of Arthur's job is that he is pursued by disconsolate performers searching for their partners or opponents. 'I can't find Mr Frew, and Mrs Jenkins said she'd be on the court at ten o'clock and she hasn't turned up, do we get a walk-over?' If Arthur is to be believed, he sends them all packing with impartial swiftness, but he is a genial man and when he reports at dinner that he told Mrs X she was cheating and Mr Y to mind his own business it is more than likely that he dealt charmingly with both. Penny, his wife, brings to our table a discreet and gentle elegance.

There is, not surprisingly, much good cricket talk; it isn't every day that one has two England captains present, as well as the distinguished correspondents of the *Sunday Times*, *Telegraph* and *The Times*. Were Jim Swanton not present we might have heard rather more about Peebles' dismissals of Bradman and lesser Australian tyros, but, as it is, Ian has proved a subtle dissector of bowling techniques and I have learnt from him. It is difficult to believe that it is twenty-two years since Freddie Brown went first to Australia, as baby of the party under D. R. Jardine, and that eighteen years elapsed before he returned as captain. It must be strange for him travelling now to write instead of play. I'd have him in my team, retired or not. As leg-break and seam bowler he would give the attack a balance it badly lacks, he bats better than any of our present bowlers, and, though giving away nearly twenty years to some of this side, he would not suffer by comparison in the field. *Laudator temporis acti*, as sporting writers would once have written unthinkingly. But conventional scholarship, classical or otherwise, has ceased to be a part of a sports-writer's equipment.

The Purser has frequently been an inspiration at the head of the table: years at sea in his particular department have sharpened his wits to the stage where he can brush off any question or voiced dissatisfaction, no matter how much to the point, with the ease of one lightly blowing a smudge of talcum powder from his gold braid. 'Otherwise all right?' he rejoins, glasses glinting, tones clipped, to any request demanding an unequivocal answer, before making an atrocious joke and passing rapidly to another subject.

We have grown very fond of him: conversationally, he has had to put up with a good many bouncers and googlies, and, if he has ducked the former with practised agility, he has struck out with simple faith at the latter, snicking them to all corners of the ship. Last night, after a couple of bottles of champagne in Peebles' cabin, he played at dinner, in the presence of only Ian, Johnny Woodcock and myself, one of the great conversational innings of his life.

My three excursions ashore have been enjoyable. At Naples Jim, Ian and myself hired a car and drove out to Pompeii, returning to eat lobsters and rice at Santa Lucia, whilst the marauding tenors of the adjacent Bersaglieri and Zi' Teresa restaurants mopped their brows and sang boldly against one another in the heat. We drank Lacrima Cristi and watched the sailing boats ruffle with the breeze as they drifted orchid-like past the landing-stage of the Yacht Club, before swinging low over the sea in a swelling line towards the two haze-mauve humps of Capri. We sailed that day at four o'clock, the bay of Naples closing in marzipan-coloured tiers of sandstone, white and green behind us, the whole harbour rocking with light. We passed the afternoon steamer to Capri, Procida and Ischia—the boat I had taken so many times in the strange, disenchanted summer of 1948—steering in close to the magic, curving coastline of Sorrento and Amalfi, before altering course for the Straits of Messina, through which we steamed in the middle watches. Most of the M.C.C. team excursioned to Pompeii, but the Yorkshiremen amongst them, Hutton, Wardle, Wilson and Appleyard, went with Bill Bowes on a pilgrimage to Hedley Verity's grave at Caserta, laying on it white roses—an act of touching piety.

We entered Port Said at dusk, a landfall I missed playing bridge with partner against Trevor Bailey and partner in the ship's competition. Ashore there, we were given numerous drinks in the Union Club, while M.C.C. players recorded messages to send to the troops in the Canal Zone. I met several naval officers, including the Port Liaison Officer with a pretty Danish wife, and a destroyer captain called Morgan, who had by some extraordinary coincidence written official letters that day to Nicholas Kempson and Johnny Church, with both of whom I had served on Rear-Admiral Hutton's staff at Buxtehude and, later, on Admiral Sir Harold (Hooky) Walker's staff when he was British Naval C.-in-C., Germany. I felt, for almost the first time in years, a disturbing nostalgia for the Navy; or was it for the war, time of tedium, fear and high happiness?

We returned at midnight, walking down the airless streets, the moonlight glinting on dusty palms, past the beseeching arms of the carpet, leather goods, postcard and basket merchants, their wares displayed in rows of boats bobbing alongside the jetties and pontoons. A few were still hauling and unhauling baskets of stuff on pulleys up the ship's side, their once urgent cries of 'What you want?' 'How much you say?' growing increasingly fatalistic and futile. The decks were deserted, the gulli-gulli men departed.

Next day we were well down the canal, the heat beating off the sand-banks, the sky stunned and colourless. At intervals, soldiers emerged out of small encampments and oases, lining up and cheering as Hutton appeared at the railings with his team. A radio message arrived on board to the effect that the pipes and drums of the 1st Battalion Scots Guards would be playing to greet M.C.C. and wish them well as we passed Suez. At four o'clock, on one of the hottest afternoons I have ever known, they came into sight, a tiny group of men dwarfed beneath us as we edged slowly by the landing-stage on which they blew and beat their brave music.

From Suez to Aden we did no more than exist, stricken with the heat. Quoit and tennis decks were empty, the swimming pool hot, salty and stale. White dinner-jackets appeared at night and a Fancy Dress ball was held. Most people were too hot to care. In the Red Sea we picked up the first smell of the East, that sour-sweet smell curdling in a warm sea breeze, a compound of spices and dust and blossom. Ever since the earliest days of my childhood in Bengal, it is a smell that from time to time returns to me in memory, mysterious and elusive and intoxicating. After Aden we picked up a welcome breeze that soothed us into Colombo, *Orsova* steaming at something over an economical speed to get us in early for M.C.C. to play an all-day match against Ceylon. *Orsova* is already the fastest ship to ply east of Suez, and this extra burst of speed is reputed to have cost the Company £1,500 in fuel. I imagine the shareholders of the Orient Line can afford it.

Anchored in Colombo, the heat came down again like a saucepan lid. Ashore, we drove to the Galle Face Hotel, a monstrously ugly building on the edge of a beach pounded by the long rollers of the Indian Ocean. I indulged in the usual ritual of travellers to and from the East, ordering silk shirts to be made up and delivered on board before sailing time that night, drank some pink gin and ate a memorable curry with Jim Swanton before going up to the cricket.

The latter was a moderate affair, the match, as is customary, drawn. Colin Cowdrey played quite beautifully, the only M.C.C. batsman to do so, and Derek de Saram, who got a Blue at Oxford in the early 'thirties, picked Wardle magnificently off his toes to square leg for six and hit him high and often to the untenanted deeps. Before the war every county had a couple of amateurs at least who batted like this, but so rare are they today Wardle must have thought himself faced by a species newly risen from the ocean.

The crowd, packed in behind barbed wire (for in their exuberance a year or two ago they set fire to the stands), seemed to enjoy themselves. Tyson and Loader bowled not at all well, the spectators cheered the local heroes from amongst palms, banana trees and frangipani, and the only refreshment was hot coconut milk. The wicket, fast and true, was prepared by a squad of groundsmen in dhotis of brilliant Schiaparelli-pink and peacock-blue, and, driving back from the match in the heavy blossom-laden air, we passed women swaying barefoot through the dust in saris of vivid saffron, turquoise and emerald, all the colours of the sunset.

Later that night, having watched from the Galle Face the sea gather up the spilling light and over a pink gin seen the catamarans bearing the deepening colours of the sky on their sails, I drove along the surf line and through the streets of Colombo at random. Wafts of sickly scent everywhere; the jangle of music, ugly and exciting in the bazaars; men squatting in the dark, all bones, like collapsed bagpipes; the tinkle of rickshaws, the brilliant interiors of fruit shops, paw-paws glowing under bulbs, lights shining over bales of striped silk and cotton. And all the time the heat something you could put your hand through.

I took off my shoes and entered the newest of the Buddhist temples. The shaven-headed priests sat around sweating in their yellow robes. The images of Buddha, products of the twentieth century, were huge and clumsy and garish, like the background figures in a fun-fair. There was a smell of ashes and incense, and in an upstairs room a sulky-looking priest was taking a class of children, intoning verses and making them repeat the words. The girls wore white dresses, white bows in their hair, which gleamed like butterflies as they turned their heads in the candle-lit shadows. A gourd was being beaten expertly somewhere outside and the plaintive notes of a flute, going over the same brief phrase again and again, broke in on the children's voices, hushed and reverent, and on the bored whine of their tutor.

On my way out I was given a temple flower, waxy red and yellow, with dark leaves like a begonia. Wilted and crushed, it is before me on my cabin table as I write.

2 Perth: Reflections on the Swan River

We have been here nearly a fortnight: a week of lovely spring weather, warm and cloudless, a few days of biting cold winds and grey skies, and now it is hot and sticky.

The last night on board Freddie Brown, John Woodcock and I gave a cocktail party; there was dancing, prize-giving, and speeches by the Commodore, Capt. N. A. Whinfield, Arthur Gilligan and Leonard Hutton. Tom Graveney seemed to go up a great many times to collect his winnings.

At the last moment, despite having long since been bored by it, one was almost sad to leave the ship. I made several friends, particularly Ursula and Bill Hayward, whom I had met with Heywood and Anne Hill in London, and Jim and Prue Holden, also from Adelaide. I would see them again later. Friends apart, my favourite character on board was a small grey gentleman who had worked his way out to Australia as a cabin boy some fifty years earlier. He had struck lucky and was now worth a fabulous sum, the exact amount of which he once whispered to me, but which I have forgotten. He had ordered from the Orient Line the best suite on the ship. Having been quoted what he considered a handsome figure, he then received a letter stating that a private bath would cost £40 extra. Displeased at this, since he imagined the bath would certainly have been included in the original quotation, he nevertheless sent off his cheque.

He had not, however, finished with the matter. His business sense had been aroused and he was determined to get his £40 worth of water. Not only therefore did he pace the ship inviting passengers to have a bath with him, as it might be a drink, but whenever he had a few moments to spare he nipped down to his cabin and turned on the taps. At various times of the day his steward would approach him and report that he had found the water running. 'How forgetful of me,' Mr de Vries would reply, shaking his head in exaggerated perplexity, 'how very forgetful.' And a few minutes later he would get up and, excusing himself, wink heavily and say, 'I must go and see a man about a tap.'

Perth is beautifully situated, the blue waters of the Swan River reaching out into the city like a spread hand. Water is the wrist of Perth, too, controlling its entrances and exits to the West; and water, bright-blue sea water specked with sailing boats and dinghies, launches and yachts, composes its character.

The centre of the town is half Spanish renaissance, half Scottish baronial: there are numerous hotels which look like cricket pavilions, each ringed with a cream wooden balcony of ornate design, and supported by rows of posts to which in the old days horses were tethered. There is an air of Sweden about the new free university (the only one of its kind in the world), of Scottish Gothic about Government House. Nearby, sham Tudor tilts up against modern flats which Le Corbusier might have designed on an off day. In suburbs like Mosman Bay, Swanbourne, Claremont and Peppermint Grove, each of which looks over the lovely wooded curves of the river as it splays into Freshwater Bay, there are sensible white villas in the French manner, with green or blue jalousies, and cheek-by-jowl to them red gnome-like structures, jerry-built shacks, unsightly bungalows. But below, the sea glitters and swells, headlands lay the shadows of their trees in water, and the sun brings to Perth a final graciousness it might otherwise lack.

For gracious is perhaps the right word for Perth: the sea comes almost up to its main street, which has an old-fashioned dignity, a wing-collar erectness, even if it soon slips over into the slovenly outskirts that were its shanty origins. It is a town of parks and gardens, playgrounds and wide streets; of tramcars and assembly rooms and extraordinary churches; of the traditional stuffily positioned next to the makeshift; of strip-lighting and arcades and Victorian saloon bars; of tall palm trees, the dead foliage hanging like sandbags to the trunks; of gulls and pelicans and cookaburras: with clear light and a sense of space. And loneliness and nothing not far off.

It is, of course, a town that, more than most, reveals its origins. It has been going exactly 125 years, being founded in 1829 by Captain Stirling; it developed slowly until the time that gold was discovered in Kalgoorlie in 1893, since when it has shot up. The Town Hall, another Spanish-Scottish creation, was put up by convict labour between 1867 and 1870. At the moment, Perth is enjoying a wool boom, and if the current speculations in oil are proved to be well-founded, it is going to spread again as sensationally as it did in the last decade of the nineteenth century. This time, however, it has town-planners and architects galore.

The problem, in such a quickly expanding city, is to decide on an architectural style, one which will look good, last, suit the climate, and, preferably, be original. Because the climate is Californian, experiments have been made with American and Spanish Colonial; and, more recently, with the functional contemporary—low angular boxes with long slabs of glass. Yet there are still areas of solid Gothic, of Edwardian gilt, of corrugated-iron: the town is built, on the American pattern, in blocks, the two or three main thoroughfares running parallel and intersected by lesser streets.

It is a hotch-potch, certainly; untidy, but lacking neither character nor charm, which, with its light and space and trees, it could not. The 'right' style will emerge, too, though I hope at no great sacrifice to the old. A city has some allegiance to its founders, to the type of men they were.

*   *   *

Since our arrival there has been some little cricket, of no great seriousness, a good deal of exploring, catching-up with correspondence and generally meeting people. A civic reception was held to welcome M.C.C., beer and sandwiches were handed out, songs were sung and speeches made. There is a fair amount, it seems, of this kind of dutiful entertainment. Hutton spoke at some length, introducing his team in turn to the gathered dignitaries, and altogether handling the whole business, as he did an awkward Press Conference held on board when we docked, with charm and skill. He has, I think, surprised many by his mellow geniality, his certainty of manner.

Nets were held on the first two days, the W.A.C.A. ground a large, engaging oval, nicely planted with gum trees and with the shallow reaches of the Swan in the background. The giant new scoreboard is more generous with information than any we have in England; there are no buildings overlooking the field of play or obscuring the skyline, and the entrance is approached through Queen's Gardens, a trim affair of lagoons, bridges, and lily ponds, with gliding swans and busy wildfowl, willows, palms and rose-bushes. Around tea-time pelicans come cruising in, motionlessly gliding in the air currents, to watch the play.

Considerable crowds arrived to observe, and were much impressed by Simpson and Graveney. What magnificent net players these two are. Hutton, Wilson, Wardle and McConnon practised at the slip-catcher, holding all manner of things with an authority that I hope does not turn out to be deceiving. The trouble is, our better fielders are unlikely to get into the Test team.

The first Sunday night I was driven down to Bunbury, 120 miles south of Perth on the coast, where the opening match of the tour began on the next day. The early part of the journey was through dry, empty country, scrub and jarrah trees alternating, small villages every twenty miles or so. Huge grey trees, the colour of elephant's hide and as creased, lay uprooted everywhere. Now and again the pale sky poured through the naked branches of gum trees, stiff as scarecrows in rough brown plains. Occasionally, wildly incongruous in this isolation, nearside trees carried advertisements hung on their trunks: Hardy's Indigestion Remedy, Relaxa Tabs for Nervous Tension, Helena Rubinstein's Waterproof Mascara.

31 PERTH: REFLECTIONS ON THE SWAN RIVER

The road is dead straight, an asphalt ruler laid over the map, aimed at the south-west. Sometimes we shot through an avenue of bungalows, each with its red jab of poinsettia, its palm trees and small lawn. Nearer Bunbury, green came back into the landscape, cattle drifted under lines of trees and along the banks of streams. We were on the edge of orchard country.

Bunbury, a timber port owing nothing, it appears, to Oscar Wilde, has recently been developing into a seaside resort: the town is a sprawl of villas, corrugated-iron shacks, gimcrack shops, petrol stations and a few hotels, but the Indian Ocean curves round it on three sides and the surf slithers in and out of a flat sea. I had my first surf bathe there, the white burning beaches stretching away for miles with only a handful of people on them.

The night of our arrival there was a barbecue—gallons of beer and a fire on which you cooked your own steak. Next morning the cricket began, surf almost brushing the boundary edge and the ring filled with neighbouring farmers. Ladies sat in the stands under parasols, and the atmosphere was not unlike a country-house match, set back a few decades, Edwardian perhaps or late Victorian.

M.C.C. batted, and Edrich, playing, it seemed, only by ear, scored the first century of the tour. I have never seen him bat worse, though trying hard to get out when past his hundred he hit some astonishing sixes. Hutton batted indulgently in the grand manner, nonchalantly driving good-length balls straight for six, till bowled by a large off-break for 59. Graveney and Cowdrey also drove with pleasant fluency, and our batting, even against moderate bowling, looked imposing. When the Country XI batted we fielded poorly and bowled worse, Tyson and Loader finding the rough approaches too much for them. McConnon took five wickets, however, and, when the country men followed on, Cowdrey four—a performance that must have surprised even his admirers when it came through on the London tapes. The match was drawn, M.C.C. still wanting, though not greatly, a couple of wickets. It was a happy game, most of the onlookers having worked on their farms or apple orchards since dawn each day and then driven upwards of a hundred miles.

I dined one night at Bunbury with Ray Robinson, who, with Jack Fingleton, is the best of Australian cricket writers. The requirements of Australian newspapers do not, unfortunately, lead to a high standard of sporting journalism. Most papers carry three or four accounts of the day's play by ex-Test players, as well as one by their own correspondent, and these, being nearly always identical, create a mounting weariness. Moreover, since Australian cities are so far apart, there is no national newspaper, and articles are syndicated throughout the six States —a fact that keeps the cable boys busy and requires correspondents to send off their copy in a series of short takes. There is, probably on account of this, no tradition of writing on sport that aims any higher than the utilitarian. Ray Robinson's books *From the Boundary* and *The Glad Season* are exceptions, though where these are marred the cause is that same crudity of spotlighting that disfigures high-pressure journalism. But Robinson really looks at cricketers, noting their physical characteristics and establishing them as human beings with a style of expression that is identifiable quite apart from technical detail. What is a pity is that his day-to-day writing is not able, for a variety of reasons both economic and technical, to bear any relation to the vivid and searching manner of his books. Fingleton was at Bunbury, too: I had last seen him in England in 1953 when we had played together for the Authors against the Publishers, on which occasion he had made a hundred and, replying to Sir Compton Mackenzie, a very good speech into the bargain.

Back in Perth I went out to the Karrinyup Country Club, writing in the cool clubhouse while Fingleton, Swanton and Woodcock played eighteen holes of golf. After banging some dozens of balls into the practice ground I played a few holes on my own in the late afternoon, ambling alongside the blue tree-ringed lake, the central hazard of the course, in the gold declining sun.

PERTH

Fremantle Docks
Australia, first and last view

City Foreshore
*Landscape
with figure*

Queen's Gardens
*Swans sometimes turn
out geese*

PERTH

From King's Park
A city writ in water

Kalgoorlie
Digger No. 1

Bunbury
Parasols, fruit-farmers, and, on the boundary, the sound of the surf

MELBOURNE

Lunch-hour
After a 'spot',
a short nap

River Picnic
Cruises daily,
songs at the piano
inclusive

MELBOURNE

Collins Street
*From Treasury buildings
to the sunset*

Flinders Street Station
Domes of discovery

Early Morning
Last day, Third Test

BRISBANE

top left: A Place to Stay

top right: A Place to Shop (Home-served, as well as home-grown)

bottom left: The Bridge to Disaster

bottom right: The Waters of Comfort

QUEENSLAND

Near Rockhampton
*One way defeat,
the other, victory*

Rockhampton
*Cricket in the
tropics*

Mackay
Coconut Palms

THE GREAT BARRIER REEF

Pandanus Palm

Casuarina

Old Age

THE GREAT BARRIER REEF

Hayman Island
Niggerheads at low tide

*Still Life, with
sea urchin and
brain coral*

The Outer Reef
*Clams, anemones,
sea-serpents,
bêches-de-mer*

Another day I had a net, after M.C.C. had finished, with Fingleton, Swanton and Woodcock, which was worth it, apart from the intrinsic pleasure, to see for one's self the pace and trueness of the wicket. I realized here how much more safely one can play in Australia at the line, rather than the pitch of the ball. Later in the week Brown, Peebles and Lindsay Hassett had nets with us, and batting to Brown I noticed for the first time how he looks up at his bowling hand just before the moment of delivery, turning his head away from the batsman until the ball is almost out. He and Ian have bowled quite beautifully this week; Ian's swan-like movements of the arms have lost little of their grace and limpidity with the years. Brown and Peebles discuss the complexities of the leg-breaker's art as Beecham and Barbirolli might the implications of Schönberg's eight-tone scale or the correct speed at which the opening movement of Mahler's First Symphony should be taken. The terms are different, but the subtleties and comparisons no less fine.

Alec Bedser, who has had a bad go of shingles, bowled a few balls at what he called 'eighth pace.' Twelve years ago at Lord's, while he was an unknown aircraftman and I was on leave from my ship, we bowled unchanged to get an Army side out for 70. We took, I think, five wickets each and I remember the game well because I was robbed of the only hat-trick of my adult life. Not only that, but I had, only the night before, arrived back from Murmansk, and a senior officer admonished me on the field for having a torn shirt. The day was heavy, the wicket green, the ball swinging late. I hit the off stump of one of the opening batsmen and had the next man l.b.w. first ball. The captain of the team, a fiercely moustached major, then arrived at the wicket. The umpire was a bespectacled and nervous lance-corporal. The major took guard, looked commandingly about him, and, stretching forward with the stiff precision of one about to take the first step in The Lancers, snicked the ball into the wicket-keeper's gloves so noisily that an appeal seemed almost indecent, an unnecessarily cruel piece of tautology. However, an appeal was lodged by the six or seven players sufficiently interested to speak; whereupon the lance-corporal, struggling between truth and duty, and rendered speechless for a while, quavered out, with half-raised finger, 'Not out, *Sir*,' addressing, *bien entendu*, the batsman, not the bowler. I subsequently somewhat lost my length, though not I hope a sense of situation.

One Sunday I went sailing in Freshwater Bay—one notes one's trivial activities because they describe what is normal to people here—and I watched, too, the final of the Inter-State Australian-rules football. Some of the 'high marking' and fielding was magnificent, but it is a game of controlled kicking and catching, with none of the lovely patterns that soccer produces, none of the bursts of speed or clear-cut tackling of rugby. The field is oval and enormous, with many players idle for long periods at a time. There are no tries, and goals are scored simply by punting through two sets of posts—inner and outer. There is no proper tackling, nor running; midfield play is scrappy and untidy. The art is to kick from man to man and field cleanly under pressure. Marking is very close, so that height is important. The game is played for four quarters of twenty-five minutes each; each side has eighteen players. It seemed to me to go on far too long, to be too much an exhibition of brawn and stamina.

Another Perth institution is trotting, which takes place every Saturday evening on the Gloucester Park track. Australians, deprived of racing during the week, cannot have too much of it on a Saturday, and when the afternoon's racing is over they go straight on to the 'trots,' where the principle is the same, only the horses are smaller and the drivers, dressed in silks like jockeys, sit behind their animals in tiny carriages known as spiders. Enclosures and grandstands, totes and bookmakers, hot-dog stalls and bars—the paraphernalia is the same as for racing. When the race begins, all lights are extinguished except those on the track itself. At first it is pure spectacle, beautiful and seemingly leisurely—a frail and magical-looking procession made out of spun glass; but as they enter the last lap the drivers speed up, the spiders occasionally get entangled overtaking, and the finish, even if contrived, is splendidly dramatic. Large sums of ill-afforded money change hands and there is general head-shaking about the way things are run. But the gambler, by nature a masochist, enjoys his misfortune. Sailing, golf, surfing, racing—that is the ritual of Australian summer. The anxieties of the age have little place in it, though even here no one can quite be rid of his private demons.

* * *

I have moved from my hotel, where my room looked out on a rubbish dump, to the Weld Club, which is excellently staffed, quiet, comfortable, and smells, as it should, of old leather. A tiger-skin is spread out in the hall and the nineteenth-century prints are all of England.

One might, at moments, be in the Athenæum; the members are, if anything, rather older, extremely kind, civilized and entertaining. The other day there was a party to celebrate one of the younger member's ninetieth birthday: Ian Peebles and I lunched the day before with the beneficiary, a sprightly gentleman who made us laugh a great deal and declared that he had been trained seventy years earlier as an ecclesiastical architect but since coming out to Perth had built twenty-five pubs for each church. His confidence in the future was such that, for the first time in a decade, he had bought a new suit. He wore a wing collar and ate greatly and I don't doubt but that he will get his century. He informed us that his father was sixty-eight when he was sired, which creates a fair span of years between them.

From my room I look out on the blue strip of river striped by the plane trees. The sun melts away behind King's Park to the west and the palm trees blacken in the clear light along the esplanade. Nightly, a kind of ballet of sport takes place on the recreation ground that runs parallel to the waterfront. Girls, fresh from their offices, jog round the boundary in running shorts. A squad of girl athletes doing Swedish exercises bend and sway like praying mantises before a male instructor. A practice cricket match on a concrete wicket swells in size as players fresh from work take off their coats and join in. A score of men in football jerseys run up and down passing a rugger ball. Their backs to the boats pulled up on the grass verge of the river, others kick to one another, perfecting their fielding. Bowls click on the smooth greens, white-suited ladies and men in separate enclosures crouching low over their woods. A sailing boat curves out of The Narrows as the evening breeze, 'the Fremantle doctor,' catches it: two trial eights are skimming into the smoother waters of Como. It is the choreography of the Antipodes. Pelicans, shag, gulls perch on mooring posts and jetties, a paper-chase of birds. Those more richly indulgent, who have sprawled out in the sun all afternoon, shake themselves and wander off in the cooler air.

Walking after dinner, which is at seven o'clock here, to the post-office with some cables, I pass down dark deserted streets. The time is nine-thirty and the bars closed half an hour ago. A man, in the Australian attitude, leans against a post smoking: a tram clangs down Hay Street. On either side the bookshops are more solidly stocked with erotica and curious manuals on oriental amatory techniques than I can remember to have seen anywhere. In Albert's, the best bookshop in Perth, I find my book on Sardinia, *The Bandit on the Billiard Table*, displayed in an illuminated window: it is nice to think of it coming half-way across the world. In Murray Street, empty save for an old man with long white beard shuffling erratically along, someone in an upstairs room is playing 'Yes, sir, she's my baby.' Feet scrape the floor on the premises of a dancing school.

Near the railway station the drunks are lurching about under the palm trees, for this is their hour. Across the bridge a thin stream of men make for Roe Street, where the licensed brothels stretch out like a series of large hen-coops along the sidings. The girls, one or two of whom are surprisingly beautiful and *chic*, lounge on verandahs behind wire netting. Outside, streams of men perambulate as though window-gazing in the Via Veneto:

mostly Italian, with a sprinkling of Slavs and Germans. Groups form up in the darkness, staring with steady concentration at the girls, who chain-smoke or read disinterestedly. It strikes one as very un-Australian, till suddenly one of the girls, an elegant redhead with hair cut in the Italian style and dangling gold ear-rings, looks up, uncrosses her legs and hisses with quiet feeling, 'My oath, you larrikins, its time you kyme in or gyve it awye.'

Coming down St George's Terrace a lonely group of Italian migrants stand together in earnest conversation. They have the air of conspirators. In Italy the evening would scarcely have begun: here the stars are upside down and the night over. All migrants, except British, are obliged to work at whatever they are directed—usually in public services, such as road-making— for two years, before practising their own trade. It is a necessary guarantee of serious intention, of good faith. Australia is desperately short of labour and therefore of houses: more houses (or 'homes' as a house is kindly called here) are needed before more people come. But there is no one to build them but the immigrants, 'the New Australians,' themselves. An Italian was reported to have said the other day that he had lived in Australia for thirty years, but that he was still a 'bloody wop,' whereas his nephew, who had been out only three months, was able, proudly, to call himself a 'New Australian.'

Near the river-front the sound of bagpipes: most nights the lonely noise of them drifts over the spongy lawns outside the club. Cars are jammed the whole way along the street kerbs, like rows of sleeping beetles, some of them in pyjama-like coverings. There is one car to four people and never anywhere to park.

* * *

The two first-class matches in Perth, against Western Australia and Combined XI, have both been won by M.C.C., something which, rather surprisingly, has never happened before. The pattern of each was identical, M.C.C. putting the opposition in on a fast flawless wicket and shooting them out for first innings scores of 103 and 86 respectively. On the two Saturday nights M.C.C. were out for scores of 321 and 311, which meant a hopeless task for their opponents. As things turned out, the first game was won by 7 wickets, the second by an innings.

Against Western Australia Statham took 6 for 23 and 3 for 68. He bowled magnificently on the first day, whipping the ball off the pitch and making the batsman play at every ball. Although he relies less on movement through the air than most opening bowlers, he is a model of how the new ball should be used. Length and direction are precisely controlled; by the end of the first over the batsman has a sizable bruise above the left pad, the ball coming in sharply from the middle stump, and from then on he knows he must get his bat to everything. There is something of archery about Statham's bowling: he aims with his left arm straight out, he is tightly sprung at the moment of delivery, and the thump down of the left foot sends the ball from wicket to wicket as straight as an arrow. He was altogether too fast for the State players, the ball bounding off the pitch so quickly that even such restricted back lifts as most of them had were too much.

Bailey bowled well too, though he suffered greatly from dropped catches. M.C.C.'s fielding has already caused a lot of adverse comment: five catches were put down on the first two days and they were staid and inaccurate away from the wicket. McConnon bowled sensibly, without getting much from the pitch, but Wardle was niggardly with his chinaman and on such a pitch he spins the ball too little with his ordinary method. In these games he should be practising his chinaman the whole time, otherwise he will be completely harmless.

For M.C.C. Hutton made 145, retiring with what was announced as 'a strained riding muscle,' Cowdrey 41 and Wilson 38. Hutton played what must rank as one of the queerest of his many innings. For a long while he batted as if on the sands, the great man on holiday, chasing and flicking at everything no matter how wide. He seemed to wish, probably rightly, to spare himself any unnecessary concentration, to reserve his long ascetic innings for the Tests. But when Simpson and May failed, and he had himself been dropped four times by slips or gully, he resigned himself to the inevitable. His last 90 runs could only have been scored by a great player: they will be talked of at Perth when the small boys present are old gentlemen. He drove over mid-off's head with a sound as mellow as the plucking of banjo strings, he advanced down the pitch and cut late or carved the ball on the half volley as its length deemed, improvising strokes that had seemed the prerogative of Bradman and Compton; and then he swung the ball half a dozen times to the fine leg boundary using his left hand only, the virtuoso loosening up with a few scales, an arpeggio or two. Hutton does not normally improvise, for he has no need to: but when he hobbled off, the members standing to him, he had showed that the classical manner is capable of adaptation, that perfect technique includes a gift for both satire and caricature.

Cowdrey again showed, when Hutton allowed him the strike, which was not often, how commanding a player he is when the ball is coming through. Playing back, his nose bisects the line of flight: driving, his hands move up the bat and the stroke is powerful and fluent. The bat finishes up brushing the left ear, the weight is exactly distributed, so that a diagram of his position, as made in Leonardo da Vinci's anatomical drawings, would find the circles and points of intersection in flowing symmetry.

When Western Australia batted again Carmody and Meuleman stayed together for nearly four hours in mid-innings, attempting nothing but the preservation of their wickets. Once they were out, Statham wasted no time in gobbling up the tail.

In the second match the State was reinforced by Harvey, Hole and Ian Johnson, all of whom had been specially flown over from the east. Hutton, Loader, Cowdrey and McConnon were replaced by Edrich, Tyson, Graveney and Appleyard.

May won the toss and put the Combined XI in on a lovely

wicket. By tea-time they were out for 86, the three Test players having contributed 9 runs between them. Bailey achieved the break-through this time, swinging the ball very late at barely medium pace, and making it float or dip from various angles of approach. Harvey, looking even paler than usual, was caught by Evans off a ball that came across him quite slowly from leg, hanging and then drifting away, a ball that achieved the finality of a 'still' taken from a moving picture. Tyson beat Hole for speed, bowling with accuracy for the first time so far, and between them the middle batting was suddenly wrecked. Statham, a glutton for tail-enders, again polished off the rest. The fielding was better.

In warm beguiling sunshine M.C.C. batted and Edrich was comprehensively yorked first ball. Simpson made 28 in his most disarming manner whereupon Ian Johnson came on and had him caught at slip first ball. Graveney stretched forward for an off-break only to find the ball move the other way and he was caught at the wicket for 0. In the next three-quarters of an hour, the pelicans gliding in over the elongated shadows of fielders and gum trees, May and Wilson added 18 runs, Johnson bowling 7 overs for 7 runs and 2 wickets. Both batsmen played him from the crease, back foot firmly anchored, while Johnson threw the ball higher and higher like some taunting pagan tempting two early Christians to indiscretion. It was a sad sight to see a stream of comfortable half volleys on a placid pitch being neglected for want of the slightest movement down the wicket. It was the epitome of the post-war English style: of course, there was all the time in the world, but usually there isn't, and if a batsman ignores runs when the ball is not turning or biting, he will certainly not make them when it is and he is left stranded at the mercy of spin and lift.

Dining with Ian Peebles and myself at the Weld Club later that night Ian Johnson remarked that he much preferred the batsman to move his feet, for then there is genuine contest between bowler and batsman, between stroke making and the subtleties of flight. When he remains immobile and strokeless on such perfect pitches, there is no struggle of wits, no exertion of the intelligence. The ball cannot beat the bat, the rhythm of the play slackens, and the whole game is becalmed. The spin bowler then has merely a nuisance value, buzzing at the batsman's patience like a fly.

Johnson, who is in the wine and spirits business, as well as running his own radio programme, is extremely likeable. At the moment he seems the probable choice as captain of Australia, anxiety about which did not deter him from defeating Hassett and myself at billiards, despite having Peebles as a partner. He is affable, eager to please but generally less robust a character than most Australian captains of the past. He is not likely to be a popular appointment with the critics, most of whom belong to the generation that believe Bradman was not an unmixed blessing to Australian cricket and who regard Johnson in some way as his mouthpiece. Sir Donald, now a selector, is still an equivocal object of love-hate to many Australians. As a race, they are not appreciative of individualists, and Bradman, while being greatly respected by the younger generation of Test cricketers, is regarded by his own contemporaries with something less than idolatry. Apart from this, the inter-state jealousies and sensitive feelings of committee representatives, all of which affect the nomination of an Australian captain, have direct bearing on the ambiguity of Bradman's position. New South Wales born, he lives now in Adelaide. Of the possible Test captains, Johnson, like Hassett, is a Victorian. Morris and Miller come from New South Wales.

Next day, in sun and ruffling breeze, May and Wilson played much better before the first decent crowd of the tour. Without looking quite as good as he can do in England May went patiently to 129, Wilson dourly to 72. May's off driving and forcing of the shorter ball to the on made their due impression, though again he played the spinners as if under some restrictive covenant. He is developing Hutton mannerisms, touching the peak of his cap twice after good strokes, tapping the pitch like a barometer, holding his bat horizontal with both hands when he runs. He also plays the good length ball on the leg stump in the same way, that is to say turning his wrists over at the last moment, the right hand on top, guiding and forcing. Wilson showed resources of character, if not of technique: he cut nicely, late and square, but drove not at all.

On the Monday Combined XI were all out a quarter of an hour before close of play. Tyson bowled still faster and more at the wicket, his run-up now being directed nearer his own stumps. Appleyard had a long bowl and is going to be all right. I have great hopes of him. He and Wardle took three wickets each and Wilson three fine catches. It is an encouraging start, however one looks at it. But we want Bedser fit again and some runs out of Graveney and either Edrich or Simpson—if neither of the latter come off I suppose Wilson might be worth experimenting with at No. 2. But unless he shows greater willingness to drive fast bowling, there will be no point in him at all.

Harvey's swoops and glides at cover must have been the envy of the many birds in the variously feathered sky. A band has played in the intervals; it should happen more often. Cricket as a spectacle needs a few reviving graces; music and pretty women watching and intelligent conversation, as there were in the nineteenth century when it was an affair of rustics and dandies.

It is no longer the habit for cricket matches to be social occasions as well, with marquees and bands and deck-chairs and bunting, and that is a pity. Art needs a warmth of surrounding to bring it to bloom. Unfortunately, modern cricket grounds are stadiums built in conformity with the unimaginative puritan conscience, demanding, and getting, dull cricket and bad catering. Perth is much better than most; it would be a pleasant ground on which to play a Test match. But this, on account of its position and smallness of population, is likely to be a matter of the distant future. In the hierarchies of Australian cricket, the influence of Western Australia is about comparable with that of Somerset in the debates of M.C.C. The 'picturesque' has no place in pastimes that have grown into industries and devolve for their survival necessarily round economics. Nor could it honestly be otherwise.

3 Notes in the Nullarbor

I'm writing this somewhere on the longest stretch of straight track in the world—east of Kalgoorlie the railway runs for 300 miles without a curve. The train is air-conditioned, diesel-hauled. In the old days—which in this country means usually a year or two ago—the journey from Perth to Adelaide took nearly a week, and the red dust came into the compartments so thickly that gentlemen were issued with special paper containers to protect their hats. Now it takes 48 hours 5 minutes, and, despite the necessity of changing trains twice owing to the fact that each State has a different gauge, is fairly comfortable. Food is not good and there is no bar; the journey would seem shorter and more beautiful if there were. Australians are ascetics, however, their civilization in its earliest adolescence, and they have the ascetic's lack of interest in, if not contempt for, the civilizing indulgences: food, clothes, comfort, the appearance of things. This might argue an overworked technocratic society, with no time for the frivolities of style. On the contrary, Australians have all the time in the world: but they belong by nature, or rather accident, to an age that does not look at things, that is democratic to the extent of admiring the ordinary and fearing the excellent, for excellence, besides making demands of its own which require imagination and discipline, creates inequalities. It is not that Australians dislike inequality: despite their often reiterated belief that every man is as good as another (with which they half-wish you to quarrel), there are quite distinct social levels in every city. But they approve of the illusion of equality, which is only fair, for otherwise they are a genial race who allow themselves few deceptions.

I left Perth at half-past three on Sunday afternoon, Percy

White, a doctor of wide renown, driving me down to the station through King's Park, its 1,000 acres of bush smeared here and there with the foggy mauve of Geraldton wax. Kings Park, founded by Lord Forrest, one-time Governor of Western Australia, is a guarantee to the citizens of Perth that, no matter how quickly their city expands, they will always be within easy reach of the bush. Most of it is impenetrable on foot, but roads, lined with gums, intersect it at all angles, and in the Spring the white spider orchids straggle across thick clusters of blue and red leschenaultia and the hedgerows are specked with the dark strawberry-patterned flowers of the red gum and the crinkled yellow coral shapes of the Australian Christmas tree. On either side of the footpaths the scarlet tassels of bottlebrush and the rubbery convolutions of kangaroo paw, the flower of which peels back from its stem like thin variously-coloured banana skins, splash the dry lizard-hued eucalypts. Through the trees the yacht-strewn waters of Melville Bay glint a dull metal against the fringe of banksia, red bottle and liquid amber that slope steeply down above the circling avenues of the Swan River. This conjunction of sudden colour and thorny disheartening undergrowth constitutes, as I later discovered, the attraction of certain Australian landscapes—one can never quite take them for granted.

After leaving we rolled till sundown through a belt of jarrah forest, the trees 'ring-barked' to accelerate their decay—most of the houses in Western Australia are built out of the hard red wood of the jarrah. Now and again a group of the shrubs known as black-boys, their pale furry spears bolt upright in the black, fronded trunks that give them their name, forced their way through the jarrah.

By 8 a.m. we were in Kalgoorlie, the black mine-stacks along Patrick Hannan's Golden Mile sticking up out of the haze like steamers run aground. We had time here to walk out to Hannan's statue along wide tree-lined roads, the bungalows and corrugated-iron shacks along them absurdly inadequate in the opulence of their setting. Kalgoorlie looks like a town envisaged by its creators as the seat of a governor; when he failed to materialize, the inhabitants, as though out of modesty or inertia, perhaps thinking it presumptuous to fulfil the early designs for their own use, settled down in temporary wooden pavilions.

Beyond Kalgoorlie the dark line of the salmon gums—one of the 700 varieties of Australian eucalypt—bisects the track, the vegetation thins out, and the landscape begins its descent into desert. A shallow sea of grey-green saltbush spills over the red soil. Gum trees wade delicately through the low undergrowth, rubbed bare in parts, with parachute-shaped blue bush flaring open amongst the silver stems of the gums. Near Rawlinna littered stones, of every shape and size, replaced the saltbush, the red light-hard plain so flat that the curve of the earth seems to press like water round it.

For the whole of that day there was no change in the landscape. At hundred mile intervals we passed railway-maintenance settlements, half a dozen wooden shacks with painted verandahs set out in line, looking as if they had been dropped down ready-made into nothingness by aeroplane. This was nearer the Australia of one's imagination, the country of Henry Lawson's poems, the dead land of swagmen, over which the early pioneers made their heroic treks, driving cattle to new stations, naming places, looking for gold and water. These places had no identity, no beginning or end. Like toy railway carriages severed from their engine on some disused siding, they faced resolutely out on the dusty thistle-grown desert. Their contact with life was haphazard and rare, radio the main thing that sustained them. By radio they ordered their provisions, and sent for the doctor; and both came by air. Over most of Australia this hardy, lonely life still exists; yet to the majority of the population, stewing in their city suburbs, it is as imaginately remote as the adventures of Ned Kelly, the bushranger, or the fabulous journeys of Burke and Wills, and Leickhardt.

The Nullarbor resembles a little the plains of Sardinia magnified a dozen times: but here, in place of the relics of pre-Christian cultures, the railway shacks represent the early pioneering life invoked by European *nuraghi* and dolmens. Even the aborigines that once beckoned for gifts of anything along this single track have been driven north by hunger into special reserves.

* * *

The lazy beauty of the old Australian place names: Bookaloo, Tarcoola, Pimba, Zanthus, Karonie, Kingoonya, and the incisiveness of the newer ones, Haig, Cook, Reid, Barton, Watson, emblems of individual men, not of places.

This morning I awoke to a kangaroo bounding along in the middle distance; later, past Wirraminna, a few came closer, almost indistinguishable against the red-brown plain. Shortly after breakfast I saw an emu, looking stiff and surprised, as though caught reading someone else's letters. But of the 'barking' lizard, reputed to make sounds like a dog barking, or the 'cycling' lizard, whose leg motions resemble the pedalling action of a man on a bicycle, of both of which the Commonwealth Railway brochure speaks so enticingly, there have been no signs.

Nearing Adelaide now, only a few hours more to go, the landscape back to a human scale. Pale, sand-coloured plains with spinifex dotted along them, sheep glimpsed through the window under spindly trees, the wind ruffling the wheat. And the cattle country swelling up into downs and hills, growing greener all the time. Port Augusta, and a chain of salt lakes stretching out to a horizon of purple trees: the Spencer gulf: and to the east, the soft moulding of the Flinders Range. Slowing down under a low grey sky, raindrops fall heavily on the unlovely northern suburbs of Adelaide.

4 Adelaide: Colonel Light's Vision

A town that is bounded by sea and mountain need not strive for other elegances: in Adelaide it is a case of gulf and hills, but the tawny line of the Mount Lofty range circles the town in a benevolent embrace and the beaches are not far off. The Torrens river forms an inner arc of water, parks continue the waterline, and every street to the east terminates in the rising foothills of Mount Lofty. The sky comes only half-way down. The centre of Adelaide, like Perth, is disappointing, and for the same reasons: there are no curves, no uniform frontages, no blending of styles. Simply a series of blocks, roads intersecting at right angles, every shop or office a different height. Skyscrapers gawk up over shabby single-storey shops, nothing seems built to last. Peasants create objects to endure, their land and lives are eternal: Australia has no peasants, nor ever has had. Houses appear to be put up on the principle that the owners will exchange them next year for new ones.

All the same, Adelaide has charm; it has been thoughtfully laid-out. The faded, decrepit-looking trams rattle out of King William and Rundle Streets, which form the central business and shopping areas, wheeling round suddenly into North Terrace, mountains at one end, the dipping sun at the other, and, along one side, Government House, the University, the Museum, the National Gallery, handsome sandstone buildings shaded by palms. Opposite these, solid and respectable, are doctors' consulting-rooms, clubs, insurance offices, banks. As in Perth, the hotels, supported on thin columns, have wide circular balustrades and potted palms at their entrances. There is an old colonial gentility about some of them, the South Australia particularly, and one expects to find guests riding up on horseback or in old jalopies rather than in Vauxhalls or Holdens (Australia's own make of car) or Sunbeam-Talbots.

Dust and metallic noonday light, jangling trams, zoos, racecourses, arcades, airway terminals and a huge modern railway station—Adelaide has the aroma of a provincial cattle town overlaid by a kind of high conservatism, but with nevertheless a *douceur de vivre* that, being purely personal, makes no concessions to such public pleasures as going to a night-club or eating in a restaurant. The absence of these things are part of Australia's puritanism—a puritanism æsthetic rather than moral. It is at night especially that one realizes how much Australian cities, despite their rapid development and access to certain modern amenities, are, at heart, country towns, dominated by the countryman's conscience. They are free entirely of those nocturnal urges that are produced by intellectual curiosity and a sedentary life.

Here, no less than in Perth, recreation is an affair of the body. Images and equipments of sport recur round the town like the theme of the Vinteuil sonata in Proust—the swinging tennis racket, the poised diver, the flash of oars, the cricket oval seen through the peeling gum trees, the polo ground, the sprinkler on the private tennis court. It is towards these that each street leads—and from the city centre you are free of commerce within a few hundred yards in any direction.

North Terrace to the cricket ground is a ten-minute walk down a broad tree-lined avenue, a walk that takes in a swimming pool, Turkish baths, a jocular round bandstand, and grassy slopes spreading to a river. Launches and rowing boats are neatly moored on either side of a fine bridge, and families sit picnicking on the banks much as Renoir or Seurat might have painted them. Light moves on water and leaf, the river bears a heavy drift of foliage, children feed the moorhens, a water-rat breaks surface. From outside, the cricket ground, with the trim towers of Adelaide Cathedral rising out of tall trees behind it, is not unlike Worcester; spires, water, swans, trees and grass form their approaches.

Beyond both cathedral and grandstand the statue of a man with proud forehead and dominating nose looks out over the city from a semi-circular eminence: Colonel Light, first surveyor-general of Adelaide. From this point—Light's Vision—he fixed the limits and central sites of the city now so beautifully contained by the Mount Lofty Hills. The statue bears an inscription:

'The reasons that led me to fix Adelaide where it is I do not expect to be generally understood or calmly judged of at present. My enemies, however, by disputing their validity in every particular, have done me the good service of fixing the whole of the responsibility on me. I am perfectly willing to bear it, and I leave it to posterity and not to them, to decide whether I am entitled to praise or blame.'

So Light wrote in his journal in 1838: barely a century later the vision hardens into stone under a faint heat haze, probably not greatly different from the way Light first saw it form in the channels of his imagination.

* * *

The match against South Australia has ended in a win for M.C.C. by 21 runs. Three victories in a row, an unprecedented start, though for the life of me I can't imagine why no M.C.C. side in this century has managed it. Yet the manner of this last success has caused such apprehension that Hutton has cancelled all social engagements on this last day in Adelaide and sent the recalcitrants off to the nets. Quite rightly, for M.C.C. have performed ignominiously against a moderate side, being rescued from dire defeat on the final afternoon by Appleyard who took 4 wickets for 6 when South Australia were only 30 runs off triumph with 5 wickets in hand and time to spare. It was a merciful deliverance, quite undeserved.

Compton, newly arrived by air, made 113 in his spryest manner out of M.C.C.'s first innings total of 246. Hutton scored 37, Simpson 26, Graveney and Cowdrey 20 each. The pitch was good for thousands, which Favell and Harris quickly demonstrated by scoring 119 in just about that number of minutes in a pre-lunch partnership. Favell, regarded hitherto as over-prone to acts of suicide for a reputable opening batsman, went on to make a century, one so full of brilliant shots and purposive bustle that it will take a good player to keep him out of the Test side. He is one of the best outfielders in the world, with a flicked, baseball player's shy from the boundary that lands the ball with a thud over the top of the stumps. In the afternoon Tyson bowled with stout heart and considerable pace so that, despite dreadfully slow fielding, South Australia were put out for 254. When M.C.C. batted a second time Hutton nobly bore the coffin of his colleagues yet again, scoring 98 out of 181 on a wicket taking some slight spin. Graveney, for the second time in the match, was out when seemingly well set. Otherwise no one managed more than 16 runs, the first three wickets falling to the pace of Drennan for 31, the last five to the spin of Wilson for 8. I lay on a bank under a gum tree and tried to pretend it was not happening. For once, this bowler's graveyard had given up its corpses. South Australia were left with the whole of the last day to make 174. The sun, on the final morning, straddled the cathedral, Mount Lofty, palms, gums and many eager spectators. By lunch South Australia, with 102 for 3 on the board, Favell 45 not out, were well on the way to victory. Hutton's spinners, who should have done the job, had let him down badly, Appleyard being hit for 40 in a short spell, and McConnon, who certainly turned the ball, bowling a really bad one in each over. With his second ball of the afternoon, however, Tyson got a very fast one past Favell to bowl him as he played back, and Hutton, when runs continued to come at a greater rate in the circumstances than wickets, then bravely recalled Appleyard. Appleyard earlier had bowled too much at the leg stump, with not enough variation of pace. Now he slowed down, flighted the ball and gave it time to move off the seam. The runs to play with were very few. But a tactic, born out of desperation, succeeded. The South Australian middle batsmen, continuing to play across the line of flight—which they had done quite satisfactorily all day—suddenly found this luxury costing them their wickets; 142 for 5 when Appleyard began his second spell, they were all out for the addition of 10 runs, Appleyard taking 4 for 6. Every batsman except the last threw his wicket away with wild indiscretion. Not one was beaten by anything the ball did off the pitch. Honest men, anticipation and the sniff of triumph was their undoing. Welcome and surprising as all this was, Hutton was left by this match with several problems. The fielding had somehow to be improved out of all recognition: that was the first problem and it was one with which Hutton never got quite strictly enough to terms. The fault was not entirely his: it stemmed from the general slackness of English county cricket, which took too little account of the great increase in tempo and pleasure which brisk, accurate throwing brings to the whole game. Neither Edrich nor Simpson were yet in form: the former too sluggish in his reactions, the latter unaccountably reckless. Roy Ullyett of the *Daily Express* produced a pertinent cartoon about this time in England, where a wave of strikes were taking place. 'When I read they're out, I don't know whether its Edrich and Simpson, or the dockers,' so the caption went. The batting of the bowlers was no less of a problem: we could not afford to lose our last five wickets for only a score of runs each innings. That again could be put against the improvidence of the county system, whereby bowlers were rather discouraged from batting longer than a few overs.

The pleasant features of the game were Hutton's own batting, and his cool resourcefulness on the last afternoon, Compton's immediate strike of form, and the dogged improvement in Tyson's bowling, which brought him 6 wickets for 99.

Hole, the main South Australian Test candidate, apart from Langley, the wicket-keeper, failed twice. He is a poor player of fast bowling, especially on the leg stump. Favell's two busy innings seem to indicate new resolutions: he swished outside the off stump only once, and lifted his head not at all. Otherwise, the South Australian batting was of moderate county strength: the bowling, apart from Drennan, a lanky young man who uses the new ball well, was slightly under it.

On my way from the ground I visited the koala bears in their farm across the road. Creatures of darkness, they were hung up asleep on small branches, dreaming at all angles, secure in their absence of struggle. Sun-doped, eucalyptus-happy, rheumy-eyed, philosophically-nosed. I envied these balls of smoke-coloured fur, complacently certain that cricket languished in the hinterland of an earlier century.

* * *

From the terrace at Carrick Hill, where I am staying with Ursula and Bill Hayward, Adelaide curves in a wide half-moon four miles below—a pink-and-white toy-like town, stuffed with trees and looking from above like a military model. Beyond it the sea fades from deep blue into colourless haze. A few ships pass during the morning, black dots pulling whisps of smoke behind them, as though on the end of strings.

Behind the house a line of downs, steeply recessed and shaped rather like the downs above my house at Clayton in Sussex, curve into a wood. The greenest piece of land I've seen in Australia so far—full and flowing and with neat groups of trees increasing my nostalgia.

Seawards, one might be looking down at the Mediterranean. The same blue, seen through avenues of cypress, the air full of almond and orange and lemon. A gum tree, nearly obscured by olives, gives the show away if you look hard enough for it: but Southern Italy has its gum trees too. I look from my bedroom over shelving lawns edged with roses and magnolia, begonia and oleander.

I wouldn't have taken this for Australia in a hundred years. Preconceptions, apart from being misleading, are usually based on single characteristics, of childish simplicity. Australia remains in the mind's eye just as it was conceived in the nursery. A land of kangaroos and koalas, of dust and desert, dingoes and water-holes. To this list, in adolescence were added gold-rushes and iguanas, swagmen boiling their billies, Melba and Bradman and *Waltzing Matilda*. But yesterday, on our way down to the sea for a picnic at Port Willunga, we drove through green, rolling country, the bold humps of the Darling foothills mauve against wheatfields pale yellow in noon sun, and the light liquid as water over paddocks, with cattle and sheep nibbling at the tough grasses, and vines sloping away from the road, losing themselves behind the thickening gums; the sunset, coming home, cracked on the hills, orange, ochre, and the waxy yellow of old paintings. Adelaide sunsets are for connoisseurs, the flow of colour miraculously controlled at its moments of greatest release—more painterly, less undisciplined than those in the East.

The final phase, an effect of glazing, when the sun dips over the edge of the world and the yellows harden into black, changes the city from an eighteenth-century painting into a late Victorian engraving within the space of a few minutes. Darkness drops like a curtain turning Adelaide by degrees into a great honeycomb of flickering light, amber, green, white, the highway to the Glenelg beaches firmer and more brilliant than all the rest. Up here at night one looks down at Adelaide, a glittering string of curves and squares in a deep nest of darkness, Orion askew and the dog-star on its back, and the heavens seem nearer than the city. Night gives to these new cities an added dimension, the illusions of age and mystery and formal beauty, which they normally lack and which are the luxuries of the past, the by-products of leisurely periods when prosperity had time to indulge its fancies and the manners to learn the proper way how. The cool of this house, with its panelled walls of English wood, the clink of ice-cubes and the heavy trail of flower scent after a long day in the sun, gramophone music, books, paintings, as well as food of an un-Australian excellence, exert a seductiveness I had never expected to find here. Had one expected Australia to be harsh and unwelcoming? No, I don't think that ever. But one had not taken into account its affinities with Europe, the constant travel of many of its people, the narrowing of the world. So it is that the rooms here bear Epstein heads on their tables, Augustus John paintings and drawings on their walls. Boudin, Berthe Morisot, Renoir, Vuillard, Goya and Pasmore dotted elsewhere about the house, form the basis of a collection which, of its size, can have few superiors in Australia. To come out of the blink and glare of the day, and moon about from room to room, from century to century, has been one of the joys of this last week.

On the way to the cricket each day I have looked in at the Australian pictures in the Adelaide Gallery. The old prints are marvellous. Robert Campbell, the Director, picked out the best of the early paintings for me and under his guidance one was able to detect, in someone like Streeton, for instance, the emergence of the first distinctively Australian pictures—landscapes painted with awareness of Australian light and contour, not out of nostalgia for England, as the earliest academic paintings had been. In Roberts and Streeton the moist blues and greens, the rounded forms, with which the first painters falsely invested Australia, are replaced by the colours and forms that are true of, and unique to, the country. Since then, Australian painting went through a period of dullness from which it has only recently begun to recover. But in the best work of Drysdale, Herman, Nolan and Friend, the shantytowns of Australia, with their empty red streets and balustraded pubs, the reality and legend of the 'wild Colonial boys,' the bush and the isolation, the glare and the dreaming, find real equivalents. It is perhaps not a style that is easily exportable, for it relies to some extent on the emotional impact of its subject-matter. The Australian interior is monotonous; even Streeton only managed to paint it for a short period. Dobell's portraits, however, most of which I have only seen in reproduction, are immediately recognizable as the work of a painter who extends beyond nationality. Probably one is wrong to look for a style that is Australian rather than personal. Painters inhabit regions of the mind before places on the map: yet most of the great painters in Europe have a style that is local as well as individual.

They belong to places as well as period. Dobell and Drysdale I hope to see more of in Melbourne and Sydney: they are not well represented here. The Adelaide Gallery, incidentally, is a model of its kind: well-lit, spacious, uncluttered, the rooms flowing into one another coolly and cleanly, so that one gets a sense of purposive movement.

Through Robert Campbell I met Charles Mountford, the explorer and ethnologist, who had just returned from a six-month trip to Melville Island, the aborigine reserve off the coast of the Northern Territory. I found him sitting at a desk covered with maps, films and colour transparencies of cave paintings. Most of these latter were done in Central Australia, where Mountford has travelled extensively: a few of the designs are abstract, the remainder symbolical in a highly involved way. Food, water, animals and human beings are suggested as well as hunting, fishing and various domestic activities. The drawing is primitive in conception, delicate and painstaking in execution. They are admirably suited to ceramics, which makes it all the greater pity that these simple lyrical motifs, evoking the vivid, secret rituals of the nomadic tribes, have been so little used. Australia, of course, has neither archæology, nor recorded past; but, largely due to Mountford and others, an attempt is at last being made to trace the racial myths, and to preserve their dignity.

Mountford showed me a great number of bark paintings, done in natural colours—ochre, black, white, yellow—with strips of chewed wood, the chewing producing an effect barely distinguishable from a brush. Designs of extraordinary delicacy and organization are achieved. The aborigines have no professional artists, all painting equally, though some better than others: they lead a complex tribal life, with elaborate rituals, fetishes and objects of veneration, and their caste system, like that of the African negro, is based on ordeal, initiation, and taboo. The women have their own initiations and hierarchies, but they are excluded from all the important ceremonies of male life. The men are well-proportioned, though, by civilized standards, thin-legged; the women, the 'lubras,' have an adolescent beauty that ends almost with maturity. Generally, they are not, despite the fact that they represent the purest racial stock in existence, physically impressive. But their meagreness of stature does not denote a corresponding weakness, for they are able to show exceptional physical stamina, existing for long periods at a time on grubs and weeds, and undertaking formidable treks. The white races of Australia have not done well by them, though under an exceptionally intelligent Minister they are now being fitted in their remote Reserves for occupations that will once more make them part of the community. Unfortunately, it has been done too late. It was not so long ago that the police were allowed to hunt and kill them like dogs. Their number now is so small that they cannot hope to survive as a race much longer. Missionaries in part clothe, feed and educate them: but by breaking down their tribal secrecies, they are removing the mysteries and pride that were the cause of their art, and the justification and meaning of their separateness. The point is not, however, that their art is exceptional, but that it exists. The aborigine has few civil rights, is not, for his own sake, permitted alcohol, and, while being deprived of all the luxuries of urban civilization, is exposed to most of its temptations. The white man is free to choose his route to perdition, and to make the journey as agreeable as possible. The aborigine is obliged to travel without even the defences of his superstition.

The subjects of the bark paintings are emus, turtles, lizards, kangaroos, snakes, warriors and trees, the various objects packed into tight emblematic designs. Each painting has a literal meaning: Mountford has captioned them in a charming way. Under a snake-pattern bark painting from Arnhem Land he has written:

'In the Dreamtime (in aboriginal belief the time before the Creation) there were no fish in the water-holes or trees to make weapons from. All these things, the legend says, were inside Bolong the Rainbow Snake. And when the aborigines killed Bolong, birds and animals were made, and fish in the rivers and even new mountains—and this was the end of the Dreamtime.'

Under a painting of emus:

'When the aborigines depict an emu they always show its broad tracks, for it cannot fly. But there is a legend telling that Dinewan the Emu once had the strongest wings of all the birds in the bush. And Goombla Gobba the Turkey Cock was jealous of her, and hiding her own wings, said to Dinewan: "Now I am Queen of the birds, for I alone am able to do without flight." Now Dinewan was afraid and went away and cut off her wings. And so to this day the Emu cannot fly because of the foolish pride of Dinewan.'

Under a cave painting of a women's corroboree dance found in the Northern Territory:

'Once in the time of the great corroboree of the Baime, when the youths of the tribe were to be made into men, there came a widow named Millin-dulu-nubba with her boys. And she was very angry because the tribes had drunk all the water in the streams before her and left her to travel alone with her children. And in her wrath she cursed them, saying, "You were in such a hurry to get here, now you can stay here for ever." And to this day the tribes believe that the ancient trees in that place are the spirits of their ill-fated fathers.'

I left Mountford with the late afternoon sun spilling over great heaps of drawings and message-sticks and pieces of bark. From him I had got the first inkling, in a month spent in Australia, of the interior past of the country, of the people who roamed the deserts centuries before the arrival of the first convict ships, and whose art and beliefs provide some kind of historic context for Australia's early Colonial history. It is a context into which too few Australians take the trouble to enquire. The reason seems to be not distrust so much as a total lack of curiosity.

Before I left, Mountford showed me an illustrated book on the paintings of Albert Namatjira, the aborigine artist who has lately won some fame, and whom the Queen visited when on her Royal Tour. They were mostly water-colours, Australian landscapes of pale gums against red plains and mauve hills, done in the European academic tradition, and remarkable considering how short a while Namatjira has been painting. Otherwise they seemed to me imitatively handled, without vitality or originality. 'Sir,' Dr Johnson said, 'a woman's preaching is like a dog's walking on his hinder legs. It is not done well: but you are surprised to find it done at all.' That, for me, expresses all there is to say about Namatjira and his associates, misguidedly at work in an old-fashioned and unsuitable style that can convey nothing of the interior life they lead, or the way they see their country. I looked wistfully at the gay, powerful cave and bark paintings scattered round us, so full of meaning and mystery, and asked if this was Namatjira's instinctive method of expression or whether he would naturally have painted in the primitive tribal manner. Mountford replied, resignedly: 'Namatjira gets fifty or sixty guineas for a water-colour; for an abstract picture like one of these bark paintings he'd be lucky to get anything at all.'

It was a sad comment, not only on Namatjira, who has picked up the tricks of his trade with astonishing facility, but on contemporary taste. I brooded unhappily in the swaying tram all the way up to Carrick Hill, resenting not those who had encouraged Namatjira in his belief that he could capture a likeness, but those who, ignorant of the aborigines' older means of communication, encouraged the idea that these pictures had anything to do with art.

* * *

Images of Adelaide, as we leave on the night train for Melbourne: the sweep of willows and poplars on the wide curve of the Torrens River, light streaming between them on trial eights and excursion launches and cruising swans. The comfortable grass banks of the Adelaide Oval, steep enough for you to watch the cricket lying down. The magnificent scoreboard above which the cathedral hoists itself through a tangle of sub-tropical trees. (These giant Australian scoreboards tell you much, but never the name of the catcher, nor, therefore, the position where a batsman was caught. And there are no scorecards as in England to refer to or to take away.) The sardine-silver beaches at Glenelg, where M.C.C. are staying—the surf slow and gentle, the light level. The sudden cool of Mount Lofty, after the airless heat of the town—gardens there have flowers and shrubs of England, the skyline is green, the air noisy with birds. In a few miles' ascent one exchanges climate and vegetation.

We trundle through the warm Australian night. From now on the cricket will be more intensive, though we could not have a narrower squeak than we had this week. Hutton has much to occupy him, and the arrival of Compton, happy as it is, increases the problems of team selection. Eighteen players is an absurd, as well as an uneconomical, figure. Yet despite our bad batting and cumbersome fielding, it will be nice to meet the Combined XI—the first real try-out—with three successive victories under the belt. Not a little perplexing too.

5 Melbourne under Water

Melbourne in Cup week: a city on a racing spree, a gambling *festa*. For Australians, gambling is a means of conversation. During a cricket match they will bet on the number of runs scored in an over, on what fielder will stop the next shot, on who takes the next wicket. At a tram stop I have heard them bet on how many passengers will alight, doubling up on how many get on. Probably this is compensation for the fact that, officially, off-the-course betting is illegal in Australia.

During Cup week the city changes hands, graziers, farmers, the men from the cattle stations, pouring in with their families. Melbourne is our first contact with a large Australian city, and, though the weather is awful, I like it tremendously. We have just missed the two big races, the Cup and the Oaks, but the crowds are still here. The Cup was won by the favourite, Rising Fast, a New Zealand horse unbeaten in seven races. Horses appear to race more frequently than in England, sometimes running on several successive Saturdays.

During the day the streets are empty. About five o'clock the buzz of traffic begins, and like a swarm of bees approaching the hive, steadily increases. The women returning for cocktail parties and balls look quite as smart as at Ascot. Melbourne has its quota of beauties. There is an effervescence in the air, a noisy excitement. At the moment, everybody one meets seems to be from the stations: I understand that when they depart at the week-end the townspeople come out of hiding and are allowed to manage their own affairs again. But there is no doubt as to who are the accepted aristocrats.

* * *

I'm staying at the Melbourne Club, comfortable, agreeably designed, greatly welcoming. I thought, after the races were over, to be quiet here and industrious; on the contrary, I have found myself drinking the clock round and invited to play billiards with eminent legislators until two and three each morning. Rain has contributed towards this, for a steady downpour has not ceased for three whole days. The match between M.C.C. and an Australian XI, which promised well, had to be abandoned at the week-end. After M.C.C. had collapsed once again on the best batting wicket yet, all out for 205 after being 130 for 2, Statham, Bailey and Bedser, taking between them 7 wickets for 167, bowled them back into a plausible position. Simpson made 74 with dash, but no great infallibility on the first day, May 45, and Graveney 22 not out. Simpson once more threw his wicket away, making a quite reckless stroke after being almost caught at extra cover the previous ball. It was an enjoyable innings all the same, full of fluent and graceful shots. The pity of it is that he has batted confidently ever since the nets at Perth: his succession of small scores, each of which has been compiled quickly, is due to a self-indulgence on which Hutton is unlikely to look tenderly. May, who, owing to the need to give even those unlikely to play in the Tests an innings, had to stand down at Adelaide immediately after having made a hundred, looked well on the way to another one, when he hooked a short ball hard to square leg. Compton was out chopping at a leg-break, but seemed until then perfectly at ease. Once he was out, six wickets fell for 32. Edrich struggled hard for 11. At Adelaide, Hutton, who was not playing in this match, brought Edrich on first change, in the hope of using him as a stock bowler in the Tests, but they were disillusioning and expensive overs. Edrich is deep in some hateful nightmare, and he will be a problem. Personally I would play him in the Tests even if he made no runs at all between now and then. His character and concentration are worth the easier strokes of his rivals: and his stature grows in a crisis, while theirs diminish.

However, I am probably alone in this, though Hutton has shown great understanding in his handling of him.

The middle batting generally is deplorable, and the old gentlemen in the club are rightly scornful. The innings ceases at the fall of the fourth wicket: the tail folds up as abruptly as a deck-chair under an obese man. The fielding, however, was better and Bedser, if not completely fit, had his first bowl of the tour. He did not get many past the bat, but he looked beautifully loose, was accurate and, in his second spell, moved one or two off the seam in the old way. This was the probable opening attack for the first Test, and it was hostile and economical. Statham took 2 wickets, Bailey 4: both bowled with fine intelligence and aim. 36,000 people watched the game on the Saturday, and with Ian Johnson, Neil Harvey, Bill Johnston, de Courcy, McDonald and Richie Benaud in the Australian XI, it was the nearest thing to a Test match so far. Harvey failed for the third time running and Johnson disposed of the middle English batting as easily and unaccountably as at Perth. Benaud looked greatly improved since he was in England: much sounder in defence, upright and fluent in attack. He also looked considerably more in control of his leg-breaks, though his action is too unvaryingly low for my taste. Archer and Drennan, who opened the Australian XI bowling, attacked the leg-stump with in-swingers and an array of short legs—a dreary attitude to adopt at the start of a match.

The loss of the last two days of this game must be a great blow to Hutton's plans, as well as a heavy financial loss. It is difficult enough keeping players in form when there is the full amount of play: this match has provided few clues, and Hutton must now decide whether to play most of the same side again or bring in the others. He has a real problem: but hard though it may be, he must put the needs of the Test side first.

I had not realized how loud and unceasing is the vocal commentary round the outer ring on Australian cricket grounds. Barely a ball goes by without drawing forth a jeer at batsman or bowler; the hubbub rises and falls, but is constant in some degree.

Nor, as I had imagined, is it informed comment. Usually, of course, it is only beer talking. Remarks rarely deviate from the expected, which is to say that theme and variation consist of 'Have a go, yer mug' for batsman, and 'Git a bag, yer mug' for fielders. These two phrases are used quite indiscriminately, as likely to be hurled at a batsman playing his first ball as at one who has hit the previous ball for six. If repetition is any component of wit, Australian crowds are vastly funny. Perhaps the Hill at Sydney is different: it could do with being so. This sounds waspish, but is unfortunately true. It may also be unfair, for the intelligent observer makes no generally audible remarks at all. It is the vocally obtuse minority who therefore carry the day.

Denis Compton, though recognized, was refused admittance at the turnstile, a bone-headed and self-righteous attendant demanding his ticket, which in fact had been left at the Windsor Hotel. Compton replied: 'Very well. In that case I shan't play. I'll go home,' whereupon he vaulted the railings and ran off to change. An endearing blow for freedom, but one which caused some consternation. Australian sports officials tend to be of literal and humourless character, guided too often by a misleading conviction that the spirit of the law has nothing to do with its application and that the issue of a uniform is tantamount to the bestowing of divine right, immune from obligations. This instance, not an isolated one, was symptomatic: a day or two later several M.C.C. players, returning from net practice elsewhere in blazers and flannels, were similarly held up, though their identity was not questioned. The constant suspicion and churlishness of minor officials could only be condoned if Australian crowds generally were a race of hooligans. This is not the case, for, if occasionally unruly, they are naturally genial.

* * *

Notes on D. H. Lawrence's *Kangaroo*. A fascinating novel, over-long and stuffed with irrelevancies, but marvellously true to the Australian landscape and character. Kangaroo himself, exponent of brotherly love as a political system, is one of the great characters of twentieth-century literature. Lawrence wrote, in 1926, about the freemasonry of the 'diggers,' of the veterans of the 1914–18 war, who conceived of a non-political organization which, by its camaraderie based on war-service, could oust the professional politicians from power. Politics in Australia is an altogether rougher pastime than in England, with different ancestry and practices. If, however, the intensely selective masonic hierarchies described by Lawrence no longer exist, nor exert the same pressure, the Returned Servicemen's League represents a modified form of the same freemasonry. All Australians who fought overseas were volunteers, and they are conscious of the rights that ought to derive from this willing interruption of their careers. Conscripts, known as 'chocos' (chocolate soldiers), were not required to serve outside prescribed areas of the Commonwealth. The R.S.L. badge is worn much as a Frenchman wears the *Légion d'Honneur* and it evokes a quiet pride of caste, at a superficial glance obtrusive to English eyes. The returned soldier, even more than the 'squattocracy' of the early settlers, owners for generations of the sheep and cattle stations, occupies a privileged place in Australian life, one which his English counterpart might well envy.

Lawrence, writing a quarter of a century ago, suggested with extraordinary prescience the subtle antagonisms that exist today behind the classless façades of Australian society—the battle between the unions and the employers, the Catholic Left Wing and the War Veteran Right, though these divisions have many inconsistencies. Lawrence, in fact, invented most of the political situations in *Kangaroo*, exaggerating the unrest and violence between Diggers and Socialists. But he seemed to understand instinctively the war between emotion and reason in the Australian conscience, and in the person of Kangaroo he created the advocate of an emotional abandonment, generous only so long as it was never thwarted. 'The old world is cautious and for ever bargaining about its soul. Here they don't bother to bargain,' Kangaroo says to the Englishman Somers. And Lawrence, in the person of Somers, rejects this mystical belief in the recklessness of love, in the religion of a comradeship that could quickly turn to unreasoning enmity.

Apart from its central examination of the divisions of loyalty in Australia, of the appeal to a growing society of different kinds of power, different labels of identification, *Kangaroo* provides descriptions of the coastal suburbs of New South Wales, of the bush behind Sydney, of the light and look of the country that no Australian writer has ever achieved.

* * *

Australian cricket grounds: one approaches them usually through gardens, the sun training, through squads of palms, on lily ponds and lakes, on petunia-bordered lawns dampening under the sprinkler. On my way to the Melbourne Cricket Ground, I walked up Collins Street, with its magnificent switchback of planes and elms, the only street in Australia which might be in Europe, across the Treasury gardens, the air smeared with roses and cedar, to where the green deepens under the Fitzroy trees. Melbourne Cricket Ground is across the railway, a vast oval, with chunky palms and grass verges forming an outer ring to it. The ground itself, unlike Perth and Adelaide, has no natural setting: its huge stands, being reinforced now and increased for the Olympic Games, bisect the sky, cutting out all outside life. Its capacity is over 120,000, the turf slopes gently, though less than at Lord's, and everyone sits in comfort. Once inside, however, one is impressed by its immensity but horrified by its ugliness. No gladiator or matador ever fought in a ring as crudely designed as this. It serves in winter as a football stadium and football has stamped its bleaker character on it. Cricket here, one feels, is a battle, not an art: statistics matter, not style. The spectacle is in the play and there is no backdrop to help it along. The Press Box is badly placed: behind wide long-on or third man.

Other arrangements for the Press in Australia make one

ashamed of English conditions. Honorary memberships are offered to visitors at most sporting clubs; excellent three-course lunches with chicken or lobster are provided free on all the grounds; service is admirably speedy. In England Press catering is generally poor and slow: moreover, visiting, as well as native, journalists are made to pay for meals, surely a needless parsimony.

In the Press Box we muster, all told, nearly forty. Relations are admirable. Before me, as I write in the Melbourne rain, typewriters pound, cable-boys scurry. Fingleton, Hassett, 'Tiger' O'Reilly, sit in a row immediately below, the years having taken various toll of their hair, but not of their wits, legend or stamina. Sidney Barnes, natty in Free Forester tie, laments his absence from the field of operations, also the fact that accredited Free Foresters should steal his thunder by wearing the same tie. Bill Bowes gazes through his glasses with an air of pity. Roberts, assistant to Norman Preston of Reuters, records the rapid fall of English wickets with honestly stricken countenance; though, a member of the Somerset Committee, he must be well used to it. Down in front, Jim Mathers, correspondent of *Truth*, fashions adjectives of explosive scorn. Rowbotham, steel-rimmed spectacles flashing, assembles his copious polemic for the *Guardian* of Manchester. To my right, Charles Bray and Crawford White, golfing cronies, examine play with the detachment suited to veterans of several tours. Preston looks over his glasses at his colleague, much in the way that Mr Pickwick observed Mr Winkle, alternatively joking and scolding—they are a fine pair, these Reuters opening batsmen. I can see Alex Bannister, master of the cynical understatement, Peebles brooding, made nostalgic by the rain for his native Inverness, the raised eyebrows of Swanton, elegant in Palm Beach suiting beside him. And next to me Woodcock, bending his head to his work, as Kilburn, hands clasped behind his back like an invigilator, surveys us all, deep in thought, nursing his admonitions for the *Yorkshire Post* with the gravity of a Canon preparing his Sunday sermon.

* * *

MELBOURNE UNDER WATER

Rain drips off the plane trees, hour after hour. Trams shuttle up Collins Street like noisy canal boats, bows breasting the leafed-over slope to the Treasury buildings. The shops, wide-paned, are deeply set like grottoes beneath the trees. People bear their umbrellas past the windows of the Melbourne Club as though part of their anatomy. Melbourne, like Perth and Adelaide, is a city of rectangular blocks, though the ups and downs of Collins Street create an illusion of curve. Parallel to Collins Street, Bourke and Lonsdale Streets, dipping down towards the sunset, are visible the whole way along their length. Streets of restaurants and furniture shops, dusty and drab and with the shabby cosmopolitanism of Tottenham Court Road. Yet they have a flavour, a garlicky, imported breath of alien vitality. Groups of Poles and Italians and Greeks huddle under shelters, hands deep in raincoat pockets. A negro hurries by, the rain dripping off his face, the colour in this damp dusk of elephant-skin. How soon, one wonders, will this transfusion of European blood, full of strange, warring characteristics alter the lazy Victorian rhythms of Australian life? Now that the pioneer, colonial flavour is rapidly disappearing, being replaced by a more closely integrated society, seeking the cities, dependent on secondary industries, the qualities that present and future generations of New Australians develop become of supreme importance. What in fifty years will Australia, no longer nursing so general a nostalgia (not without complex inhibitions) for the home country, represent in its ideals and affections? Today's paper publishes revealing figures about migrants. Since 1945 430,000 alien migrants, in addition to 416,240 British, have settled in Australia. The alien migrants figure is made up like this: 93,000 Italians, 71,000 Poles, 58,000 Dutch, 29,000 Germans, 25,000 Yugoslavs, 20,000 Russians and Ukranians, 18,000 Greeks, 13,000 Hungarians, 11,000 Czechs, 10,000 Lithuanians, 9,000 Americans. What will the 'home country' be then?

It is said that most migrants shed their former nationalities as naturally as a snake its skin, becoming quickly more Australian than Australians themselves. In certain places, though, cells develop—of Germans, of Dutch, of Greeks—in which facsimile European existences, with the customs and smells and dialects of the past lovingly cherished against isolation, are constructed as self-contained as in a honeycomb. But Australia has always been a country haunted by a sense of exile, its robuster citizens resolutely turning their backs on the sources of nostalgia, determined to find in their new continent a sustaining myth, a unique nationality. So it will continue to happen. Only now in more complex and absorbing ways.

Collins Street, storm-washed and deserted, has tonight a moving melancholy, its sweeping trees, Indian-blue at dusk, seeming to sail into the frail sunset like ships cast from their moorings. Across it Swanston Street and Elizabeth Street trail skyscrapers, general stores, and churches that might have been built by the Catalan architect, Gaudi. Lower down, reached by arcades, dim lanes and clubs and solicitors' offices form courtyards of dignified gloom, the watery tints of sunset spreading like transfers over shining cobbles. There are several of these secret dead-ends, smelling of printer's ink and beer, like the courts off Fleet Street. Being Sunday, nobody is about, the day of rest here more deathly even than in England, for papers are forbidden, only a few being smuggled in furtively from Sydney. Flinders Street railway station, squeezed in alongside the Yarra River, looms over Princes Bridge, an enlarged elongated Edwardian music-hall of a building in yellow stucco with coroneted green domes. Beyond this central block, Melbourne sprawls through parks and gardens into large areas of gardensuburbs. Australians hitherto have not taken to flats, so their towns move outwards rather than upwards. To inhabit a suburb is a mark of distinction, not of despair. Because of this, cities tend to have an area out of all proportion to their population.

The rain swilling down the gutters, the Sunday abstractedness, the afternoon *cafard*, induce a paralysing inertia. The leather and brass and padded quiet of the Melbourne Club exaggerate this, nor is it dispelled by a dinner of turtle soup, *filet mignon*, Hunter River claret and brandy of incendiary sharpness. All the same, these senior clubs of Australia deserve an elegy. They provide good food, varied conversation, and an attention to the details of service, which, without being obtrusive, are not offered by Australian hotels—or by very few of them. The Melbourne Club has a cloakroom of such delicacy that mirrors placed obliquely allow one to observe whether the various compartments, partly screened in anyway, are occupied, without need to approach and thereby risk disturbing members. The members of the clubs, unlike most Australians, seem to care about their meals. 'I look upon it,' Johnson, I believe, wrote, 'that he who does not mind his belly, will hardly mind anything else'—or words to that effect. If he had no passion for clean linen, Johnson at least maintained a respect for the pleasures of the table.

* * *

Monday is better, still raining, but the digestive juices better for their rinsing. Unfortunately, further exploration of Melbourne will have to wait till our return in the New Year. Only frogmen are abroad today. I should like to have walked along the river, but the barges are all tarpaulined and the railway goods-yards gleam as wetly as in a French film. These hotel-confined days are murder for cricketers, so early on in a tour. Later they have their uses. But now everyone is anxious to be about and doing, and this delay is bad for nerves. It makes the tour seem a long while getting under way, too.

6 Approaches to Sydney

We left Melbourne on the night train, changing at Albury into sleepers, and jogging noisily northwards out of the Victorian rain. By dawn we were under clear skies, green slushy paddocks stretching away from the track to the pink foothills of the Great Dividing Range. The pale stems of gums, their branches like sprays of nerves, hardened in the mounting light, the sun coming up fast over the eastern spurs and glinting over sudden pools and overflows.

The outskirts of Sydney: miles and miles of bungalow suburbs, whole districts one-storey high, looking as if they had been lopped off by a butcher's knife. Each house with its patch of lawn, its washing hanging up to dry, its goat tethered under a smoky jacaranda. Raw red tiles, squat ugly boxes of cement, verandahs with pale piano-leg fluting. A girl lay out in a patch of sun, drinking coffee in her pyjamas. Chalked upon a wall in huge letters was the sentence TERROR AND VIOLENCE IN SOVIET RUSSIA. Sydney bridge, a smudge of distant silver, appeared momentarily through the smoke, then was lost as the train plunged into tunnels. Warehouses, signal-boxes, liver-coloured side-streets jerked out their advertisements. Leaving the compartment I noticed that it cost £10 to pull the communication cord.

* * *

The match against New South Wales, played in lovely weather, followed the familiar pattern, the scoreboard during England's innings resembling its usual over-indulged, still digesting snake—neither head nor tail, a huge bulge in the middle. In this instance the bulge was provided both times by Hutton and Cowdrey.

M.C.C., sent in to bat on the first day by Miller, lost four wickets for 38 on a wicket that was early lively, but with scarcely more juice in it at lunch than bitters in a pink gin. Hutton and Cowdrey made 102 and 110 respectively, whereupon the last five wickets subsided for under a dozen. The pitch, watered overnight, in the first hour was greenish, and Crawford, a tall, thin young bowler of high action and some pace, made the ball swing away considerably, occasionally very late. Edrich and Simpson were both brilliantly caught at slip, May, for whom Miller at once produced Treanor to bowl leg-breaks, taken at the wicket, and Wilson caught off Miller. During their partnership of 163 Hutton and Cowdrey scored almost at a run a minute, using their feet, Cowdrey more than Hutton, to drive the leg-breaks of Benaud and Treanor, and push away the quicker bowling of Davidson and Crawford. It was batting of honourable lineage, unruffled and commanding, with every short or over-pitched ball being hit to the boundary, as though no alternative existed. Timing and placing alike were perfect, Cowdrey the more correct and economical in his positioning of the feet, Hutton making up for a slight shuffling of his left foot, which moves twice to get to the right place, by the inclining of the body and the pointing of the left shoulder. Driving to the off, Hutton's body from shoulder to knee follows the arc of the bat as loosely and gracefully as a sail. Hutton finally was bravely caught by Davidson at short extra cover, Davidson, as he was to do several times later to Hutton, clinging on to a fierce hit. Incidentally, Hutton in this innings was struck nastily on the knee quite early on. M.C.C. being all out for 252, there was time for Bedser and Tyson to bowl one over each at the end of the day. Off Bedser's Morris, as though enraged by the cherry-redness of the ball, produced four exotic and audacious strokes that brought him 14 runs. Next morning he was soon out, seemingly off-colour and out of touch, Bedser duly claiming his 'rabbit.' Watson, a schoolboyish figure engulfed by his cap, playing in only his second state match because of an injury to Briggs, the regular opener, was joined by Miller at 50 for 2. Miller, in the proconsular manner one had thought never to see again, barely bothered to shake the hair out of his eyes before hitting Bedser several times high and hard to the mid-wicket fence. Thereafter he made a series of glances that slid the ball as smoothly as off a billiard shot to the fine-leg boundary. The rich, green outfield, as flawless as any I have seen, had a baize-like nap on it. Having scored fifty, Miller square-cut the next thirty or so of his runs with the exactness of a practised executioner. Wilson caught him eight feet up, one-handed at mid-wicket, for 86. He never once batted like this in England in 1953. Watson, dwarfed physically but in no other way, delighted a huge crowd, packed close and as variously undressed on the Hill as Brighton beach on a Bank Holiday, by scoring run for run with Miller. He gets resolutely behind the ball, drives it pleasantly through the covers, but scores mostly by leaning away and lashing square off the back foot with vigorous follow-through. When Miller was out, Watson, growing ever redder in the face, went happily to his century, his first in any class of adult cricket, and an occasion that was later reported to have brought him to tears. If true, there were few signs of them for, after one or two obligatory swishes, he got his head down again and batted out the day. He must now join Favell as a Test possible. M.C.C.'s score was passed before tea, and though De Courcy, struggling for a Test place, declined to bat in dubious light in the evening, New South Wales finished up 290 for 4. Next morning Tyson, whose improvement these last weeks has been consistent, again bowled with great life and accuracy, and N.S.W. were put out for 382, a lead of 130. With a day and a half to go, M.C.C. made yet another appalling start. Hutton, having enterprisingly decided to experiment with two new opening batsmen, this time sent in Cowdrey and Wilson. Wilson was yorked for 0, fourth ball of the innings, by Crawford, and at 39 Simpson, who was dropped when 0 at the wicket, had his middle stump knocked back. May hit a no-ball for six, but soon after drove Treanor accurately to De Courcy at close mid-wicket. Edrich, marching in as doggedly as to a court-martial, which, for him, batting must now resemble, played more recognizably and, with Cowdrey batting as if in continuation of his first innings, M.C.C. reached 138 for 3 by stumps—8 runs on.

The last day was anti-climax, but a welcome one for M.C.C. Though Edrich was out for 37 at 158, Cowdrey and Hutton together made the game safe. Cowdrey reached his second century, joining A. C. Maclaren, Rhodes and Sandham in the small company of those that have scored two hundreds in a match against N.S.W. Hutton, going in No. 6, made 87 without apparent effort, and the tail, with no great responsibilities, ensured that N.S.W. would not get within distance even of moral victory. Set to make 198 in two hours, they settled for 78 for 2.

Cowdrey, after an indifferent innings or two, seems now to have shed a becoming, but inhibiting, modesty. He played throughout his two centuries without a shadow of uncertainty, the margin for error as negligible as in Hutton's own technique. His on-driving was exquisitely balanced, the bowler and mid-on, or mid-on and mid-wicket, bisected as though dividers had been placed between them, and the exact spot marked. He showed complete certainty of what, and of what not, to play on the off, hoisting his bat in commanding silhouette to anything moving away. The manner in which a player lets a ball go by is a nice test of æsthetics, as well as of judgment. Cowdrey leaves a ball more splendidly than anyone playing in cricket today, with the possible exception of George Cox. Whereas Hutton covers up thoughtfully, quietly resting for a few seconds before the next ball, Cowdrey strikes an attitude. Hutton, of course, has no truck with elaboration: his style is reduced to essentials, beautiful in the economy of its technique. His scores to date have been 145 (retired hurt), 37, 98, 102, 87: preliminary innings, when it seemed his wish was not to tire himself. Alas, he has had no alternative: each innings has been, if not a Test match innings, one in which his side's prestige was gravely threatened. It is grossly unfair, and one can only marvel humbly at him.

Cowdrey's comment on receiving congratulations was simply: 'I was batting each time with Hutton'—as if that was somehow quite enough to explain his success. In his eyes it probably is. More's the pity that Hutton's batting has not the same effect on others.

Sydney Cricket Ground, its superb playing surface apart, because that I did expect, was a pleasant surprise. I had imagined the Hill vast and bare; instead, the fine scoreboard is flanked by lush green banks, neither ugly nor intimidating. Stands and pavilion are eccentrically various in architecture, domes and pagodas painted in greens and pale blue, and flags fluttering gaily from them. From the Press Box, which looks from a considerable height up and down the wicket, you can see, across intervening palm trees, the distant bay where Captain Cook first landed. In front are the clock tower, stands and waterwheel of the Show ground. Inside, the atmosphere is dignified and genial, the seats sprinkled with the colour of women's dresses—women form much larger a part of the crowd here than in England—and the flavour of the cricket rather like Lord's on a sunny day.

* * *

Hutton's problem thus far has been whether to keep his successful batsmen in form or to persist with his failures, the second being the more numerous category. On the whole, he has inclined to the latter, with the result that no single batsman except himself has gone to the wicket truly in form. May, after making a hundred at Perth, has played little; he failed twice in this match, and must now be back where he started. Graveney, who has yet to make a score of 35, was incomprehensibly not picked here, but is surely a Test probable. He will have batted only once in a month. Compton, too, could well have done with some practice against Miller. Eighteen players is an impossible burden for any captain: it has been increased by Hutton's inability, through no fault of his own, to arrive at a probable estimate of the Test side, and to keep their needs in mind, regardless of human kindness. Hutton has obviously wanted to play Edrich, though whether he ought to persist with him after scores of 0, 0, 2, 7, 11, 7 and 37, the last score made at No. 5, is a matter of opinion. Wilson, the best fielder we have, has lately made 9, 4, 9, 0. Simpson, the alternative No. 2 to Edrich, has not often made runs with Hutton, who, in any case, is no great advocate of back play against the new ball. Simpson, as if aware of this, has batted with a kind of desperate charm. Cowdrey's success at No. 2 complicates matters still further, for, however he fares against Queensland, it is asking a lot of him to open the innings against Lindwall and Miller in his first Test match.

The bowling is another matter, for with Bedser gradually warming up, we have four quick-to-medium bowlers in Statham, Tyson, Bedser and Bailey, all of whom have done more than enough to deserve a place at Brisbane. Tyson has taken 5 and 4 wickets in the first innings of the last two matches he has played in, and he will be hard to leave out. Statham and Bailey have bowled exceptionally well. If we had five reliable Test batsmen one could play all four and add Wardle, who in his only long bowl, at Melbourne, looked more likely to seal up an end than either Appleyard or McConnon. Wardle has still to make double figures, nor has he bowled much, but he is an astute defensive bowler and Hutton tends to think of slow bowlers largely in that way. Myself, I should like to see him try his chinaman more, and take wickets. Hutton's reluctance to use Appleyard resulted in the second new ball being wasted both at Adelaide and here. Appleyard has, for some reason, constantly attacked the leg stump at medium pace, which seems an error of judgment for, since Hutton is virtually committed out of necessity to playing six batsmen in the first Test, Appleyard, using flight and spin, could still be the all-purpose bowler who would provide a varying contrast to Statham, Bedser and Bailey. His fielding has brightened up a lot.

Generally, M.C.C.'s fielding against N.S.W. bordered on the mutinous, Evans needing as many and as long arms as an Indian idol to deal with the throws that came wildly above, wide and short of him. On present form, we can expect to give away 20 or 30 runs a day in the field to the Australians, and to miss a similar number in our own running between the wickets. We can ill afford either.

However, we shall go to Queensland undefeated, albeit by the skin of our teeth, and with basic problems still to solve.

* * *

Again Sunday, but the sun shining and the air fizzy as soda. Sydney has a bustling, noisy vulgarity intoxicating after the dismal rain-filled afternoons of Melbourne. Today, however, the streets are empty, the light beating off the panes of closed shop-windows and deserted pavements. This time we are here only for six days. First impressions are of the hardness of the light, the congestion of the narrow streets, which, even the central ones, follow the old bullock tracks down to Circular Quay, the charm of the dockside houses, the ugliness of the new ones. Elizabeth, Castle, Pitt and George Streets form the main rectangular block, within which are shops, cinemas, hotels, banks and offices. Sydney has developed upwards more than Melbourne, though despite the efforts of Governor Macquarie and his quarrelsome architect of genius, Francis Greenway, order and ambition have had no place in its growth. Greenway, trained in the late-Georgian style of the west country and deported in 1812 for forgery, produced, in his five years as Civil Architect of the Colony, a number of buildings that survive today, mutilated most of them, as the first examples of genuine Australian architecture—brilliantly adapted to situation, materials and climate, harmonious and elegant. He and Macquarie planned to redesign the city on a spacious and grand scale, but unfortunately Greenway's temperament and indolent, demanding character caused them to disagree, the plans were shelved, and their successors, economical and visionless men, showed no desire to implement them. Yet, mean and dowdy though much of Sydney is in conception, and impossible though it is not to regret the squandering of such unique opportunities, it remains a city to fall in love with. Greenway, in St James Church and the Hyde Park Barracks (now the Law Courts), has left his mark on its centre, which, despite overcrowding, has an alternating solidity and vitality, crudeness and occasional miraculous proportion, to be exciting. 'Love still has something of the sea'—Sedley's one good line—and it is the sea, flashing and ferrying, that holds Sydney together. King's Cross, Woolloomooloo, Miller's Point—there is enough of what is loosely called 'Old Colonial' here to show how agreeable much of Sydney must have looked. The sea, too, reaches into the city, bearing the smell of brine, and tar and sacking. Funnels of ocean-going liners breach the gaps between the palms as intimately as chimneys, and the hoot of tugs, the departure sirens of ships, mingle with the jangle of trams and traffic, part of daily life. Amongst the brashness and crush of contemporary Sydney, it is impossible to lose the feel of the old, pioneering days—of the arrival of the racing wool clippers, of Captain Philip landing from the *Supply* in Sydney Cove, of the cattle-trekkers and the convict-masons (of whom the Lieutenant-Governor, Ross, wrote: 'I think it will be cheaper to feed the convicts on turtle and venison at the London Tavern than be at the expense of sending them here), of the saloon brawls and the covered-wagons and the gold hunters. All this seems to me to be in the air of Sydney, as evident to the senses as the lemon-gums and flame-trees, the pink iron-bark and wheel-trees of the Domain.

* * *

A city of banks and shipping offices, the warm malt smell of beer drifting out among flower-stalls and kiosks. Within a few yards of my hotel in Castlereagh Street the slim green spire of St James's Church halts one in the midst of the traffic. Five minutes' walk takes you to Hyde Park, where, as in London, impassioned orators cry in the night, or to the Botanic Gardens, where Moreton Bay fig trees, like giant magnolias, splay over a steep green slope to the harbour. In the shade of one of these sticky, umbrella-shaped trees, with their large shiny leaves, you can lie out and gaze at the ferries splashing from Port Jackson to the north shore suburbs, to Mosman and Cremorne and Manly, to Curl Curl and The Spit. The water is a smoked blue, the cars hum over the bridge four lines abreast, and beside you the skyscrapers of Macquarie Street—the Harley Street of Sydney—rise up behind orderly palms. Alongside them, squat colonial buildings, their elaborate wrought-iron balconies stuffed with plants, taper down to the sea.

Nearby, Greenway's old convict barracks, the original proportions spoiled by additions, and Sydney hospital, lead you to Queen's Square, where the trams to the 'Cross' swirl round in a circle like merry-go-rounds. Hyde Park itself, with its benches and flowers and fountain, is bisected by William Street making its long climb up to King's Cross, the capital of New Australia, where immigrants have recreated Europe out of nostalgia. The air smells of garlic, the inhabitants dress as if in Montparnasse, the delicatessen shops and cafés stay open far into the night, and Australian is a foreign language. Girls wear horse's tails and trousers instead of the psychotic hats and white gloves of Castlereagh Street. South of King's Cross, tilting on the Surry hills, the old honeycomb suburbs of grimy wooden shacks, corrugated-iron roofs, and unpainted verandahs, are jammed together in tight disorder. The tram to Sydney cricket ground jangles through them, dipping and twisting to show segments of other hills, tomato-tiled and compressed as in a cubist painting. Further out, the recreation grounds are linked together as firmly as elephants' trunks and tails, ovals in single file, with cricket going on against backgrounds of gum trees and beeches, cathedrals, churches, synagogues and cinemas. Oases of green exist all over Sydney: Rushcutters Bay Park and Belmore, Randwick racecourse, and, nearer the centre, the Domain, its neat lawns overlooked by the National Art Gallery and the Mitchell Library, the Law Courts, Parliament House and Sydney Hospital.

These are all Sydney, yet not Sydney: for Sydney means the harbour, that great starfish of water, with its 152 miles of bays and points and coves and inlets. Along it, houses of every shape and size hug the foreshore, which, from the mile opening at The Heads to the inner reaches of the Parramatta River, is, as the crow flies, only sixteen miles. Nowhere in the world do so many people live poised above the quick blues of an ocean: not in Rio de Janeiro nor in San Francisco, not in Singapore, nor in Naples.

* * *

Today, a long Sunday of unbroken sun, we have cruised through every inlet between the bridge and the ocean. The Cricketers Club of New South Wales, hosts for the day, provided a launch, inviting M.C.C. and correspondents for a harbour picnic. Some two dozen of us, Cowdrey, McConnon, Appleyard and Andrew among the players, Geoffrey Howard, George Duckworth, Arthur Gilligan, Lindsay Hassett, and various writers, participated in an orgy of oyster eating. When these ran out, heaped plates of chicken and prawn were laid out in the sun and cases of beer hoisted from the hold. We ate, drank, sun-baked and rested, meanwhile nosing gently into shark-proof beaches and past headlands, their names sufficient litany to any who know them: Farm Cove, Woolloomooloo Bay, Potts Point, Double Bay, Point Piper, Rose Bay, Vaucluse, Watson's Bay; and on the north shore, Manly, Clontarf, Chinaman's Bay, Taronga Park. We crossed between North and South Head, anchoring awhile in Middle Harbour, and walking on the white sands to digest the excesses of lunch. By early afternoon scores of yachts were twisting in the breeze like clumps of orchids, each clump graded in size, V.J's, 16-footers and 18-footers, streaming up towards their various starting points.

The race of the day, for Sunday is racing day, was the M.C.C. Cricket Tourists Handicap for 18-footers, and through the melting afternoon we followed them from buoy to buoy, Lindsay Hassett opening oysters with professional skill, spinnakers of every colour billowing out around us. The harbour, however, is not the exclusive preserve of sailing boats, and a dozen ancient ferries, in the style of the Mississippi steam-boats, pursued them urgently, so laden with passengers and low in the water that those on the lower deck found it necessary to remove their shoes. An innocent might imagine them pure devotees of the lovely arts of sailing; but, in truth, each ferry carries quantities of beer, blares out canned music and echoes to the shouts of bevies of bookmakers, whose turnover on these outings is reckoned in thousands of pounds.

In the westering sun the harbour begins to lose some of its garish, picture-postcard qualities. Bungalows, villas and baroque residences glow like Japanese paper houses under their halters of green foliage. Headlands, with their tight curl of trees, acquire shadows and softnesses. In the day Sydney harbour is all dazzle: rinds of white beach, blistering stone, the busy commerce of boats. When the sun dips, it hauls down the perspectiveless cruelties of this southern light, softening harsh outlines with pools of graded shadow. By day Sydney displays an extrovert prettiness, a clean vitality: at night it acquires romantic beauty.

* * *

The newspapers, at the moment, debate as hotly as an election this week's referendum on whether the N.S.W. licensing hours should be extended from 6 p.m. to 10 p.m. As I write, voting is about even.* The situation at present is that the working man leaves his place of employment at five o'clock, goes straight to the nearest beer counter, and crams as much beer down his throat in an hour as he can manage. Last orders are taken just before six, and by ten-past all glasses have to be removed. The common practice is for a man to line up six or seven 'schooners' before the bar is closed, then to drink them one after another in the ten minutes left to him. The consequences

* The 10 p.m. voters won by a small majority, and the hours have been accordingly altered.

of this are not difficult to imagine. Last night five men were curled up in five successive doorways just behind my hotel: the time was half-past seven. In Melbourne a week ago a man, arrested for drunkenness, was reported to have drunk forty beers in seventy minutes. (He excused himself by saying that he was 'trying to get to a party.')

This evening ritual, known amongst Australians as the 'six o'clock swill,' is supported by two large and powerful groups: the brewers and the Methodists, 'wowsers' as they are called here. The brewers own the pubs, drab drink shops of the Dickens era, and the way things are, can sell as much beer between five and six as they could hope to between five and ten. By doing so, they save in overheads, at the same time being absolved from the effort of having to make their places of business agreeable.

The Methodists support them, as usual for the wrong reasons —namely, that later closing will mean more drunkenness. They encourage housewives to believe that, if the licence was extended, their husbands would stay away from home, and family life be further disrupted. The price they pay for this myth is that they come home drunk. Social life ceases at dusk, and the neon-lit streets of Australian cities are turned into illuminated tombs. If you are staying in a hotel, you may have drinks up to almost any hour in your bedroom: but you may not drink in a public room, such as a lounge; so should you have a guest, he or she must virtually drink on your bed—a positive incitement to immorality.

Naturally, every intelligent Australian wants the extension, even though the next phase might be one of its abuse. But once the change was made, and drinking became a social activity, not a furtive debauch, hostel-keepers would have to improve their premises and compete for custom. Sooner or later, the change will come; but, as in Victorian England, it has to battle against vested interests and obsolete moral codes, which, in the name of purity, merely encourage dissipation.

* * *

At night the harbour flashes and winks, a pale haze of light like a great mosquito net hung over the city. The stars are hard as tinfoil, the motifs of the sky repeated in water. Ferries drift gently as fireflies through the soft heavy-lidded dark. Trams sway noisily up William Street, past the rusted tenements of Bourke Street. The moon coats the few remaining Georgian-Colonial cottages round Miller's Point with colourless varnish: down here streets tip up at all angles from the harbour, the iron lacework, brought out as ballast in the convict ships, glinting on the balconies of condemned houses. The bridge is a dark weight overhead, and across the quays of Walsh Bay and Darling Harbour the lights of Balmain flick on and off between the funnels of liners. No one disturbs these paper-thin stage sets, deserted except for the rare cruising car. Yet these empty vistas of weather-boarding and overhanging eaves, of delicate columns and fluted wooden verandahs curving away in formal lines under the throbbing stars, retain, more than anywhere, the essential flavours of early Sydney—the Sydney of Verge and Greenway, of Watts and Lennox and Lewis, creators of an imperial dream under an ambitious governor, who, 12,000 miles from his capital, built out of a convict settlement a city splendidly opposed to the modest intentions of its responsible Ministers. Sydney was a fluke metropolis, whose luck failed to last: its Georgian pioneers were flattened by the second wind of Victorian prosperity, and now it has no past, but only a future, which its architects must dream without ever looking backwards.

7 North to Brisbane

The players flew yesterday north to Brisbane where I have just arrived after nineteen hours in the train—the result of a pious resolve made in Perth that I would travel the breadth of Australia by the slowest route possible. I believe that in a new country one should always do this the first time. Probably from now on I shall fly, but at least I will have seen what much of Australia looks like.

In a train, too, one learns about people. From Perth to Adelaide I shared a compartment with a retired bootmaker from Sydney. He had saved up for a six-months holiday to see the Australian continent at his leisure; alas, it disappointed him, for I saw him at Sydney Cricket Ground three weeks after we first met, and he confessed himself thankfully home. He was a rough, frisky, knowledgeable man, with a hatred of women. 'Proper ratbags,' he informed me when we were hardly out of Perth, 'I let one under my guard once, Ruby she were called, and she fell heir to a posh hotel. Worth £20,000, my oath, but I wouldn't marry her if she were worth a million. Not knowing what I do now.' But he wouldn't say more, though I tried hard to elicit the particular deceptions he nursed in his imagination. I did learn, however, that his misogyny was not derived from early romantic disillusion: he was sixty-nine now, and Ruby, it transpired, had occurred only five years earlier. At each station at which we stopped, he hurried out for reinforcements of beer, recounting in between swigs at the bottle the exact scores of various of his heroes in Test matches at the turn of the century. 'That Druce, aw, he batted well at Sydney in '97, Monty Noble got him leg-before for 64. Aw, I remember that well, Trumble got him second hand for 18. Aw, we gave you a lamming then, Joe Darling took 160 off of Richardson, Briggs and Hearne, easy as pie. Ranji, batting No. 7 in the first Test, feeling crook 'e were, gave Ernie Jones and Trumble a terrible drubbing, 175 'e were afore McKibbin had him caught Gregory, aw, I remember that, my oath, and in 1901 before Christmas Barnes and Braund ran through us like a dose of salts. Albert Relf, I remember 'm well, and, aw, that Lilley was a keeper. Trumper 'e were me favourite though . . .' I had the Playfair *Book of Test Records* with me and he dared me to doubt his figures. 'Don't take me word, look it up, strike me down before God if Foster never retired with the 'flu at Melbourne Second Test in 1903, naw, you can't catch me. I'll lay yer 10–1 Clem Hill was bowled Braund for a duck at Sydney in the second innings 1901.'

He had been to England once, with the A.I.F. in 1918, and knew all the pubs round the Elephant and Castle, and even more about the genealogy of the Royal Family. A splendid fellow, I grew greatly fond of him, even though he snored vilely and was occasionally sick; his parting words to me were: 'Well, Lord Byron, don't let the ratbags get at you: aw, yer'll love Sydney, I'll bet yer do.'

In this train to Brisbane I have bunked beneath an engineer Warrant Officer, who trained hereabouts during the war. He pointed out to me the lonely hilltops on which he had bivouacked, the forest where a twenty-foot tree python had curled round his arm, the valley in which an opossum had jumped accidentally on the trigger of an N.C.O's rifle and fired it, to the great consternation of itself and others.

Admittedly, this journey has not otherwise been especially stimulating: the track is narrow and bumpy, and sleep was out of the question. Also in Australia the landscape changes slowly: one need only look out of the window every two or three hours. Even then one may pick up an identical view. At 6 this morning —having left Sydney at 7.40 last night—we de-trained, as the military say, for breakfast at Coff's Harbour. Then, for ten minutes, we circled a calm bay with two humps of rock at either end of it, our last view of the sea, for immediately we turned inland and climbed steadily. It was slow going, cattle country, with ghost gums rising here and there over coarse grass, gradually giving way to steep, thickening forests. Not far off, the mauve rocks of the Great Dividing Range presented and removed themselves as we seemed to revolve on a lathe, the track softly floating on mattresses of purple weed, known as Paterson's Curse. Sweating, bare-chested men working on the line, New Australians mostly, doing their two-year penance, cheered ironically as the train grunted past, away from them into the bush. We stopped once or twice at small towns, dairying or timber centres, their single, wide road edged with the vivid gardens of iron-roofed bungalows. Casino and the Clarence River were almost obscured by foaming jacaranda trees, frothy blue umbrellas over houses built on stilts, a design that has the triple merit of allowing the air to circulate beneath them, of keeping away the white ants and providing garage space. Sometimes a ti-tree, its foliage spattered white like a blown-up cauliflower, thrust through the gums, or a pink orchid tree hung like a parasol against the rolling line of blue hills spilling along the horizon.

On the Queensland border it began to rain. Over the pole-supported suburban homes and steel bridges of Brisbane, clouds curled like a giant octopus, emitting at regular intervals slow, heavy drops of liquid.

* * *

The Queensland match, which was drawn, produced the dullest cricket of the tour. Rain was partly responsible, reducing Saturday's play to under two hours, but Queensland batted with painstaking tedium and the match was not very cleverly handled. In fact, it was not handled at all. Hutton did not play.

The start was as usual: M.C.C. 18 for 3, after being put in on a comfortably-paced pitch, with a spot just short of a length at one end. Cowdrey, who went in with Simpson, pushed Lindwall for 4 off his legs before edging the next ball, a swinging half-volley, to the wicket-keeper. Bailey, appearing at No. 3, was bowled off his pads in the same over for 0, the ball starting outside the leg stump and hitting the middle and off. At the other end, Archer bowled, and May was unlucky to get one that kicked as he played back, the ball curving gently off the shoulder of his bat to gully; 18–3–0. However Simpson, for once not batting like a man with a high temperature, and Compton, happily at ease, produced strokes of a kind that Queenslanders, judging by their own batsmen, can rarely have seen. They were together at lunch, by which time the occasional demons of noon had departed, they saw the 200 up, and both reached hundreds that were as enjoyable to watch as they were technically faultless. Lindwall bowled with lovely run-up and control, swinging late and not despising the bouncer, three of which he bowled to Compton in a row. Two leg-spinners and a slow left-armer were hit by each player to all points of the compass, Lindwall and Archer becoming lesser powers as the sun mounted. When Simpson reached his hundred, each of our probable first five Test batsmen had done so: yet every M.C.C. innings has depended absolutely on two players. Simpson, even when hitting, betrays no effort: he is a most beautifully co-ordinated player, his timing and balance removing all angularities of movement. His strokes truly flow, there are no distinguishable stages to them. Compton, in comparison, is natural in a different way, a batsman of invention, of imagination and power and resolution. One is never aware of Simpson, the man, at the wicket. Not that he is colourless or coldly correct. But his vast human fallibilities are controlled by a style of such smoothness that the man is submerged by it. Compton batting is always a person first, a cricketer second, which makes his success or failure always a matter of human concern. It has taken him four years since his knee operation to return to the heavily-guarded gates of greatness. In youth, Compton's batting was free and lovely as a sailing boat freshly catching the breeze. He played county cricket as one indulging children on the sands: he dreamed a little in the slips, was forgetful and romantically vague. Yet, in Test matches, his great achievements, like those of Hutton, were for losing sides. He batted in shadow with a mastery of technique and a resourcefulness that came surprisingly from one whose arts seemed a charming endowment, rather than the fruits of study. But Compton has never lacked character: grace has only been the sugaring, not the essence, of his style. Then, like Icarus, he flew too close to the sun and his wings melted. But, unlike Icarus, the sea cooled him into new life, streamlining him, tempering his metal. In 1953 in England he laboured patiently and nobly for runs, when before it had been they who had sought him out. He put to flight the evil geniuses, and the Sirens returned once more to whisper to him from their distant rocks. In the West Indies that winter they called louder, more seductively: against Pakistan he made runs as on the beach. Now he is like one called back by gods who, having run out of heroes, fondly recall an old favourite. But gods, alas, are creatures of whim, on who one does ill to rely.

The rest of the Queensland match resembled more than anything the third day of a county game, when there is nothing at stake. Compton and Simpson were out at the same score, 232, M.C.C., apart from a stout 30 by Bedser, then throwing away their hard-won advantages. Three players scored 276 of their 304 runs. One has ceased to expect anything else when the fourth wicket falls, one now just waits for the bump.

On the Saturday it rained. *L'anatomia presuppone il cadavere;* anatomy presupposes the corpse, as D'Annunzio observed, and there was little corpse to dissect that day. On Monday Queensland took very many hours over scoring 288, and, though M.C.C. lost Cowdrey and Andrew for 8, there was by then little interest left. Wilson, who added scores of 4 and 0 in this match to his previous failures, must now have written himself off. He has resisted many wooings to success, though a stalwart and nice man. May and Compton thrashed some bowling, which, in Lindwall's absence with gastric trouble, was of the country house variety. Bailey tuned himself up with 51 not out. It is, one often feels, scarcely worth his while batting except in

Test matches, for friendly cricket exposes his flaws without summoning up his virtues. The game petered out, with Wilson and Simpson opening the bowling in the Queensland second innings, and Compton signing autographs with his back to the wicket during play. It was fair comment.

Brisbane hardly looks a Test match ground. From the Press Box, sections of it are not without unpretentious charm. Weeping fig trees curve round a wide arc of banked grass, spattering it with their shade, and Mount Gravatt, a tight curl of forest, rears up in the distance between two covered stands like a negro's head. People lie out on the banks, blobs of white against green and blue, in the manner of a Frith painting. The pavilion, however, has roughly the dignity of a lavatory, and the members' stands, separated by wire-netting like hen-runs, are ugly to look at and uncomfortable to sit in. Beyond them, rows of dingy corrugated-iron shacks emphasise a kind of prisoner-of-war atmosphere. Perhaps when full it will look better.

* * *

This afternoon, two days before the Test is due to begin, Hutton announced his team in this batting order: Hutton, Simpson, May, Cowdrey, Compton, Edrich, Bailey, Evans, Tyson, Bedser, Statham. Six batsmen, four pace bowlers, no spinner. The last two days, when the wicket should take spin, will therefore be no use to us. Hutton has virtually committed himself to putting Australia in if he wins the toss. Should Australia survive the first hour we shall be in trouble, for they have the spinners to make England's batting on the last day a painful affair. It is not the kind of gamble I care for, for whoever wins the toss Australia will surely bat first, which on the face of it is not cricket sense. Graveney was not considered for the side, for he has been ill with stomach trouble. McConnon was hit in the groin during the Queensland match and is in hospital. Wardle has scarcely looked the part. Evans, though selected, is at the moment in bed with a temperature and violent headache, and by no means certain to play.

Australia's team is: Morris, Favell, Miller, Harvey, Hole, Benaud, Archer, Lindwall, Langley, Johnson, and Johnston, with Davidson the probable 12th man. Ian Johnson is captain, Morris vice-captain.

Hutton has been much criticized for the inclusion of Edrich and the exclusion of Wardle. About Edrich he has shown great courage, which deserves to be rewarded. If a slower bowler were to play I should now have preferred Appleyard. Hutton's argument is doubtless that a good seam bowler who can cut the ball is worth more on a wearing wicket than an untidy spinner who does not genuinely spin. And none of our spinners do. But our bowling, if not immediately successful, will be fearfully monotonous. We shall need to catch all our catches.

It is a great moment. Excitement here is tremendous, and it will not be only the players who will have butterflies in the stomach when the first overs are being bowled.

8 The First Test Match

November 26 — December 1

AUSTRALIA

L. Favell, c. Cowdrey, b. Statham	23
A. R. Morris, c. Cowdrey, b. Bailey	153
K. R. Miller, b. Bailey	49
R. N. Harvey, c. Bailey, b. Bedser	162
G. Hole, run out	57
R. Benaud, c. May, b. Tyson	34
R. Archer, c. Bedser, b. Statham	0
R. Lindwall, not out	64
G. Langley, b. Bailey	16
I. Johnson, not out	24
Extras (b. 11, l.b. 7, n.b. 1)	19
Total (8 wkts. dec.)	601

FALL OF WICKETS. 1—51, 2—123, 3—325, 4—456, 5—463, 6—467, 7—545, 8—572. Did not bat: W. Johnston.

ENGLAND

L. Hutton, c. Langley, b. Lindwall	4	l.b.w., b. Miller		13
R. T. Simpson, b. Miller	2	run out		9
W. J. Edrich, c. Langley, b. Archer	15	b. Johnston		88
P. B. H. May, b. Lindwall	1	l.b.w., b. Lindwall		44
M. C. Cowdrey, c. Hole, b. Johnston	40	b. Benaud		10
T. E. Bailey, b. Johnston	88	c. Langley, b. Lindwall		23
F. Tyson, b. Johnson	7	not out		37
A. V. Bedser, b. Johnson	5	c. Archer, b. Johnson		5
K. Andrew, b. Lindwall	6	b. Johnson		5
B. Statham, b. Johnson	11	c. Harvey, b. Benaud		14
D. C. S. Compton, not out	2	c. Langley, b. Benaud		0
Extras (b. 3, l.b. 6)	9	Extras (b. 7, l.b. 2)		9
Total	190	Total		257

FALL OF WICKETS. *First innings*: 1—4, 2—10, 3—11, 4—25, 5—107, 6—132, 7—141, 8—156, 9—181. *Second innings*: 1—22, 2—23, 3—147, 4—163, 5—181, 6—220, 7—231, 8—242, 9—243.

THE FIRST TEST MATCH

Bowling Analysis

ENGLAND

	O.	M.	R.	W.
Bedser	37	4	131	1
Statham	34	2	123	2
Tyson	29	1	160	1
Bailey	26	1	140	3
Edrich	3	0	28	0

AUSTRALIA

First Innings	O.	M.	R.	W.	Secong Innings	O.	M.	R.	W
Lindwall	14	4	27	3	Lindwall	17	3	50	2
Miller	11	5	19	1	Miller	12	2	30	1
Archer	4	1	14	1	Archer	15	4	28	0
Johnson	19	5	46	3	Johnston	21	8	59	1
Benaud	12	5	28	0	Johnson	17	5	38	2
Johnston	16.1	5	47	2	Benaud	8.1	1	43	3

AUSTRALIA WON BY AN INNINGS AND 154 RUNS

* * *

First Day: Australia, put in by Hutton, are 208 for two after a day of placid batting and much cruel English misfortune. Evans was not after all fit and Compton can take little further part in the game. Hutton, having won the toss, turned a blind Nelsonian eye to the wicket's evident lack of moisture, hoping, doubtless with hand on heart, that pace might at the pinch compensate for nature. It did not, and England must now bat fourth against a formidable array of spinners. When Bedser prepared to bowl the first ball of the series to Favell, one was conscious of how many miles had been travelled, how many weeks spent in preparation, for just this. The shirt-sleeved, chattering crowd lying out on the warm green slopes or under the fig trees suddenly quietened. Bedser loped up under sierras of high cloud, Favell took a good length ball high on the pad, and the hollow in the pit of the stomach stirred. Favell pushed one run off the over, and then Statham flashed two in quick succession past his off stump, the second coming back enough to make Favell shoot a hurried confirmatory look at his wicket. Hutton allowed Bedser and Statham only three overs apiece in this first spell which, though it cost very few runs, must have been disturbing; the ball neither moved in the air nor lifted. Tyson and Bailey therefore bowled with it as red as an apple, which meant that the full resources of England's attack had been produced within the first forty minutes. Morris drove Bailey sweetly for four past cover, and Favell square-cut and glided him twice more to the fence, with not a fielder needing to move. In Tyson's second over Morris turned him neatly on to the end of Hutton's fingers at leg slip: the ball was pitching perhaps two feet in front of Hutton, but was slow from the bat. Tyson proceeded to whistle a couple over Morris's head, the breeze from the second one blowing out his cap; whereupon he handed it to the umpire, probably deeming that a safer place. With both opening bowlers soon on again, Favell and Morris had done their job. Favell, though Statham twice more found his bat bidding the ball a late farewell outside the off stump, looked ominously assured: and Morris, shuffling not at all, hit a no-ball from Bedser between two alarmed ladies with parasols, patently at that moment discussing other things. The fifty came up in an hour and a quarter, and it looked to be the first of a good many. In fact, Favell was out a run later. Statham pitched one short, Favell swung, getting it high on the bat, and Cowdrey, just backward of square-leg, plucked a lovely catch forward of his instep. 56 for 1 at lunch was not long in being doubled, for while Morris pushed for the most part unhurriedly at Bedser, Miller cut late and square, glancing from time to time into an arc as untenanted as the Nullarbor plain. Having hit another no-ball from Bedser as high as Mount Gravatt for six, Miller passed Morris in the mid-forties, causing Bailey to switch his field and concentrate on the leg stump. It was an old tactic with many successes behind it; it worked again in the familiar paradoxical way, Miller chopping a ball outside his off stump hard on to his wicket. His 49 runs had been made in most princely fashion. He was largely out through hurry, not surprisingly, for Edrich had bowled an over of long hops at the other end and Miller is no ascetic. Harvey's arrival preceded by only a few minutes the news that Compton, who wrapped his left hand round a paling when chasing a boundary before lunch, had fractured a metacarpal bone and would bat in this match only in dire necessity. One felt now that no one less than a Captain Bligh could keep England afloat for six days. Hutton is not that. Soon after tea Morris, his score 55, hooked a short rising ball from Bedser high and straight to Bailey fielding with back to the fence at long leg. The catch was unaccountably dropped, though had Bailey not split open a finger playing against Queensland he would not have been fielding there at all. Next over Morris snicked Tyson ankle-high between wicket-keeper and first slip, a shot that brought him four runs. It was hot enough at this stage for Simpson and Edrich to have recourse to caps, which sat them strangely. Tyson patrolled the boundaries in floppy white sun hat as though butterfly catching. Neither of our fast bowlers like fielding near the wicket, which means they get a lot of running about and Hutton a lot of unfair criticism. Yet oddly Australia did not ride the wave. Morris, having banished all the old ghosts, fell to a kind of sleeping sickness. Harvey played often and missed often, Statham in addition forcing him to numerous uncomely jabs. Neither has lately been long at the wicket, and they seemed satisfied to be there at all, which is not befitting men named Harvey and Morris. Harvey did, in fact, shake himself free for some minutes at the end, but mostly he played like a man not long out of convalescence.

* * *

Second Day: Apart from a brief period in late afternoon, when three wickets fell for 8 runs, Australia's batting was the logical extension of what had taken place on Friday. Four wickets fell as against two, and 295 runs were scored as against 208. The five hundred went up in the last over of the day, and Australia are probably worth seventy or eighty more on Monday morning. England will therefore have to bat for three and a half days without Compton. It is especially disappointing that so early in the match there is nothing but this to hope for. Misfortune in this instance was given a considerable shove by circumstance. Morris, who reached 153, gave chances at 0, 11, 55 and 89; Harvey, who made 162, was dropped at 58, 72, and 102. In addition, both might have been run out by more accurate throwers. Only two out of these seven chances could be called comfortable; but all were of the kind that Australians habitually take.

Morris's century was his eleventh in Test cricket, Harvey's his twelfth: somewhat surprisingly, it is only Harvey's third against England, Morris's eighth. And Morris is now third to Bradman and Clem Hill in Australian Test aggregates, which one would not have expected of someone who has of late failed so frequently.

Although runs came at a fair pace from the first, it was some while before Harvey's innings moved out of its sickly origins into full health. Morris, whom May failed to hold at second slip as soon as the new ball was taken, looked, despite much buffeting, the more leisurely player. Harvey, still stabbing at Statham, was not long in flicking Bailey off the leg stump low down to Bedser just astern of him; but Bedser needs them these days at least knee-high. Edrich came on for Bailey rather than Tyson, though the second new ball was not yet adolescent, and 22 runs were scored off two overs. Morris slashed three fours in succession past cover, which Tyson chased, his sun hat bowling along the ground after him. Harvey loitered rather, while Morris swung Bailey off his toes high into the crowd. Morris's cupboard skeletons had put on flesh and blood now, and he looked a man who slept at nights.

Lunch was taken at 299 for 2; afterwards, with stands and grass slopes so close packed that the fig trees were pressed into service, Tyson bowled steadily with shortened run. The sun streamed down on women with coolie hats, and men with cocked paper ones and burnouses of handkerchief. The conviction that this Woolloongabba ground was a rest-camp for foreign legionaries was upset by Cowdrey suddenly clasping a fast snick to his stomach. Morris had driven at Bailey and got only an edge. His innings had been a long ascent in its early stages, an achievement of character rather than of the imagination. But today it had been born of the sun. At twenty-past two Harvey pushed Bedser for four to square leg to reach a century that was essentially exploratory; in the same over Bedser failed to hold a hard hit made on the rise. Hole, weak against pace, especially just short of a length on the leg stump, was not subjected to it, nor given a forward short-leg, in which position he is more often than not caught. Instead, he was able to show many handsome off drives, and to cut frequently. Four hundred were up before tea, and when the new ball was taken by Tyson and Bedser, Harvey drove both bowlers with noisy rattle to the fence. Several times, too, he glided Tyson with so sensitive a touch that he seemed loath to remove the shine. The partnership was worth more than a hundred when Hole, going for a second run, unexpectedly found a return from Tyson too quick and straight for him. Seven runs later Harvey, pulling a long hop from Bedser savagely to square leg, was wonderfully caught by Bailey, who flung himself to his left and held the ball as it was pitching. Archer hung his bat out and steered Statham to Bedser in the gully, which, though giving the scoreboard a more comforting look, led one to gloomy reflections. Lindwall was not long in dispelling these, driving the ball smoothly and swiftly past cover point. Medium-pace bowling is meat and drink to him, and he is a batsman of Rabelaisian appetite.

Hutton today could have had only slight hope of a break through with the new ball; when this did not come there was little he could do except set a field, and encourage his bowlers to bowl to it. It seemed on occasions that he was slow to block the gaps pleasurable to different players, and his handling of the bowling was not always easy to follow. Today the freshest and most successful bowlers when the new ball was due were Bailey and Statham; but, in fact, Tyson and Bedser used it. Not probably that it made much difference, for by then the equation of runs *versus* time seemed one that only Australia was in a position to work out.

* * *

Third Day: In the hour and a half before lunch Australia scored 98 runs. Hutton bowled Tyson and Statham for an hour of this time, and Lindwall and Benaud swung their bats heftily at the line, if hardly the pitch of the ball. No matter, for both are players from the front foot and if they missed occasionally they connected often. Lindwall slashed Statham to leave cover stationary, and Benaud hit him on the rise for six over long-on. The bowling was never of bad length, but it was of nice pace to be hit if the intention was there. The ball came through at a predictable height and, though defensive fields were set, Tyson and Wilson (substituting for Compton) on the fence were kept toiling. Long leg seemed hardly the place for a fast bowler in the circumstances, but Tyson covered the ground, threw heroically, and came in to bowl with great heart. Once, too, when bowling, he stopped a hard drive from Lindwall in the middle of his follow-through and hurled the wicket down, all but running Lindwall out. He had some belated reward when Benaud, trying to turn him to leg, cocked up an easy catch to cover off the edge. Langley made himself at home with cuts and glances that seemed both to surprise and please him, meanwhile Lindwall hustled to fifty with another four off the conveyor belt past cover. Bailey brought one back to hit Langley's leg stump at 572, the first time in the match that ball had eluded bat to hit the wicket. Johnson, his crinkly hair gleaming, entered upon his first innings as captain of Australia, and he sent Bailey quickly sailing over mid-on for four; Cowdrey dropped him at gully, a gentle catch, in the same over. The last twenty minutes were unwilling comedy for England. Johnson struck Bedser for six and then twice off successive balls was dropped a yard in from the boundary. Johnson, unconsciously assuming the role of pantomime dame, departed for the pavilion on the second occasion, not surprisingly believing he was out, since Cowdrey,

FIRST TEST, BRISBANE: K. R. Miller driving Bedser for six during Australia's innings of 601 for 8 declared. Bedser, who took 1 wicket for 131 runs, played in no further Tests, and this picture, with the one below, says all there needs to be said, from England's point of view, about this disastrous match

R. T. Simpson, bowled by Miller for 2, also played in no more Tests during this series. In England's first innings, the first three wickets fell at 4, 10, 11; in the second, Simpson was out at 22, Hutton at 23. The Brisbane Test made quite plain that Lindwall and Miller, with Archer in support, would provide a new ball assault that only a solid, reliable opening pair would be able to withstand. This pair was never found: only at Adelaide in the Fourth Test did England get off to a reasonable start

SECOND TEST, SYDNEY: T. Graveney, c. Langley, b. Johnston, o. Not till the fifth Test, when, with the Ashes safely retained, he made a gorgeous hundred, was Graveney able to make good the manner of his failure in this innings. The evident exuberance of appeal was customary among the younger Australian players; often it bore little relation to the probabilities

above: M. C. Cowdrey pushing Benaud away to mid-wicket during his second innings of 54. His partnership of 116 with May was one of the turning-points of the series

below: A familiar sight when Statham was bowling. Archer hit above the knee as the ball whips across from off to leg. Archer, 49, was top-scorer in Australia's first innings

above: W. A. Johnston, c. Evans, b. Tyson, 11. The end of a last-wicket partnership of 41 between Harvey and Johnston, and with it victory for England by 38 runs

below: P. B. H. May, b. Lindwall, 104. This early break-through by Lindwall with the second new ball seemed to put the match within comfortable reach of Australia

THIRD TEST, MELBOURNE: R. Benaud, b. Tyson, 22, during the second Australian innings, in which Tyson took 7 wickets for 27. Benaud, hooking at a short ball outside his off stump, pulled it on to his wicket

above: G. B. Hole, b. Tyson, 11. Hole, with his high flourishing backlift, was much too late on a full toss. This was in Australia's first innings when, in reply to England's 191, Australia lost 4 wickets for 65. *opposite:* R. N. Harvey, c. Evans, b. Tyson, 11. The vital first wicket on the sensational last morning of the match. The cracks on the pitch, as can be seen, reopened. Harvey flicked Tyson round the corner, and Evans, moving very fast, took an astonishing catch

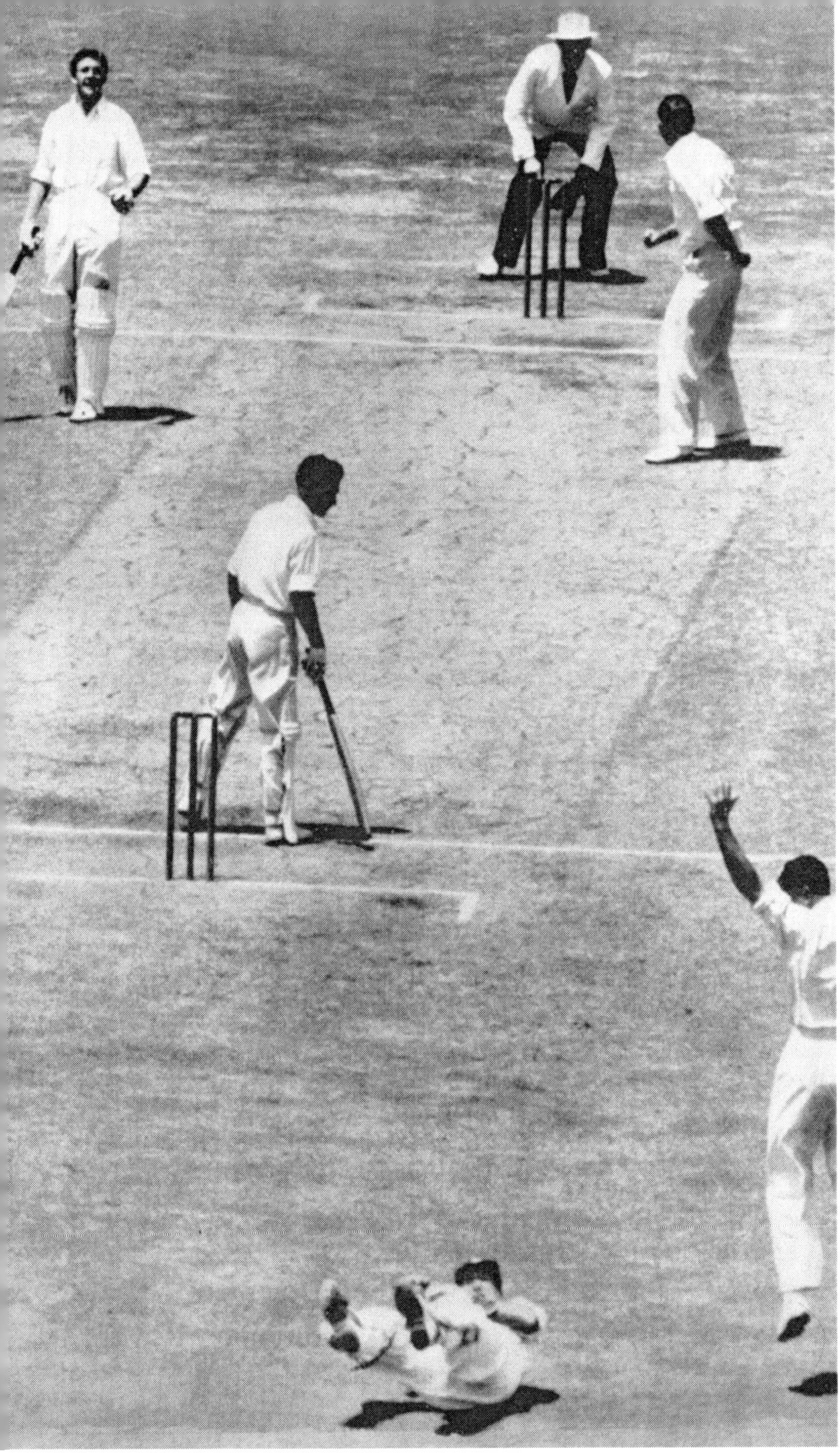

FOURTH TEST, ADELAIDE: *above:* L. Hutton, c. Davidson, b. Johnston, 80. This was Hutton's best Test innings, ended, for the third time in the series, by Davidson's superb catching. In this instance, Hutton pulled a long hop hard to Davidson, standing murderously close at short leg

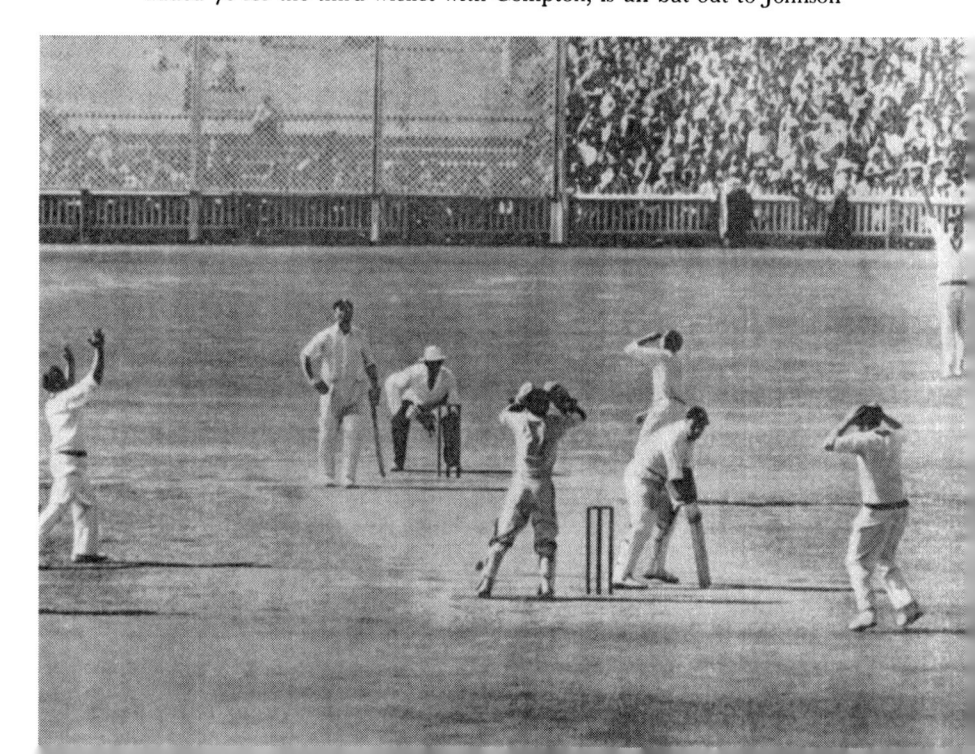

below: Australian fieldsmen fail to hide their anguish as Cowdrey (79), who added 70 for the third wicket with Compton, is all but out to Johnson

the fielder, had his back to him. A piece of theatrical funny business which Hutton interrupted by recalling him to the stage. The six hundred was up, however, and it being lunch-time Johnson allowed himself the luxury of declaring.

Hutton, a lonely figure struck down by as many disasters as any overworked hero in Greek mythology, took four off Lindwall's first ball in the direction of gully. The seventh was of good length and Hutton, playing neither forward nor back, was beaten off the pitch and caught low down by Langley. Edrich strode out next, marching as if to a brass band, and he, too, steered his first ball past gully to the boundary. Simpson managed two to third man off Miller before being bowled by his fifth ball, an in-swinger which went away off the pitch as he shaped to turn it. May snicked a single off his pads, and Edrich played at, and missed, two of steep lift outside the off stump. A memorable over. Lindwall, frisky as a racehorse, then bowled May off his pads. At 11 for 3 Cowdrey began his first innings in a Test match. Miller was replaced after three overs by Archer, two of whose three opening long-hops Edrich hooked for four. The brave martial music of these shots had barely subsided when, pushing forward at Archer, Edrich got the thinnest edge and was snapped up by Langley. Lindwall bowled with melodious run up, multiple changes of pace and sudden bounce at Cowdrey, who took a few on his broad beam but continued to position himself firmly behind the ball. Lindwall had a fair breeze behind him, enough to keep the fig trees swaying as dutifully as the *corps de ballet* in *Les Sylphides*, but his arts as a swing bowler come from the full length that permits the ultimate variations of swerve. Miller, less lovely to watch, bowled as one who had mastered and grown bored with technique long before birth. When Johnson took a turn Cowdrey twice moved down the pitch to him and drove him high and straight over mid-off. By tea fifty had been scored, Cowdrey cutting Archer sharply between the slips. Subsequently, Johnston bowled in place of his captain, and Cowdrey leaned him several times with checked swing past cover. Twenty-eight of his first thirty-two runs came in boundaries. Bailey defended for an hour, then hit Benaud, who bowled with indulgent length, for four fours in the space of five minutes; an overthrown five off Johnston, also to the benefit of Bailey, took him to thirty. The funeral march had turned into a gallop, rather as if some irreverent urchin had put a squib behind the coffin. Lindwall was recalled to restore top-hat and grave demeanour, and Johnston attacked the leg stump on a nagging length. The pace noticeably slackened, but the hundred went up at five to five, by which time the partnership was worth 75 runs. The ball was not now often beating the bat; the corpse might even have stirred a little under its lid. For the last half-hour neither batsman made any attempt to score, a policy that usually breeds trouble, altering, as it does, the natural rhythm of stroke-making. Cowdrey, tormented as though by a mosquito, finally snicked a spinning half-volley off his boot in the last over of the day to Hole at slip. He seemed not to realize he was out; and subsequently doubts were raised about the rightness of the decision. Still, a half-volley is a half-volley and at any other time Cowdrey would have hit it for four. He is not a comfortable defensive player, bringing bat and pad so closely together that they brush, and stopping the bat at an inward slant of 45° with an unpleasant effect of pawkiness.

If, however, he lost his wicket owing to the convention under which he has grown up, that the last thirty minutes of the day are sacrosanct, any scoring shot attempted being a kind of indecency—then, this apart, and the convention being responsible (though the opposite used to be the case, tired bowlers made free with), his innings was of perfect modulation, a warming proof of temperament.

* * *

Fourth Day: England, after many ups and downs, finished the day requiring 281 runs to make Australia go in again. To put it more practically, they have two full days to bat, with the wickets of seven able-bodied men and Compton to fall. Bailey saw England's first innings through till lunch; which was followed by the customary dismal start, Hutton and Simpson being out for 23. Edrich, who was missed twice, and May then batted with courage and no little fluency, their unbroken partnership reaching a hundred in the last over of the day. As yet, the pitch has remained blandly accommodating. One or two have kept low, and a handful have turned; but, by and large, it is still a wicket anyone should be happy to bat on. Johnson before lunch and Miller after it bowled with purpose.

The sky was overcast this evening, with a cool breeze scuffling the wastepaper up the green, deserted slopes. The weather men talk of rain, but not very convincingly. Bailey this morning played as one who had batted throughout the hours of dream and was finding reality no more disturbing. Tyson for a while prospered, driving Johnston twice through the covers; but, when 25 had been added, Johnson pushed one between bat and pad. Bedser struck a bold four to mid-wicket and Johnson then bowled him in identical manner. Australian batsmen of the lower order move their feet; England's do not, and Bedser's clockwork lunge was left arrested in mid-air. Bailey made two late cuts off Johnston for four, pushed him several times past short-leg, and hooked him violently to the fence. Johnson made him stretch unavailingly, but in return was driven on to the bank between long-on and mid-wicket, a stroke that not only put up 150, but was worth a hundred pounds, a local business man having offered that sum for the first six of the day. He can hardly have envisaged Bailey as recipient. Andrew looked to be enjoying the feel of Lindwall on the middle of the bat; but pleasure was interrupted when he came down a shade late and was bowled. Benaud took over from Johnston, and Bailey leaped out and hit him first bounce over mid-on. Statham showed signs of keeping Bailey company till lunch but, having hit Miller straight for four, went into his customary state of euphoria. Though Bailey might be batting yet, Statham swung three times wildly at Johnson and was rightly bowled. It was the kind of irresponsible cricket for which a small boy would have his ears boxed. Statham had done the same thing at

Melbourne recently, when Graveney was not out at the other end. Attention to detail has long ceased to be the mark of the English county cricketer, who knows it all without ever having bothered to learn. A bowler rarely troubles to bat, or a batsman to bowl. Thus do we lose Test matches. Compton, sympathetically cheered, let a kindly ball from Johnston pass his off stump, allowing the innings to last till lunch—which had not at one time seemed probable. Thereafter Compton pushed nobly at Johnson for ten minutes that were painful to behold. Bailey, having pulled Johnston for four, brought merciful release by being bowled. He batted 4 hours 21 minutes for 88, his highest as well as his most accomplished Test innings. Not once did he look like getting out. At two o'clock, therefore, weather dullish and sultry, Hutton and Simpson, in unspeaking isolation, walked out past where Lindwall, the new ball glinting in his hand, menacingly rotated arms and shoulders, rehearsed phrases of his run. Neither batsman cast him a glance. The chatter stilled. Hutton once more took four off the first ball, this time to square leg; but, playing too soon at the seventh, cocked it up only a foot or two short of Johnston fine of the umpire. Simpson, despite a blow on the ankle from a fast full toss from Lindwall, played serenely. Hutton flicked Lindwall off his legs for another four, and Simpson turned him twice through the short legs. Having taken 0 for 17 Lindwall was probably on his last over when Hutton snicked him just short of second slip, who misfielded; Simpson, without apparent urgency, went through for a run, but Favell, retrieving the ball, threw the wicket down with Simpson sickeningly out. One run later Miller, having changed ends, had Hutton l.b.w., playing early and across a much slower ball. Edrich was immediately dropped at second slip off Miller, bowling with ill-concealed magnificence; but he rose up on his toes like a conductor bringing in the violas after a long rest to cut Archer late for four, off-driving him for another. May quickly settled to powerful drives both sides of mid-on, and, soon after tea, 50 went up. Edrich was missed by Hole at slip, but otherwise, for the first time since last summer, seemed not to require the services of a prompter. When 32 he hit a no-ball from Johnston magnificently for six with continuation, rather than change, of stroke. From that moment on he grew, ball by ball, into the batsman of familiar portrait: it was as if, like Cephalus, who, after disguising himself to test the fidelity of his wife Procris, daughter of Erechtheus, eventually revealed his identity, Edrich, too, felt the testing period to be over. He smote a half-volley to the cover-point boundary, reached his fifty with an off-drive that ended with the bat brushing his left ear, and late cut Archer twice to the fence. May warmed the fingers of cover and extra, but failed to find the gap. With the hills turning mauve as the light began to retreat into the sky, Johnson seemed to fret somewhat. He switched his bowlers, bringing on Benaud: a costly experiment, for three overs from him produced 24 runs. Lindwall indulgently watched the play from slip and short leg, rather as a shark observes the antics of pilot fish, unhurriedly getting up a hunger.

* * *

Fifth Day: Logically and inevitably, this ill-starred match was lost at eleven minutes past four, Harvey making a magnificent running catch on the boundary off Benaud. The margin of England's defeat was an innings and 154 runs; or, rather, they failed by six and a half hours to save the game. Defensive cricket is never easy to play three days in succession, and once England's batsmen stopped making shots they were doomed. Edrich and May were both out within three-quarters of an hour in the morning, and, though Bailey again demonstrated the placidity of the wicket, only continuous rain could have robbed Australia of victory. In fact, low grey clouds piled up steadily before lunch and a heavy squall drove the Australians unwillingly in between half-past twelve and one. Afterwards, however, it lightened and the last five wickets fell on a cool afternoon with only a sprinkling of witnesses. So deserted were the green slopes under the impressive premises of the Bengal Chutney Company that a solitary squatting gentleman was able to strip to the waist, turn his trousers up and enjoy a leisurely sun-bath with no one a cricket pitch's length either side of him. For the first twenty minutes Edrich and May raised faint hopes by taking Lindwall and Johnston safely in the middle of the bat. Lindwall was accurate and intelligent at no great pace; Johnston bowled all lengths. Edrich late cut Johnston for four and slashed a full pitch for another; May then disposed of a second full pitch rather straighter. Lindwall was probably due for a rest when he moved one in rather low to get May l.b.w. Edrich pushed Lindwall for two past the short legs to make England 150, a score as meaningless in the circumstances as the obscurest of Egyptian hieroglyphs. But Edrich was moving into the ball, drawing it into the middle of his bat as though edges did not exist; moreover, he scored easily in the arc between cover and mid-off, for some years untravelled territory for him. So it was a shock when suddenly he swung at a faster ball from Johnston and was bowled. Probably it was not quite short enough to hook, and it hustled through, capsizing the last lifeboat as it did so. Edrich hit thirteen fours and a six; nor did he make the problems of batting appear as difficult of solution as he is sometimes wont to do. Normally, it is of Edrich's determination that one is abidingly made aware: but these 88 runs reinstated him as a batsman of gifts, as well as character. Five minutes later the rain thickened from a drizzle to a downpour, lasting exactly till lunch. Afterwards Cowdrey and Bailey faced Johnson and Johnston, each of whom bowled round the wicket to three short legs standing very close. Cowdrey, either badly advised or reasoning unfortunately, decided to make strokes only when essential: mostly he took the ball on the pads or dropped it down a foot in front of him. Runs admittedly were of little account, and the longer the new ball was delayed, in a way the better. But it is psychologically a bad policy. The bowler can experiment as he likes without fear of retribution, while the batsman tends to stiffen up, eventually so mesmerized that he can barely tell good ball from bad. Runs on the board, whether they matter or not, are like dry sherry: they create an appetite and a good humour. Watching Cowdrey was akin to seeing a healthy monk depriving himself of needed sustenance through adherence to some self-imposed devotional discipline. His asceticism caused his downfall directly, for checking a stroke to a well-pitched ball from Benaud he ruefully saw it spin off the inside of his half withdrawn bat on to the stumps.

Bailey, the match now well lost, hit Johnston for three illustrative fours and cut Benaud late to take England to the respectabilities of 200 and the extravagance of another new ball.

Lindwall, therefore, returned and Tyson played both him and Miller admirably off the front foot. His left elbow and right hand are both too low for much elegance or power square on the off, but he gets properly to the pitch and when he keeps his head down the ball travels. Bailey had little of the strike for several overs, during which Tyson scored 25 runs; he seemed, therefore, rather out of touch when Lindwall mixing in-swingers and out-swingers, in one over had him dropped on the leg side by Langley and then brilliantly taken low down on the off. Bedser and Andrew were not long at the crease; nor Compton, who generously, but surely unwisely, decided to bat. Statham laid about him for some minutes, finally carting Benaud high to mid-wicket where Harvey, running in from long on, held him, in baseball fashion, at eye-level.

The crowd thereupon sauntered out to inspect the pitch, paying no heed to Johnson leading his team off the ground on which he had vowed never to play cricket again. Against South Africa in 1952 Ian Johnson, in company with several other Victorians, was pitilessly barracked, because no Queenslander had been chosen for the first Test, and Jack Ryder, then chairman of the selection committee, was a Victorian. Johnson was dropped after that match, and did not tour England. This match, his first as captain of Australia, also marked his return to Test cricket. If the result made it seem a compensatory gift from the gods, it was one which Johnson received in silence. No applause greeted the Australians as they returned to their ignoble dressing-room: it might have been the end of a drawn grade game.

All the same, for Australia it was a heartening match. Morris, Harvey, and Hole, uneasy starters to the season, must all now expect to make runs, which they cannot truly have done before play started. Miller and Lindwall have stepped firmly out of the encroaching mists of legend to confront yet another generation with the reasons of their skill. At full pace, they are not detectably slower than when last in England. They are splendidly unaffected cricketers, natural athletes who delight even as they destroy. The Australians are a beautifully balanced side, both in bowling and batting, which England is not. Persistence will need to overcome nature, if we are to pull back from one down.

* * *

This is no match for a long post-mortem. The fates were against us from the beginning. The wicket failed to produce its opening hour of liveliness, vital catches were dropped, Evans was unfit, and Compton, at peak form, turned into a passenger. One can look at it as retribution for declining to bat after winning the toss on a wicket on which you could literally sniff a big score before play began. Against this, Hutton's policy was forced on him by the weakness of our early batting, and the odd reluctance of our spin bowlers to try to spin the ball. The fast bowlers had a thankless task and stuck to it well, but none of them bowled a full length with the new ball. The Australians, allowed to play back, were given that vital extra second or two to see the ball that Lindwall and Miller never permit. The English bowlers, Bailey excepted, used the new ball defensively, as if fearing the very stroke that Miller and Lindwall, with their contrasting dissipated and formal methods of delivery, use all their arts to entice. A back stroke against Lindwall is a rarity—he demands to be driven, and the reluctance of English batsmen to do this enables the late swing to find the edge of stationary bats. Miller, cutting the ball off the seam, swings late and achieves steep lift.

However, the lessons are there to be learnt. Had the Furies not flashed their frightful eyes at Evans and Compton we should not, despite the many fielding lapses, in all probability, have lost the match. Hutton's batting failures were psychologically understandable: out to a bad stroke in the first innings and clever tactics in the second, he batted like one imprisoned by bad thoughts. Had Johnson won the toss he would certainly have batted, and the saving of the game could have been set about without the sickening sense of guilt that must have accompanied Hutton on each of his short visits to the wicket.

No-balls in this match cost us around 50 runs, dropped catches 200, slow running between the wickets another 30. These must be attended to. Bailey possibly will have to go in first at Sydney with Hutton, as he did quite successfully in the West Indies, though the probable absence of Compton from the second Test will make our batting even more rickety than it already is. Appleyard, despite Hutton's wish to keep him in reserve for Adelaide and Melbourne, where the wickets are more likely to suit him, must take the place of one of the fast bowlers—whose shock value has lost most of its threat. Next time, the toss, should he win it, must not be an embarrassment to Hutton. He must hope to bat first with an easy conscience, having at least one bowler able to make use of a wearing pitch. Australia, despite their large score, did not in the early part of their innings bat convincingly. Morris and Harvey can scarcely ever have missed so many balls at which they played. Lindwall's innings should have been cut short early on. Only Miller and Hole batted really well. Though the Australians have every kind of bowler, a fact that enables Johnson to make the best of any sort of pitch, the slow bowlers did not seem a worry. Johnston bowled many more bad balls than he did ever before. Benaud's length is variable; and, if only English batsmen would use their feet, Johnson ought to be taken care of on covered pitches that cannot be expected to take a great deal of spin.

Edrich thoroughly justified Hutton's (and my) faith. Cowdrey, so long as he does not allow Johnson and Benaud to bowl to him on a good pitch with three men squatting off his hip, as he did in his strokeless second innings, will, when Compton returns, give our middle batting a much-needed solidity. Defects of judgment are comparatively simple to remedy: flaws in character or temperament are not, and Cowdrey's will be always an asset to him. An exceptionally nice person, he has become in these last few weeks a Test batsman to be reckoned with.

Hutton, during the next fortnight, will be confronted with as many problems as faced Hercules as he set off from Mycenæ along the bay of Argos after consulting the oracle. They are psychological, as well as technical, for the threat of fast bowling must once more be made real to Australian batsmen. The difficulty of judging how much our necessarily depleted batting can be damaged still further to add a slow bowler, is not an easy one to solve. Wardle and Appleyard are, in any case, rollers and cutters of the ball, not, in their present mood anyway, wrist and finger spinners like the Australians. Hutton, despite the urgent need for change, has no new menu to put before batsmen who must go in now with the pleasant assurance of men who, having eaten well off simple fare at a restaurant once, are confident of doing so again—once more, it will be *table d'hôte*, not *à la carte*, with no unfamiliar flavours to digest.

Hercules, it is said, suffered greatly during his life, but once he had performed his self-imposed tasks of redemption, he was escorted by Jupiter's four-horsed chariot into the assembly of the Gods. Hutton's place, in the assembly of cricketing immortals, is secure. But the next month will test fully his ability to inspire confidence in others. He has led, hitherto, largely by the example of his own prowess: now he will need to demonstrate similar qualities of resource off the field.

* * *

Brisbane for me has been inextricably mixed up with the misfortunes of the Test match. I cannot see it now as a city separable from the anti-climax of those five wounding days. I remember driving, soaked in perspiration each morning, over one of the various bridges that link Brisbane to its sprawling suburbs, returning each evening to the air-conditioned room in Lennons Hotel where, over a plate of oysters and a bottle of Chablis, I composed my gloomy messages. The days were hot and sticky, though less so, I believe, than usual. Sometimes, when I had finished, I wandered by the muddy river, where the tugs and steamers lay moored in the silvered shadow of the fig trees; on occasions I dined with Ian Peebles at the Queensland Club, lying out after dinner in its long boat-like verandah chairs, sipping at whiskies and soda while the date-palms bent in the hot wind and the poincianas shivered under approaching thunder. Club members in tropical suits, pure inventions of Somerset Maugham, drifted in from the shadows, shedding cigar-ash among the bougainvillea and poinsettia.

My diary tells me of other things: of a reception at Government House, which took us most of the evening to find; of a long day spent with Freddie Brown at Surfer's Paradise, a great curve of white beach backed by Norfolk Island pines and hideous bungalows, where we bathed often and ate huge steaks at a barbecue in the evening, driving the sixty miles back in a solid glow-worm of traffic. I remember a solitary evening with Leonard Hutton in Lennons, the Australian team boisterously happy a few tables off, and a party in Norman Preston's room, with George Duckworth singing to wake the dead in a feathery pink hat. I went, also, more than once to The Oasis, a charming swimming pool fifteen miles out, its clipped lawns and oleander trees bearing large notices announcing that 'Wrestling and all forms of undue familiarity between couples are not permitted.' I acquired an affection for the Brisbane sunsets, when, for an hour, this harsh, tinny town flows with peachy light, and the trees along its winding river raise black branches against lilac hills. But mostly when I think of Brisbane it will be of drinking beer late into the small hours with John Woodcock and Ronald Roberts, brooding over the mishaps of the day, regretting the ifs and might-have-beens. Denis Compton joined us sometimes, his left hand in plaster, a perpetual reminder of the maddening cruelty of that first morning. He is patient in adversity, much more philosophical than any of us. All the same, it was not the happiest of times.

9 Rockhampton and the Barrier Reef

I flew from Brisbane in a D.C.3 some 350 miles north to Rockhampton, where M.C.C. were due to play their first match ever in the Australian tropics. Five miles south of Rockhampton a signpost, labelled Tropic of Capricorn, points one arm to the Torrid Zone, the other to the Temperate. We came in to land half an hour before sunset, circling over swamps and gum trees, with ibises darting in the shadow of the wings. That night I slept under a mosquito net, sweating through sleeplessly until the dawn. For Rockhampton is separated from the north-east Trades by the great humps of the Berserker Range, and even at night the town, as a consequence, swelters without relief. It is not, as I discovered next day, an unsightly town. A river runs through it, also a single-track railway line; the latter, unprotected by gates, allows the trains to shunt past the main street in charmingly informal manner. Houses, supported by stilts in the usual Queensland style, stretch along the river bank amongst hibiscus and poinciana; banana trees, mangoes and palms shelter the roads that run southwards past the pale sandstone church into the bush and northwards to the foothills. The town itself, a little honky-tonk in character, boasts many saloons through the swing doors of which tough men in cowboy hats push their way, as if looking for a fight, a girl, a game of dice or a rodeo. In fact, the mountain-framed Show ground, where a two-day match against a Queensland Country XI was played, is normally used only for the Agricultural Show. The pitch, which had never had a ball bowled on it, was prepared in the Botanic Gardens and transplanted in 18-inch sods. The outfield, on which various kinds of cattle had left their cards, was dry, dusty and uneven.

The match, which began lightheartedly enough, ended in an innings win for M.C.C., but not before Hutton had asked for a quarter of an hour's extension of the agreed playing hours, a singular request that subsequently caused unfavourable comment. Hutton and Edrich put on 112 for the first M.C.C. wicket, May made 61, Wilson 74. The heat was very great, the sun, directly overhead, beating off white palings and seven-barred gates. A holiday-happy crowd cheered, drank lemonade, ate steaks at barbecue counters, and mopped their brows. One would not have been surprised if they had fired revolvers into the sky or twirled lassoos. After play, the Mayor held a reception in a beer garden: Hutton, in splendid fettle, incited flushed and beaming old gentlemen to make speeches, a habit Australians need no encouragement to indulge. He himself in reply sprang on to a chair and declared with great good humour how glad he was to be in Townsville, a town several hundred miles north. Lapses of memory are permitted to great men, and the good citizens of Rockhampton took this roguish irony with innocent comprehension. On the morrow, Hutton remembering his whereabouts, the Queensland countrymen were bowled out twice, Appleyard taking 7 wickets at the second attempt.

* * *

M.C.C. travelled south after this match to Melbourne, playing a one-day match against the Prime Minister's XI at Canberra on the way. I, however, flew northwards, in the excellent company of Sam Stott, one-time Signalman, R.N.V.R., now following both the sun and the cricket, for a fortnight's holiday on the Barrier Reef. I had looked forward to this from the moment that I knew I was going to Australia.

Taking off at breakfast-time, by noon we were in Mackay, one of the great Queensland sugar towns, a circle of wooden bungalows ringed off from the crimped green cane fields by coconut palms. It was Sunday, the heat heavy over empty streets. Officials of Australian National Airways—a Company of meticulous efficiency and courtesy—drove us out to the new harbour, where sailing boats curled out towards a string of mauve islands, and fishermen in the lee of tramp steamers hauled up bream as fast as they could throw their lines out. A cricket match was going on in the Botanical Gardens, the boundary shaded by firs, fig and dazzling acacia trees. Couples strolled through tall avenues of coconut, or picnicked against the trunks of the coral-pink Leichhardt, a ghost gum named after the explorer, and one of the most exquisite trees in the world. A leg-break bowler, his run so suddenly sideways that it looked as if he was stepping over a snake, took five wickets in three overs while we watched. Then a swarthy fellow, disdaining gloves and pads, carted him twice for six amongst the scarlet chandeliers of poinciana, hitting his wicket next ball attempting a cut that felled all three stumps, and almost the wicket-keeper too.

In late afternoon we took off for Proserpine, flying low over lion-coloured hills and lagoons, the westering sun buttering our wings as we came down over miles of gum trees, landing in a circular clearing and bumping up to a solitary hut barely visible in the dusk.

From here, we drove twenty-five miles through the bush to Cannonvale, the quick darkness eased only by the dull light of occasional shacks. Winged insects smacked against the truck windows, and the pale trunks of the gums gleamed, as the headlamps probed them, like the limbs of giant albinos.

We swung down towards the coast, the sea-smell deepening. A red, papery moon hung over the Pacific. Off the quays a launch with motors running waited to take us out to the invisible islands.

* * *

Hayman Island, where I spent ten days, has an interesting, rather saddening history. Shortly after the war the entirely laudable idea was conceived of building a hotel in Australia that would compare with anything in the world. Such a thing had never been imagined before. A site was selected on Hayman Island, the most northerly of the Whitsunday Group, and the services of an imaginative architect, Mr Guildford Bell, engaged. At considerable expense and labour, the Royal Hayman Hotel was slowly constructed, finally opening its portals in 1950. Elegant white lodges, with private telephones and bathrooms, were separated from a curve of white sand by nothing more than the thickness of sliding glass doors. Behind these lodges, each of which was set in its own patch of lawn amongst magnolias and alamanda, the island carried its thick forest steeply up to a granitic skyline nearly a thousand feet above sea level. Other islands, larger and smaller, encircle Hayman, reducing the horizon and holding back the severer assaults of the south-east Trades. The hotel possessed a swimming pool, two tennis courts, numerous terraces, an excellent chef. The moon-shaped bar looked out through coconut palms at an expanse of turquoise sea that drew back at low tide to expose a vast coral reef. In the daytime, launches took guests on cruises to the Outer Reef, on fishing trips, and on excursions to the lesser islands: nearer home, they could choose between aquaplaning, swimming, and fossicking on the reef. Oysters from adjacent rocks could be taken for the picking. At night, there was dancing in the cleverly simulated tropical darkness of the cabaret room. The basic tariff was four Australian pounds a day.

Unfortunately the idea has not worked out. The reasons were complex and symptomatic. Australians, generally speaking, neither like nor appreciate the subtler refinements of good living. Those who have money have mostly made it the hard way, and see no point in such indulgences as uniformed waiters and French wines. Evening dress was required at Hayman, and Australian men, apart from disliking formal clothes, tend to feel uncomfortable in sophisticated surroundings. There are, of course, many exceptions to these generalizations, but not, unfortunately, enough to have made the Royal Hayman Hotel, at its original level, a paying proposition. The average Australian —and Australia is one of the few countries in the world where the term 'average' possesses validity—likes to have his beers before dinner, and then soak them up with as little fuss as possible. The American millionaires, whom the proprietor doubtless also had in mind, did not come either, for one reason or another. They have their own playgrounds in the Caribbean, and Florida and Hawaii are very much nearer. Hayman Island is a long way from anywhere. The British, who might also have been prospective clients, were at that moment involved in bitter domestic struggles; in any case, few of them had ever heard of Hayman Island.

After it had been running for some months at an impractical loss, the original plan for the Royal Hayman Hotel was reluctantly scrapped. The tariff was cut by half, a less demanding clientele was sought. This inevitable conclusion was accelerated by the series of tragic happenings which took place on June 25th, 1952. On that particular day Sir John Northcott, Governor of New South Wales, visited the island, Mr Ian Cutler, manager of the hotel and a former A.D.C. to the Governor, previously having requested tourists from neighbouring settlements to leave the jetty free that morning, and not to land. His request was disregarded, and soon after the Governor's arrival a large party arrived from South Molle. Cutler was on his way back to the jetty in the gaily-striped little train, rather like the Emett railway in the Festival Gardens at Battersea, that serves to bring guests, luggage and supplies the quarter-mile from pier-head to hotel, when he saw the trippers making their way ashore. He stopped the train and asked them to go back. He then continued on his way, loaded the train and began the return journey.

No one later seemed very clear about what happened next, or how it came to happen. It is enough to say that the party of trippers paid no attention to Cutler's warning, and that three of them were somehow hit by the train and knocked into the sea. One of these, a man aged sixty, cut his head on the coral and died immediately. Within minutes Cutler was set upon from behind and thrown into the water beside the body of the dead man. He sustained injuries that required several painful operations.

This is not the place to go into the rights and wrongs of it. Others, in any case, have done so.* But the facts are common knowledge. Cutler, still on crutches, was committed for trial at the end of October on a charge of having unlawfully killed Thomas May. The jury on this occasion failed to agree and were discharged. A fortnight later a new jury, after being out for four hours, returned a verdict of Not Guilty. About who had attacked Cutler, no evidence was forthcoming. The South Molle party were kept for several hours together in their launch awaiting interrogation, and nobody subsequently professed to have seen or heard anything. It would be surprising had it been otherwise.

During my stay on Hayman I spoke to several of the staff who had worked in the hotel in its hey-day. All, without exception, regretted the change. The island has, however, retained its beauty; the hotel, though less richly furnished, is elegantly designed and extremely comfortable. Most days I had the swimming pool, illuminated at night, entirely to myself. Three former English sailors make drinks expertly in their chromium bar. Outwardly, apart from the cuisine and the present non-stop blare of commercial radio, little has altered. The beach and the reef are at your window. You can still fish and aquaplane and charter a launch to anywhere you want. Or you can lie all day under a casuarina tree and sun-bathe. Hayman in many ways continues to offer the perfect life. But it is always sad to see the failure of a daring and imaginative conception: not because exclusiveness is necessarily a thing to be respected, but because quality is.

* * *

I was fortunate in that my first day at Hayman coincided with tide and weather conditions ideal for a visit to the Outer

---

* Alan Moorehead has described the Hayman Affair brilliantly, and in much greater detail, in his book *Rum Jungle*.

Reef. It can happen that these do not exist for periods upwards of a week, and even then boats frequently have to turn back. A launch had already been chartered, and in company with thirty others I set out early the next morning.

The Great Barrier Reef, running for over 1,250 miles from just south of Gladstone on the Queensland coast to a point east of the Torres Strait, between New Guinea and the Cape York peninsula, is the largest coral reef in the world. Its area is 80,000 square miles, and it contains more than 600 coral islands, not counting thousands of smaller reefs and shoals. Of the whole lot, under a dozen are inhabited. It is not a continuous line, but consists of two series of coral reefs, an outer and an inner, with shallow or deep interrupting channels, the majority of the reefs being completely covered, except at low tide. Within this broken barrier, which runs parallel to the coast at varying distances between five and fifty miles, are various groups of islands. Some of these, like Heron Island in the Capricorns, are known as coral cays, low-lying, oval, and surrounded by large coral ramparts. Those that have a central lagoon are called atolls. Their size depends on their age; few of them are larger than Heron Island, which is a mile in circumference. Hayman Island belongs to the more considerable category of island, those that were once part of the mainland, and which formed their reef by tiny coral polyps stretching upwards to the shallow warm surface as the land sank. Mostly they resemble floating mountain ranges, settling heavily into the sea like crocodiles, with the water breaking at throat level. They are thickly forested, predominantly with gums and pines, and below their great granite cliffs, small sandy bays dangle like aprons.

It was past several of these that we made our way, the sea deep blue and the sun splaying over it through a layer of high white cumulus. The reef that had been chosen as our objective was twenty-seven miles out, a journey of three hours. It was almost noon when, with the islands lost behind us, we sighted the reef. The whole way across we had been accompanied by an escort of gulls, while deep-sea garfish, dolphins and Spanish mackerel shot high-spiritedly across our bows. Lines were trolled from the stern and it was not so much a question of how many you would catch as of how many you could bother to pull in. The surface of the sea shivered as though a vast tarpaulin, containing millions of sea-creatures newly let out of school, was being rippled under it.

At first, the reef was no more than a lightening of the blueness: as we came up to it, the deep crisp blue flattened out into satiny strips of peacock and turquoise. Gradually the area of these strips increased and as we patrolled slowly parallel to them, black coral boulders began to protrude through the top, continually growing, until it seemed that a ridge of hills was about to break surface. In fact, these 'niggerheads,' which are chunks of coral broken off the main structure of the reef by storms, are comparatively small, but, enlarged by an illusion of light and angle, appear huge. The next thing that one noticed was the sea breaking on the far side of the reef, the long Pacific swell petering out on steep protective precipices that pointed in all directions.

It was not long before the coral itself appeared, looking in the distance no different from any flat stony beach when the tide has just gone out. The launch anchored as close to the reef as possible, and a boat was lowered, returning from the reef several times to pick up more passengers, each of whom clasped a glass-bottomed tin and a stout stick. This procedure was not without disaster, for an elderly man, who had long set his heart on this trip, fell down the gangway and broke two ribs. An American, who had travelled 3,000 miles to see the reef, decided at the last moment, as if in poetic compensation, that it was not the place for him, and also remained on board.

The rest of us waded ashore from the dinghy in batches, splashing through the deeper outlying pools to the grey, limestone centre. Already those who had gone in the first boat-load were reduced to tiny blobs in the distance. The pale shell light is such that everything stands out with brilliant clarity against it. Though the tropical sun was directly overhead the harshness of its rays seemed to have been absorbed by wisps of faint, cotton-wool cloud.

An hour and a half is about the length of time for which you can walk about on the reef without being cut off by the tide. Sometimes people leave it too late, panic, and hurrying back over sharp and projecting pieces of coral, cut themselves badly.

It is impossible on the reef not to be amazed, first and foremost, by the fact that one is there at all, leisurely walking about and talking fifty miles out in the Pacific, with no land in sight, and the frilly line of breakers rustling in round you like paper on a baking dish. That basic feeling of unreality never leaves one, though soon it is submerged by the extraordinary excitement of seeing, larger and brighter even than in reproduction, the coral gardens that, through childhood, transfixed one in the colour plates of encyclopædias.

The reef resembles, more than anything, I suppose, the interior of the human body, especially the head, as it appears on the charts in doctor's surgeries. This does not make it sound wildly exciting. But, though the greater proportion of the hard coral is of the meandrine or brain type, in the pools that form about it or in the cup-like depressions natural to coral itself, the most fantastic and exotic kinds of marine life are on display.

For the first few moments, intent on keeping my feet, I noticed principally the round, brown coral, pitted like brain cells. Extremely smooth, these are scattered about as if for the express purpose of acting as stepping stones. Around them were softer, rubbery varieties, some looking like the human heart, others like entrails or fœtuses, still others like sponges, mushrooms and cauliflowers. Dotted among these were delicate honeycomb structures, like children's doll's-houses seen from the top with their roofs off. You can, however, describe the coral how you like, for there is no shape or texture that you can imagine which is not there somewhere. At intervals I trod on alcyonarians, looking like yellow boxing gloves tied together. Above the water, brittle antler-shaped corals branched out in clusters of pink, lavender, rose, green and yellow, some with tips of a different colour to the branches. Gales cause havoc to these staghorn coral, breaking them off and leaving them on the coral rock like fallen candelabra.

It is some while before one gets used to the idea that not only are the inhabitants of the pools alive, but so is the coral itself. In the daytime, unfortunately, the polyps retreat into their porous lime-stone cups, for they feed only at night; if therefore one wishes to see the radiant colours of the living coral one has to seek it out at night by torchlight. But though the coral tends to seem beautifully inanimate, nothing else does. Each step one takes through a garden as colourfully interwoven as a Victorian glass paperweight, causes something to spit out, glide away or draw itself abruptly in.

After half an hour I had grown familiar with clams of every shape, colour and size. Out of the water their sinuous mantles have a dull gleam, but, below surface, examined through glass boxes, they glow like living jewellery. Half-open in their encrusted grey shells they tighten their brilliant double lips over anything you put into them. All round me, the mantles glistened like coloured velvet—blue, green, purple, bronze, sometimes in two- or three-coloured strips. One was constantly being told tales about 'giant' clams, reaching a length of four feet and weighing as much as five hundredweight, that had closed over the legs of divers and drowned them; but, although I saw none as large as that, I poked my stick into several that could comfortably have taken my foot.

More exotically patterned even than the clams, sea-anemones went out like coloured lights as they felt one's approach. From a few yards off, you could see them lying like underwater flowers against fringes of seaweed, usually some minute, gorgeously-coloured fish ready to dart out from their protection. Then, as you came nearer, the anemone curled back into the underside of the coral, the fish flicked away into a clump of staghorns.

These tiny anemone-fish, of which the demoiselle is the prettiest, work in conjunction with the anemone, leading all sorts of marine prey into the anemone's tentacles, and sharing the victims. Certain pools were throbbing with evident life, clams discharging water like geysers, coral snakes sliding over the backs of scuttling crabs, three-inch, glazed-blue demoiselles with gold tails being sleuthed by persistent yellow-and-white striped suitors, garmented like footballers. Here and there, a pool lay relaxed and silent as a formal garden. Each brand of dense, or soft, coral seemed to have contributed some part of the arrangement, usually completed by a large blue sea-star, straddling the pool like a plump bather floating on his back. Sea-stars, like nearly everything else on the Barrier Reef, grow to extraordinary sizes; often of handsome colour, they tend as a rule to have an over-indulged, blown look.

By the time the launch had begun to hoot, the reef was steadily contracting, warm buoyant water running gently in with the noise of a low-pressure hose. The party had split up, some of them the whole length of the reef apart, which must have been half a mile, and they came leisurely in, moon-walkers stopping to peer in pool after pool, unable to tear themselves away.

I suppose I saw the Outer Reef under as favourable conditions as it is possible to do so. Certainly those conditions were not repeated during the next fortnight and no other expeditions to my knowledge left for the reef during that time. Some things, of course, I did not see: the stone fish, for one, a slimy, wart-covered creature with vomit-green mouth that pulls itself along like a slug. Fortunately, probably, for it is among the most poisonous fish in the world, the pain from contact with one of its thirteen, needle-sharp spines usually causing death from shock or asphyxia, before the victim even has time to die from the paralysis and complete loss of red corpuscles, which are the basic consequences of the stone-fish's sting. Nor did I notice any sharks, the mysteriously-transmitted warning of whose presence causes the Red Emperors, the peacock-coloured parrot-fish, the demoiselles and coral trout and Harlequin Smilers suddenly to evaporate. The effect is equivalent to shaking up a kaleidoscope. When, a little while later, one looks down again, the tightly-organized sections of colour are still there, but they are not the same ones. Only those creatures that adhere to the coral remain.

I missed one other marine drama, a common phenomenon of the Reef: the ritual attack of frigate-birds on foraging gulls. The methods of these high-soaring air-pirates are symbolic of the ruthless parasitism of reef life. The frigate-bird, poised motionless high above the coral, waits around till it sees a gull on its way home, its beak full of fish. Selecting one that has foraged well, it dives vertically on it at tremendous speed, leaving the gull no alternative but to disgorge its capture. The frigate-bird continues its dive, picking up the fish with incredible dexterity in its own beak before they reach the sea. Then it climbs happily back to its wind-perch up aloft, to wait the arrival of the next diligent housewife. This parasitical procedure is not confined to frigate-birds alone; it extends to almost every living species on the reef, gulls included, who themselves prey on terns and smaller birds, in much the same way as the frigate-bird does on them.

Though I made no further trips to the Outer Reef, I spent many afternoons on the coral reefs between Hayman and Hook Island. Each island has its own coral platform projecting under the surface like a kind of under-skirt. On these you can swim or walk waist-high in water for considerable distances; eventually you reach the edge, a sudden precipice dropping to a depth of anything up to a hundred fathoms. Much more of this coral, exposed daily at low tide, is dead, for coral cannot long survive in fresh air. The rains on the Reef damage the coral almost as severely, for fresh water is as lethal to it as fresh air. Except for this the island coral-pools are no less absorbing than those on the Outer Reef.

The most conspicuous objects on these coral platforms are the bêches-de-mer, which lie about in hundreds, usually across one another, looking more than anything, from a few yards off, like the black velvet ribbons that stream from the straw hats worn by girls in the pictures of Renoir or Berthe Morisot. In fact, they are sausage-shaped, heavy with water, which, as you handle them, drains out, leaving them slack and reducing them to half their original size. If you prod long enough, they will eject a kind of sticky thread, that winds round and round their bodies until they are tied up like a parcel. Most of the time, they rest limply on one another, as if inanimate; but now and again I would see one crawling laboriously across a pool, its tube-feet contracting and expanding. In an afternoon's reefing I used to see several thousand. Before the war, the bêche-de-mer industry was the second largest on the Barrier Reef, the Chinese, who spent up to £30,000 a year on them, using them as a basis for various soups. Recently, however, the Chinese have inclined to spend their money on other things, and bêche-de-mer fishing, commercially speaking, is virtually extinct.

No two days on the reef were ever the same. Certain afternoons seemed to be especially favourable for the student of crabs—pale-blue soldier-crabs, marching along the sand in battle formation, hundreds at a time; fur crabs, their shells luxuriously swathed, waddling off like middle-aged women on their way to a theatre; sand crabs, always out of sight, but the sand above their tunnels dotted with ventilation shafts; spider crabs, bearing self-made seaweed gardens on their backs. These reef-crabs, like the mantis shrimps and bright-painted lobsters one met in deeper water, have cerulean undersides, faintly mapped with pink.

Coral rocks, beneath their sharp mauve crust of oysters, are similarly coloured. Sea-urchins, balls of sinister black quills with five, differently-coloured button eyes among them, sometimes rolled out from under them or from projecting bits of brain coral. Singly, or in grotesque quartets, they rolled over and over across adjacent pieces of slimy, weed-covered coral biscuit, marked with sea-star patterns, as though belonging to a proprietary brand, before subsiding clumsily in the sand.

As one sloshes about knee-deep in water, there is a constant popping of seaweed, a geyser-like eruption of clams. Searching, perhaps, for a cowrie, or a sunset-coloured spider shell, one's eye would be caught by a crab half-way into a helmet-shell, by a baby octopus no bigger than a postage stamp, or an exposed patch of lavender coral. I never found one of the beautiful bailer shells, so-called because the natives use them to bail from their canoes, which fishermen occasionally brought back from Arkhurst Island, across the bay. But I did find a graphis cone, fetchingly mottled on the outside, orange inside, one of the most poisonous shells in the world. Not long ago, a man picked one up on this reef, remarking after a few moments that his hand had gone completely dead. His friends noticed a dull, bruise-coloured mark on his flesh, but imagined him to be exaggerating. Some minutes later, he began to circle aimlessly, complaining about a fog in his head and asking where he was. Within half an hour he was dead. Inside the graphis cone is a sharp-toothed tentacle, secreting a deadly venom, which, when the creature is aroused, shoots out of the shell.

In England, one is accustomed to thinking of shells as being empty, as objects in themselves; on the Reef, one learns that every shell harbours a creature, and that most of them are slowly moving from one place to another in search of food. The coral itself, unable to digest plants, lives entirely on animals. In turn, every single one of these teeming millions of creatures fancies one or other of its neighbours, using every conceivable kind of subterfuge and decoy to entice it. Every morsel of weed or sea-plant desires and is desirable to something else; whatever one catches and cuts up, contains some other species in its belly.

Nor is this struggle for survival, with its nocturnal plot and counter-plot, confined to the sea only. Death-adders lurk along the granitic spine of Hayman, in dry weather slithering down the red hill in search of water. They, too, take their toll of insects and lizards, not even scorning to present themselves in the white lodges of the guests.

In late afternoon I used often to hear the whooping of foxes, a noise like a child's top running down, and watch the goats, deposited on the islands originally for shipwrecked mariners, miraculously scrambling, as if on high heels, over the coral.

Yet, despite this unceasing marine warfare, the islands and waters of the Barrier Reef rarely give the impression of anything but unruffled content. Like most human illusions, it is one we preserve as long as possible for our own comfort.

* * *

The rains are not generally due over the Reef before early January, but half-way through my stay at Hayman the weather broke, and from then on the sun made only phantom appearances through low, stationary cloud. For a few hours at a time it rained; then, around sunset, the light filtered over the coral flats, the sky flooding behind Whitsunday and Long Islands, and the surrounding hills turning a smoky purple. Before night finally descended, strips of ochre and heliotrope widened behind the line of pandanus palms and casuarinas alternating along the foreshore.

At dawn and sunset the cockatoos, rosella parrots and currawongs are at their noisiest. Hayman is full of these birds, never silent for one moment of the day. The currawongs, black and rapacious-looking with white markings on their tails and Jewish-shaped beaks, make an indescribable noise, a kind of discreet, trilling belch, both resonant and gay, quite unlike the sound produced by any other bird. Despite their appearance, they are beautiful in flight: one awoke to them and went to sleep with their incessant chatter in one's ears.

The hour before dark was my favourite. If the tide was out, flotillas of gulls stalked importantly about between the upturned boats, inclining occasionally to peck juicy morsels out of the coral. The sea was quiet, as if in prayer for the battles ahead of it. At intervals, flights of white cockatoos would tear out of the coconut palms or poincianas, or curlews circle in the oyster light, crying plaintively.

The last, sunless days I spent hours lying on my stomach at the end of the jetty, watching schools of parrot fish and pike twist among the pier-stakes. Twice I saw green turtles surfacing sadly in pairs, soon flippering away as if in disappointment at the weather. Sometimes I rowed over to Black Island, where golden orchids, shaped like coral, grow right down to the rocks. The only shark I saw, though they were reported every day, was a dead one that drifted ashore one afternoon.

At dusk, I would return in time to see the huge, black, island butterflies shaking themselves out of the coral-tree in front of my window. On certain evenings, on my way to the bar, I would notice the albatrosses, looking like small aeroplanes, gliding in the air currents over the fading water.

The people in the hotel, almost as interesting as the specimens on the Reef, would need a novel to themselves—Americans collecting shells for mid-Western museums, Czech table-tennis champions, fruit-machine addicts, underwater fishermen, beach-combers with classical educations, Sydney waitresses on holiday—but I have been on the Reef long enough already.

10 Proserpine to Mascot

The islands float away on a sea of greenish milk: so numerous, it seems that they were flung there like pebbles from a great height. Our launch, *Miramar II*, points her nose between mauve haze-hung headlands, their vegetation a mass of tight foliage under cracked bald ridges. A dawn of leaping fish, the air wholesome, the cool sun climbing. All round us, private islands, islands for sale, as manageable as kitchen-gardens. Water, most likely, is a problem, but not money, nor clothes, nor food. Nearly all are uninhabited, going almost at cost price, which is to say, for next to nothing. Imagine a white villa set against coconut palms, a crescent of coral beach, a line of casuarinas. A vineyard, paw-paws, figs. At night, strolling among the drugging scents of poinciana, magnolia, frangipani, hibiscus. Parrots, cockatoos, currawongs. Goats to pose against the skyline. A sailing boat, a motor-launch. Goggles and a spear. The Outer Reef only three hours into the Pacific; the coral shelf, the most exotic club in the world, at your feet. And sunsets, those slow, lethal cocktails of the tropics, that bind you to a place as surely as ever love does. What would there be to fear? Why don't we stop all the nonsense of our lives, pack up, once and for all, and buy our island?

The launch, taking us away for ever, sidles in to Cannonvale, the Whitsunday islands, with Hayman further to seaward, lost in sea-dazzle. The bus jolts through the brilliant cane-fields, setting us down in the melancholy clearing of Proserpine airport, not guarded fortunately by three-headed watchdogs. We race at the gums, the ghost gums of Australia, stalking in skeletal procession under us, scattering their ash. Flying at 4,000 feet in our D.C.3 we pass over nothing, nothing at all. No cattle, no houses; only swamps, gum trees, river-beds, hills. What would finally turn one away from this lovely coast of Queensland is that, though different in shape, its islands are all alike. Progressively, they dull one's faculties, for landscapes need, if not the reality of people, at least the idea of human life. It is not so much the Australian past that one misses, but the present. The past, since its nature is to be fragmentary, can be imagined: of the present we demand proof. Australia, æsthetically as well as economically, needs more people.

We land at Mackay; then, an hour later, tilting over the gun-metal wriggle of the Fitzroy River, at Rockhampton. The airfield, stifling and dusty, drives one longingly back into the air. Two hours later, we sight Brisbane, laid out like a town-planner's model. The river snakes its way to the sea, the bridges flash against their dark lining of fig trees. At roof-level the suburbs seem to be waddling away on their stilts, off, in aboriginal fashion, on 'walk-about.' The rows of palms wave like feather-boas, the western sky suddenly occluded. A storm brews up beyond our port wing-tip. We bump down amid ominous rumblings into the atmosphere of a boiler-room.

At Brisbane we change planes, forsaking our genial run-about and climbing steeply out of Eagle Farm on the four mighty motors, with reversible propellers, of a Douglas Super Skychief. Seats are foam-rubber padded; the fully-pressurized cabin changes its 1,300 cubic feet of air every three minutes. Warmth is maintained, and noise reduced, by the use of laminated mica and fibre-glass.

At 16,000 feet we straighten out, purring southwards over cushions of white cloud. Our speed is 300 miles per hour, vibration negligible, sensation nil. There is no land visible, nothing to reassure us that we are on the planet Earth. The man in the next seat tilts his chair back as if at the dentist, mouth wide-open, eyes shut. He snores gently; the hostess offers me a sweet, forbearing to pop one between the adjacent rows of teeth. There is, on the Reef, a shell which perfectly resembles an upper denture.

The clouds are veined like marble; only the striations are not land, but intervening sky. The wings gleam pink-bronze, scuffed by wisps of cloud. This cloud non-land, beyond reach of the birds, which has the perfection of classical sculpture—movement trapped at a split-second of tension into stillness—possesses a futile power of intoxication: it is not hard to understand how pilots, bored by invulnerability, aim their machines at the sun and keep on going. The great suicides have done this, not out of foolhardiness, but as fatalistic acts.

Looking at my map, the sign *Fasten Seatbelts* flicking on for'ard, I see that I have travelled 1,200 miles today.

But I have nothing more than a thirst to show for it. No sense of exploration, no discomfort either. Flying has a certain clinical fascination, but is without flavour, aseptic. It is not travel, for it leaves no residue behind it, nothing to identify, or separate one flight from another. For the passenger, wonder is soon ousted by boredom.

We are aimed at Sydney now, dropping down past Lake Macquarie through white cloudfields thinning out over the dark bristle of trees, shaped like a clothes-brush, behind the surf of Manly. To port are the red roofs, the blue inlets of Watson's Bay, Vaucluse, Rose Bay, Mosman. Lights thicken down the main avenues, the sky-signs the colour of nougat-sundaes. The green turns to mounds of sinking velvet, spattered with nests of coalescing light. The fine gold tracery of foreshore throbs, doubling itself on water. Blocks of flats lean their yellow, honeycombed stalks of cement against the dark. Pylons and mastheads and lighthouses flash their lemon arms.

We turn our great wings earthward, towards the moving traffic, the wrangle and pleasure of life. At Mascot we touch the ground, regaining, Antæus-like, our strength from contact with the soil.

* * *

The evening papers announce the teams for the Second Test. Keith Miller and Ian Johnson have been declared unfit, so Morris will captain Australia. Burke comes in for Johnson, Davidson for Miller. Hutton has replaced Simpson with Graveney. Appleyard and Wardle are amongst the twelve from whom the team will be chosen, Compton still not in the running. Bedser's name is last on the list. Can it be that they are thinking of dropping him? Either Wardle or Appleyard must now play. If Hutton decides on both, then Tyson or Bedser must stand down: and Tyson has this last week bowled exceptionally well against Victoria. It will be a nasty decision. Up to this Test, Bedser, Miller and Morris are the only three to have played in all postwar Anglo-Australian Tests. If Bedser does not play, then Morris will be the sole survivor.

Hutton, I hope, will not this time pick his team, and decide whether to bat or field, without regard to the wicket. One of the touring captain's real advantages is that he can delay the selection of his side till the very last minute, without administrative inconvenience. It is a pity, with a party as badly balanced as ours, to throw this advantage away.

11 The Second Test Match
December 17 — 23

ENGLAND

L. Hutton, c. Davidson, b. Johnston	30	c. Benaud, b. Johnston	28
T. E. Bailey, b. Lindwall	0	c. Langley, b. Archer	6
P. B. H. May, c. Johnston, b. Archer	5	b. Lindwall	104
T. W. Graveney, c. Favell, b. Johnston	21	c. Langley, b. Johnston	0
M. C. Cowdrey, c. Langley, b. Davidson	23	c. Archer, b. Benaud	54
W. J. Edrich, c. Benaud, b. Archer	10	b. Archer	29
F. Tyson, b. Lindwall	0	b. Lindwall	9
T. G. Evans, c. Langley, b. Archer	3	c. Lindwall, b. Archer	4
J. H. Wardle, c. Burke, b. Johnston	35	l.b.w., b. Lindwall	8
R. Appleyard, c. Hole, b. Davidson	8	not out	19
J. B. Statham, not out	14	c. Langley, b. Johnston	25
Extras (l.b. 5)	5	Extras (l.b. 6, n.b. 4)	10
Total	154	Total	296

FALL OF WICKETS. *First innings:* 1—14, 2—19, 3—58, 4—63, 5—84, 6—85, 7—88, 8—99, 9—111. *Second innings:* 1—18, 2—55, 3—55, 4—171, 5—222, 6—232, 7—239, 8—249, 9—250.

AUSTRALIA

A. Morris, c. Hutton, b. Bailey	12	l.b.w., b. Statham	10
L. Favell, c. Graveney, b. Bailey	26	c. Edrich, b. Tyson	16
J. Burke, c. Graveney, b. Bailey	44	b. Tyson	14
R. N. Harvey, c. Cowdrey, b. Tyson	12	not out	92
G. Hole, b. Tyson	12	b. Tyson	0
R. Benaud, l.b.w., b. Statham	20	c. Tyson, b. Appleyard	12
R. Archer, c. Hutton, b. Tyson	49	b. Tyson	6
A. Davidson, b. Statham	20	c. Evans, b. Statham	5
R. R. Lindwall, c. Evans, b. Tyson	19	b. Tyson	8
G. Langley, b. Bailey	5	b. Statham	0
W. Johnston, not out	0	c. Evans, b. Tyson	11
Extras (b. 5, l.b. 2, n.b. 2)	9	Extras (l.b. 7, n.b. 3)	10
Total	228	Total	184

FALL OF WICKETS. *First innings:* 1—18, 2—64, 3—100, 4—104, 5—122, 6—141, 7—193, 8—213, 9—224. *Second innings:* 1—27, 2—34, 3—77, 4—77, 5—102, 6—122, 7—127, 8—136, 9—145.

Bowling Analysis

AUSTRALIA

	First Innings					Second Innings			
	O.	M.	R.	W.		O.	M.	R.	W.
Lindwall	17	3	47	2	Lindwall	31	10	69	3
Archer	12	7	12	3	Archer	21	9	53	3
Davidson	12	3	34	2	Johnston	19.3	2	70	3
Johnston	13.3	1	56	3	Davidson	13	2	52	0
					Benaud	19	3	42	1

ENGLAND

	First Innings					Second Innings			
	O.	M.	R.	W.		O.	M.	R.	W.
Statham	18	1	83	2	Statham	19	6	45	3
Bailey	17.4	3	59	4	Tyson	18.4	1	85	6
Tyson	13	2	45	4	Bailey	6	0	21	0
Appleyard	7	1	32	0	Appleyard	6	1	12	1
					Wardle	4	2	11	0

ENGLAND WON BY 38 RUNS

* * *

First Day: There was a violent thunderstorm during the night, and, though the drizzle that succeeded it stopped about breakfast-time, the weather was not conducive to gaiety. Nor was the light good. Driving to the ground, one might have been on one's way to Old Trafford. By eleven o'clock, modest crowds were streaming through the avenue of heavy palms that links the city tramlines to the cricket ground; the gates, however, were not open, and they were obliged to wind themselves on to the end of a queue well-equipped with raincoats, parasols and umbrellas. Twenty minutes before play was due to begin the sun came out, the audience permitted to enter. The rumour was that Bedser, regardless of the conditions, would not play: it turned out to be correct, and there were few who did not think it folly. It looked just the day for him, the atmosphere heavy, the wicket a genuine green-top. Hutton, however, lost the toss, and Morris, most bravely in view of Brisbane, put England in to bat. Had Hutton won this, the nastiest of tosses to win, Bedser's absence would probably have obliged him to choose to bat in any case. Yet, despite the wicket's apparent greenness, Morris was taking some considerable risk. His action showed how little he thought of England's two spin bowlers. Hassett, sitting next to me at lunch, subsequently committed himself to stating that it was not a risk he would have dared to take.

Hutton and Bailey, therefore, came out with stoical countenances, Lindwall going through his habitual unloosenings, the umbrella-field folding round the striker. Hutton took guard, warily eyeing the arc of five slips and two close fine legs, chewing slowly. Thus does a keeper, entering the cage, sense the tiger.

Hutton, in the first over, turned Lindwall for two off his leg stump with loose wrists and delicate application of the guiding hand, a stroke to calm nerves. A few balls later he leaned a full toss past gully for four. Archer bowled tight at the other end, just short of a length, which is the right foil to Lindwall, who barters runs for wickets generously in his opening overs. Without either third man or deep fine leg, any stroke that beats the close arc is worth four runs. Morris provided Lindwall with his usual 'Carmody' field, and Lindwall, keeping the ball right up, moved it a lot both ways. Lindwall works up gradually to full pace, preferring to let the shine do the work for him in the early stages, and his first three overs were not fast. Hutton nowadays prefers to steer away, rather than hit, the widish half-volley, with body not truly over the ball, and Lindwall generally attacked this area. Bailey played Archer with dead bat and back foot outside the off stump for three successive maidens. Johnston then came on for Lindwall. The first half hour was weathered, with fourteen runs scored, all off Hutton's bat. Lindwall, however, had retired only to change ends, and now, in his first over from the Noble Stand end, a breeze blowing in from cover, he sent Bailey's middle stump somersaulting. The ball dipped in late, and Bailey, late down on it, was yorked. May is always an agreeable sight at number three, for while not being incapable of airy waves outside the off stump, he gives an immediate impression of impending assault. Moreover, he encourages, with his full swing, the idea that the fall of the first wicket was of little account. He was not long in, though, for, after several firm strokes, he drove at an in-swinging half-volley from Archer with insufficient control, and the ball shot off the inside edge straight at Johnston's midriff fine of short square leg. Graveney, next man in, for some minutes made no sense at all, straddling his legs as if playing leap-frog and withdrawing his bat at the last second. Lindwall found various edges subsequently, Graveney pushing and missing at both him and Archer, and taking the ball on the thigh when it came down the line of the leg stump. Hutton, smoothly efficient early on, was rendered strokeless by a combination of misery and accurate attack. So it continued till the interval, at which England were 34 for 2 after ninety minutes of increasing discomfort. Archer had bowled seven overs for four runs and one wicket. This was the first of four successive gloomy pre-lunch sessions for England.

Graveney looked better for his lunch, playing Lindwall firmly off the front foot and once driving Johnston with elegant swing past cover. He is, however, a player of yacht-like character, beautiful in calm seas, yet at the mercy of every change of weather. There are no obvious faults in construction, but the barometer has only to fall away a point or two from fair for way to be completely lost and the boat broached to, if not turned for harbour. Lindwall bowled two magnificent overs to Hutton, varying swing and pace, adjusting them each ball as he attacked one stump and then another. Hutton was never allowed to let one go by with certainty, nor did he receive a ball of length short enough for it to have straightened out. The trajectory was full and gradual, the ball holding up at the end of its flight for the breeze to drift it across. Hutton played thoughtfully and without impatience, but there were no pickings at either end. A whole hour more passed before Hutton turned Lindwall through the short legs to send up the fifty, which had taken 150 minutes. Lindwall wound up with two bouncers of great savagery that curved Graveney back like a sapling, and then demanded his sweater. Davidson bowled in place of him, which meant that two left-handers were in operation, Johnston wheeling away at varying speeds from the other end. Davidson was lively and quick off the pitch, but the ball usually went straight through after pitching. Johnston alternated between floating the ball away towards the slips, and digging it in, rather quicker, just short of a length on the leg, two fielders crouching off the batsman's hip. Together, with the score 58, they took the vital wicket: Hutton flicked at an in-swinger pitching on his legs and Davidson at leg slip flung himself yards to his right, catching the ball right-handed (the wrong hand for him) grass-high. The stroke was technically perfect, the ball kept well down and steered fine of the wicket-keeper. Hutton stood bemused, uncertain of what had happened, much as an actor might, who having delivered a line with cutting irony, finds it answered with words not in the script. Slowly, very slowly, he walked from the wicket. Before he can have got his pads off Graveney joined him, pushing out at a ball from Johnston that, pitching a foot outside the off stump, was proceeding towards third slip. Graveney helped it on its way and Favell, a puppyish fielder, frisky in the chase, took a low tumbling catch.

Cowdrey and Edrich were therefore obliged to start again from scratch, rather as if beginning the innings, but with the knowledge that none were to follow. Neither looked unduly disconcerted. Cowdrey glided Johnston still finer than Hutton had done, the pupil instructing the master as it were, and received four runs. Edrich pulled a no-ball from Archer to the square-leg boundary, and his bat continued to make healthy noises. Cowdrey, calm and relaxed, was disposed to treat the bowling with no more than the deference expected of youth. Twenty were added: then Archer, who had taken Edrich's wicket at Brisbane, got one to lift abruptly on the off stump and Edrich, already in position, could not avoid giving Benaud a gentle catch at gully. Tyson arrived, and Lindwall could hardly get his sweater off quick enough. His eagerness was pardonable, for he quickly knocked back Tyson's leg stump. Evans, who for some weeks has played any ball on the off as if handing point his bat to hold, moved back to, and inside, a half-volley from Archer, and was caught by Langley. Three wickets had fallen for four runs and Archer, in ten overs and one ball, had taken three for eight. England at tea were 94 for 7, Cowdrey 18. Benaud dropped Cowdrey in the gully to the tinkle of teaspoons, but it was of small account, for Cowdrey, trying to force Davidson, was caught at the wicket five runs later. He had played admirably, but the ship was too badly holed and he was obliged to try and salvage what he could.

Appleyard put the hundred up, displaying a model forward stroke before Hole snatched a low fast snick at first slip. Wardle, who had been cavorting about as though wearing someone else's glasses, stabbing his bat a yard inside or outside the ball, now suddenly saw Johnston plain and with great good spirits hit him for 17 in one over. Four came from a strapping cover drive made on the hop, two upper-cuts sent second and third slip on futile chases to the boundary, and three hefty swings, made with bat and legs as far apart as the human frame can stand, just cleared the field for 2, 2 and 1. Benaud, running back, got his hands to one of these, but, to the delight of the Hill, failed to hold it. Statham, soberly professional at the other end, cut and drove when opportunity offered, but was largely content to observe Wardle with the good nature of one who had long outgrown such crudities. The 150 went up, and Morris began to bear the air of a stage manager who sees two comedians inserting unrehearsed jokes in an act already running late, and only reluctantly engaged at all. Eventually Burke caught Wardle at long-on very quietly, but not before 43 runs had been added in twenty minutes for the last wicket. No sooner was the ball pocketed than a great bundle of clouds, gathering for some while, sent the players off at the double, as fast as they had run all day.

With only half an hour left, Australia seemed safe till the morning. But the rain departed as rapidly as it had appeared, and finally Hutton had time to give Statham and Bailey two overs each. Morris and Favell scored 18 with discourteous hurry, until, with two balls to go, Bailey made one lift on the leg stump and Hutton at leg slip picked the ball politely off Morris's glove. It seemed almost too unobtrusive to have really happened.

* * *

Second Day: Favell and Burke set off at such a gallop under the loose grey clouds of noon that it looked as though England's 154 would be overtaken before lunch. Tyson was good for only two wild overs, and Statham was glanced and cut by both batsmen. Favell was quick to detect the length of the ball, and he lay back and thrashed anything at all short. Burke had a pale air of permanence about him, and he offered few edges. Fifty went up in forty-four minutes, and the field was unflatteringly spread for two fast bowlers reckoned to be as quick as any in the world. Hutton switched Statham, and brought Bailey on at the opposite end from the evening before. Bailey, by adroit and systematic attack on the region of the off stump, first halted, then drove back Australia. He kept a precise and determined length at no more than medium pace, pitching the ball on roughly the same spot, but using his bowling crease so variously that the angle and margin of swing altered constantly. There was little short enough to hit away off the back foot, little quite full enough to drive. As the ball pitched, it ran away towards the slips, so that the forward stroke had to be made outside the line of flight. Now and again Bailey, bowling a faster one straight, had Burke shuffling behind it in a hurry; and sometimes, after Favell had pushed forward to several in a row, one came back sharply at him, causing him to jab it down awkwardly in front of short leg. Both felt for, and missed, the ball that was delivered, with surprising bounce off the seam, as obliquely as possible.

Rightly enough, Bailey in the end dismissed them both, caught off identical strokes by Graveney at second slip. Favell departed at 65, leaning forward and getting an outside edge, and Burke at 100, immediately after lunch. Graveney held Favell ankle-high and Burke more easily at shoulder level.

Harvey was an hour over six runs, two of his scoring shots sending the ball skimming past the heads of May and Cowdrey in the gully. He seemed, however, to have settled down for the day when Tyson, whom Hutton had brought on for Statham, made one kick sharply. Harvey, already into his stroke, could not withdraw in time, and Cowdrey took as simple a catch in the gully as Benaud had done to remove Edrich from a similar ball. The lunch score of 100 for 2 had become 104 for 4. Tyson, bowling with admirable control and much fuller length from a shortened run, now made the ball both lift and break sharply back from the off. Hole, like many modern Australian batsmen, curves his back and bends his knees at the wicket, but he drove Bailey with so splendid a stroke to the cover boundary, having cut imperiously between slip and gully from the start, that patriotism and pleasure were made to struggle for supremacy. He had made only 12, several late cuts bringing no more than one run each, when Tyson slanted his leg stump. He is not happy against real pace. His back lift, circular rather than straight, is high, and he was no more than brushing pad with bat when the ball was through him. Benaud, morally bowled numerous times before scoring, was badly dropped when playing Tyson with the break into Graveney's hands at short leg. Bailey, in a spell of seventy minutes between lunch and tea, had both Benaud and Archer scraping forward and missing so monotonously that the stomachs of the three slips must have been turning over continuously with ungratified apprehension. Had Archer's bat possessed whiskers, it would assuredly have forfeited them several times over.

Nevertheless, they were together at tea, albeit poised as precariously as curates on a dowager's Regency chairs. Statham, returning for Tyson, had Benaud l.b.w. with a ball that both came back and kept low: but Graveney's missed catch had cost 20 runs. Appleyard had his first bowl of the series and, after several introductory balls of quality, was struck for four and six successively by Archer, who, wretched so long, seized on him with the relish of one who suddenly sees a familiar face in a hostile, crowded room. The second of these unexpected blows took Australia past England's score.

Archer was moving out of the precincts of banditry into the quiet suburbs of middle-order respectability, when the new ball became due. Davidson, his partner since tea, had helped him to add fifty in the same number of minutes, though both were frequently defeated. Nevertheless, in the intervals they made bold and imaginative strokes, Davidson driving splendidly to extra cover, where Hutton was slow to put a fieldsman. Australia's lead was fattening disagreeably when Davidson hit across a ball from Statham and lost his leg stump. Archer, one short of his fifty, was then beautifully caught by Hutton at third slip, Tyson having not long before taken the new ball. Lindwall drove and cut his way into double figures, the ninth Australian to do so, before he swung at a tired bouncer from Tyson and obliged Evans to catch him off his glove. Things had moved at so rapid a pace that, were Johnston or Langley to get out quickly, England would be faced with seven or eight minutes' batting. Hutton, therefore, commanded Tyson to bowl down the leg side, which he did, to Johnston's keen disappointment, even beyond the range of the latter's one-handed sweep. With exactly ten minutes left, Bailey rattled Langley's middle and off stumps in the manner of one who could take a wicket whichever ball he wished. Australia, all out for 228, were 74 ahead. But, due primarily to Bailey, who had taken the first three wickets, England were not out of it. They had attacked, and, if they were to have any hopes of winning the match, they had to continue to do so.

* * *

Third Day: The pattern was little different from that of England's first innings, though the recovery came earlier and was longer sustained. Bailey once again looked devoid of shots, lasting this time for forty minutes, but without ever seeming likely to do other than delay the inevitable. Hutton had no alternative to Bailey to open the innings with him; a week ago he and Bailey had put on ninety for the first wicket against Victoria.

Yet, watching Bailey now against Lindwall and Archer, his unsuitability was painfully made evident. An opening over of half-volleys from Archer was patted gently back, with only two fielders in front of the wicket. An opening batsman must be able sometimes to drive the over-pitched ball, and Bailey, for all his solid virtues lower down the order, holds his bat in such a manner as to preclude the free swing of the left elbow. He made of his bat the usual barricade, but, with Hutton ruminative, that was too unambitious in the circumstances. In Archer's fourth over, the first three having been maidens, Bailey failed to get behind a ball that moved away late off the seam, providing Langley with the simplest of catches. He endured for forty minutes, during which, apart from hitting a full toss from Lindwall for four, he made the scoring of runs appear well-nigh impossible.

May at once forced Archer several times hard to mid-wicket, thereby encouraging Hutton to a more sprightly gait, which is what often happens. Hutton glanced Johnston for four, drove him firmly past cover and then turned Archer a shade uppishly through the short-legs for four more. Fifty came up, the lead was cut to twenty-four, and English hopes rose with the sun, that was now free of cloud for about the first time since the match began.

At 58 the left-arm combination of Johnston and Davidson was at work, Lindwall having bowled very fast, but with little swing, for three-quarters of an hour. Johnston had not long changed ends when Hutton, checking a stroke made well away from the body at a wide half-volley, succeeded only in steering it towards Benaud's head in the gully. Hutton does not always drive with his left foot at the pitch, preferring sometimes to hit it later and squarer, with arms extended. He was not over this ball, which was thrown disconcertingly into the wind. Had he continued the stroke, he would probably have cleared Benaud and got four runs to third man.

Graveney, having narrowly avoided edging his first ball, similar to the one that took Hutton's wicket, groped forward, left leg down the line of the leg stump, at the third, also pitched on or outside the off stump and leaving him. This ball, bowled over the wicket and moving diagonally from leg to off across the batsman's body, is one that Johnston has bowled thousands of times. Graveney was well inside it and Langley took the catch almost apologetically. Over cold lobster at lunch the talk was not surprisingly of how long the match could now last— talk that was soon made to appear absurd by Cowdrey and May playing Lindwall and Johnston in bright sun but cool breeze with an ease of manner that betokened innocent digestions. May scored continually in the area between square leg and mid-on; his bat swings naturally across his body, and anything not well pitched-up outside the off stump he was able to force into that space. When Archer came on, he hooked him hard for four. Bowlers tend to pitch short to May, for he lays into the over-pitched ball with uninhibited savagery. Davidson took over from Lindwall, and Cowdrey drove him sweetly several times through the covers, as well as once to the sightscreen. Bat and pad come down as one when Cowdrey drives, and so truly is his not inconsiderable weight distributed that he seems never to need to do more than lean quietly forward. His natural instinct being to play off the front foot, he is less quick than May to move back on his wicket and force the shorter ball through gaps on the on-side. He is, therefore, for the moment, the easier player to pin down.

At 118 Benaud came on to bowl the first of seventeen overs, interrupted only by tea. Cowdrey and May had raised the score by sixty before he began, but he quickly found a length, and Cowdrey especially found himself restricted to forward strokes that had not the power to beat a deepish ring of off-side fielders. Johnston bowled also to a field set half-way to the boundary on both sides of the wicket, and, though every so often both batsmen moved their feet and hit the ball hard through them, the safer shot was the checked forward push. Harvey, Favell and Burke, however, are not fielders to encourage the repeated stealing of runs. Lindwall after tea had another long, foxy and accurate spell, bowling with constant changes of pace, sudden venom and ancient guile. By five o'clock, nevertheless, a hundred had been added, all of them along the grass, since Graveney's dismissal. Cowdrey for a short while looked to have tired, made restless also by the fact that there was under half an hour left for play. He reached fifty, however, not long after May, who seemed sensibly to be encouraging him to further assault, rather than to withdrawal. But, with the score 174, the time ten-past five, Cowdrey, going down the pitch to a googly from Benaud, failed just to get there. Continuing his stroke, he lifted the ball, which went high and straight to Archer at long-off, the only occupied place behind the bowler. Wretchedly disappointingly as the fall of Cowdrey's wicket in this manner was, to others as patently as to him, he and May had set, through their wise blend of patience and aggression, a new value on any runs that were to come. For three hours, in their contrasted styles, they had batted with unforced authority, the one upright, flowing and lithe, the other powerful with the gentleness of strength. May split the air with the noise of his strokes, Cowdrey the field with the ease of his timing. There was little to choose between them in the correctness of their technique, the natural assertion of their breeding.

It was to be expected now that Edrich and May would settle for survival. But not a bit of it: Edrich began by hooking Johnston for four, off-drove him for another, and then, swinging violently at a no-ball, unsighted Langley who let it speed through to the rails. In the next over Benaud dropped one short, and Edrich, with forearm only, pulled him for the swiftest four of the day. May, finding Edrich's mood as infectious as it was surprising, hit Johnston wide first of mid-on, then of mid-off. When the field dropped back he pushed him for singles. Thirty-three runs were scored in twenty minutes before a perspiring Morris was able to lead his team to shelter. This was champagne, when one had prepared for indigestion tablets.

The pitch, having sown its wild oats on the first two days, appeared during the afternoon to have acquired a taste for domestic calm. However, the new ball would be due when play began in the morning, which meant that May, who was two short of his first century against Australia, and Edrich would need to see the shine off. England at 204 for 4, 130 runs ahead, had still a long climb to make.

* * *

Fourth Day: May reached his hundred off Lindwall's second ball, turning it for two past Johnston at backward short leg. This innings of crisp drives, powerful on-side placings and, most important of all, a certainty suggesting that he knew himself the equal, if not the superior, of Australian bowling, marks the end of May's first Test period. Henceforth, however, he will need to throw off his present unhappy characteristic of being a second innings batsman. He should by nature be the architect of a match, not its restorer.

During this first over of Lindwall's, bowled with the old ball, drizzle began to block out the sky over Botany Bay, thickening quickly, and sending everyone scampering in as soon as it was finished.

Twenty minutes later the headlands of the Bay were once more visible over the cabbage-tree palms behind the pavilion, and play continued. Morris, because of the wet outfield, delayed taking the new ball, using Johnston and Davidson in the meantime. Edrich played Johnston agreeably through the covers for four, and was then all but caught and bowled by Davidson, who bowled steadily for half an hour.

At twenty-past twelve, the real moment of crisis, Lindwall took the new ball. He bowled two out-swingers fairly wide: the third ball, swinging in, pitched on the middle stump and May, watchful for the out-swinger was late on it and yorked. It was Lindwall's first wicket of the innings, costing him fifty runs. May had appeared perfectly comfortable, though Johnston and Davidson, attacking his off stump at a good length, never allowed him to get going. The loss of this wicket, caused by Lindwall's control over the new ball and his understanding of the psychology of the batsman faced by it, put an end to the possibility of a commanding English score. Australia were again on top.

Tyson made several reassuring forward strokes to Lindwall; then, moving forward to make another, he found the ball shorter, and momentarily perplexed, hesitated. The ball lifted steeply and, before he could do more than turn his head away, hit him on the back of the skull, shooting down to fine leg as knowingly as if it had come off the centre of the bat. He went down at once, throwing his arms back helplessly. It was a sickening blow. Lindwall's bouncers are not of the childish, 'telegraphed' variety common to most fast bowlers. They pitch only just short and get up almost straight. Tyson is not at the best of times quick on his feet, and he was on the wrong foot anyway to duck. He was eventually led off by two ambulance men, patently uncertain whether in heaven or hell, but with a very bad headache whichever it was.

Evans was dropped at slip by Hole first ball, holding his bat out as in an Edwardian photograph, well away from his body. On the stroke of lunch, what seemed the ultimate disaster occurred. Edrich, concentrating resolutely on keeping his wicket, moved forward and then drew his bat away from a slower, shorter ball from Archer, going well wide of the off stump. He was in position far too soon, however, and his bat dropping as he let go his right hand, turned the ball on to his stumps. The score was 232 for 6, England 158 ahead.

During lunch the opinion was that Tyson, who had been taken to hospital for an X-ray, was unlikely to bat or bowl again in the match.

Evans wasted no time in placing Archer politely into Lindwall's hands at third slip. He was barely half-way to the pavilion when Tyson, pale, but not otherwise visibly shaky, strode out past him. He was nobly received, and played quietly and efficiently, driving Johnston for four to extra cover and Archer straight, before Lindwall bowled him for the second time in the match. Wardle hit Lindwall to the square leg boundary and was then l.b.w. Five wickets had fallen to the new ball and only forty-six runs been scored; which meant that, with the last pair together, England were 176 runs ahead. With the pitch as placid as it had been all day, this seemed at least a hundred short of a reasonable proposition.

That looked to be the opinion of Statham and Appleyard, who, with the modesty of bowlers pure and simple, played unobtrusively for some overs of considerable swing from Archer and Lindwall. Appleyard again revealed a forward stroke of some merit, and a bat of such pallidness that one feared it would get sunburned. However, it had its longest outing yet, its owner even cutting Davidson for four with a stroke of governessy severity. Statham, by habit, is a batsman of adventure and hazard, but he seemed for once quite interested in the technique, as opposed to the more esoteric sensations, of batting. He placed his body behind Lindwall's good ones, declining to lift his head or sweep round towards the square leg umpire. He smote a half-volley all along the ground to the sightscreen, and cut Lindwall hard down past gully for another four. Pleased with these strokes he repeated them off Davidson for a similar number of runs. Lindwall demanded his sweater, Davidson was encouraged into his. Statham continued to slant the ball through the slips by skilfully angling his bat. He was the first to lose patience, though, swinging wildly at Johnston when it was beginning to look as though he had found an individual kind of orthodoxy rather attractive, and snicking the ball to Langley. Appleyard was left caressing his bat like a bridegroom. Forty-six runs had been put on, which brought the contribution of the last English pair to 89 for the match. The first wicket partnership in both innings had been more than doubled. More important, it showed that it was worth while for the last few batsmen to take a little trouble. Runs scored for the last wicket, a fact that English bowlers have been slow to learn, count just as much as any others. Langley in the two English innings held five catches and let through no byes. He is a wicket-keeper whose considerable virtues lodge behind a rubicund, homely and undemonstrative exterior.

At twenty minutes past three Australia began their fourth innings, needing 223 runs to win. It was not generally thought, on this wicket, to be a task likely to extend them. Statham's first over, however, bowled into the wind, was of such liveliness that most preconceptions were quietly shed. His second ball swung in sharply, and Favell, covering his middle and off stumps, was hit firmly on the pads. A confident appeal was disallowed, the ball perhaps rising enough to have frisked over the bails. The fourth ball lifted, and Favell, with a semi-circular scoop, steered it wide of Edrich a foot above his head. Edrich, though he got both hands there, could not hold it and the ball went through his fingers for two. Favell was within an inch of being bowled two balls later. The last ball of the over skidded off the inside of his bat for four to fine leg, Favell anxiously seeking its whereabouts. Altogether an over which, since it was without reward, seemed likely to dishearten any bowler. Tyson, downwind, worked up a fine speed, but Morris pushed the ball confidently into vacant regions round square leg and, when Tyson bowled him a full toss, sliced it between first and second slip to chip the paint from the pickets. A black spaniel, seeing no fielder, squeezed on to the field, retrieved the ball, and cantered elusively about as if reluctant to allow Morris another go at it. In Statham's next over, the last before tea, Morris seemed to take leave of his senses. He went to hook a good-length ball, missed, and was appealed against for l.b.w. Next, he slashed vainly at out-swingers three times in succession. Finally, despairing of contact, he swung well above a ball only fractionally short on the leg stump. It kept low, hitting him on the pads. This time he was out. Harpo Marx could barely have dreamed up such antics.

At 37 Favell, possibly curious, after his earlier good fortune, about Edrich's abilities, guided an away-swinger from Tyson straight at his head. Edrich, standing deep, held a much faster travelling ball with both hands clasped together in a boxer's acknowledgment. Favell's habit, playing a good-length ball on the off stump, is to move back along the line of the leg, his bat at the moment of contact showing itself more to the sky than to the bowler—a common fault among players who place their feet for the cut. Harvey played at, and was only a thickness of oil off, his first two balls from Tyson, both of which lifted over the off stump. Subsequently, he made certain of getting well behind the ball, not scoring much, but slowly establishing a right of tenure. After half an hour of high-spirited attack, Statham and Tyson were rested, Appleyard and Bailey coming on to concentrate on Harvey's leg stump. Anxious for another wicket Hutton called up Wardle, who bowled two maidens to the intransigent Burke, before bringing back Tyson and Statham for a final assault. Harvey, however, was now proceeding without trace of uncertainty, and, having seen the fast bowlers off, found time to take two fours off Wardle in the last over of the day. Thirty-five runs only were added in eighty minutes after Favell's departure, Harvey making 26. Australia, 72 for 2, needed 150 more. England could hope for nothing from the pitch.

* * *

Fifth Day: The first overs bowled by Statham and Tyson confirmed the worst fears of the night before. The pitch was corn-coloured, the light excellent, and Harvey and Burke played each ball in the middle of the bat with time to spare. The Hill was not much over a third full, the stands rather less so: a few sunbathers lay stripped to the waist on either side of the scoreboard. A light breeze ruffled the flags and Australia, one imagined, would be high and dry by tea-time.

Burke has so little backlift, and, generally, preserves an air of such immovable detachment, that it was some time before one became aware that a yorker of exceptional speed from Tyson had uprooted his off stump. Two balls later Hole's middle stump rattled against its fellows; the ball was of similar pace, perhaps a couple of inches shorter. Tyson, using a run now little longer than Tate's, dropped his shoulders and hung his arms loosely in his habitual follow-through. But the stumps were awry, and the slips leaping like salmon as Hole disconsolately made his way past them: 77—4—0.

Benaud joined Harvey and, playing solidly off the front foot, looked disagreeably less out of composure than might have been expected. Tyson kept up a tremendous pace, forcing Harvey back on his stumps, so that, although he was putting the middle of the bat to the ball, he was detained at one end. Benaud took runs here and there from Statham, earning each one. With the score 100 Hutton rested Statham and brought on Appleyard to bowl into the wind. Benaud pushed forward at his first ball, which hung a little before turning in between bat and pad to shave the leg stump. He seemed to prefer the pace of the others, which he thumped hard to mid-off. Appleyard is not, nevertheless, a safe bowler to drive indiscriminately, for he varies his pace and makes the ball hold up at the last second, before dipping into the batsman. Just such a ball Benaud, fancying a half-volley, attempted to sweep to mid-wicket six runs later. He swung early, therefore across, and sent the ball swerving high to square leg. Tyson stood under it, gazing upward and weaving anxiously from side to side. Palpably it drifted and equally obviously Tyson misjudged it. At the last moment he lunged forward on bended knee, extending his hands as for the sacrament. The ball found them, miraculously.

At lunch Australia were 118 for 5: forty-six runs had been scored in ninety minutes, 105 more were wanted. At five minutes to two, with the total 122, Tyson bowled a ball very fast and slightly short outside the off stump. Archer leaned away as if to cut, but his bat was still ascending when the ball broke back and shattered his wicket.

Harvey was being kept as much as possible from the bowling, both Tyson and Statham forcing him to play back off his ribs with three men a pitch's length away on the leg side.

At 127 Statham, bowling into the wind, hit the shoulder of Davidson's bat, and Evans, who had not been taking the ball cleanly, made several yards to snatch the ball with both hands outstretched from in front of second slip. He rolled over and over but kept his gloves aloft. Davidson himself might have caught such a catch; not conceivably anyone else. The ball flew from the bat-maker's name as if it had come in contact with a spring.

Lindwall took eight off the rest of that over, mostly through the covers. A single by Harvey then brought him face to face with Tyson. The first ball came sharply back from a length and Lindwall did exceptionally well to stop it. The crowd had visibly stiffened, musing, as perhaps, was Lindwall, on the possibility of something very fast, straight and short. The second ball pitched about six inches in front of Lindwall's off stump, which it hit long before Lindwall had gauged its length; 136—8—8, Tyson 5 for 54.

The scoreboard at this point showed a certain confusion, due to an unprecedented number of people being required at the Members' Gate. In consequence the name of Dr F. Rosati found itself temporarily inserted into the batting order in the only vacant space, which, however much it might have dismayed its possessor, seemed exceedingly sharp practice.

At half-past two, the score 145, Statham hit Langley's off stump with an in-swinger, breaking the base off. Johnston therefore emerged preceded by an umpire carrying a replacement— an embarrassing accompaniment for the batsman, obliged to walk fifty yards in a file of two. Australia were 77 runs behind.

Johnston stabbed at his first two balls: the first nearly removed his off bail, the second got him the benefit of the doubt after an appeal for l.b.w.

Harvey now threw off the protective colouring he normally wears at the wicket and decided on all-out attack. It was later suggested that he might well have done this before; in fact, he was given no chance. Prescience lagged behind events.

He soon made up for it. His timing magically returned to him, and he hit the ball away off the back foot almost regardless of its length on both sides of the wicket. He scuttled for threes and twos when he wanted them, and declined long singles. Hutton did his best to prevent this sudden monopoly of the strike, but the accuracy and speed of his fielders let him down again and again. Johnston, rarely asked to play more than two balls an over, was not above despatching them one-handed to the long-leg boundary. Twice he treated Tyson thus.

After eighty minutes' onslaught against the wind, Statham came off. Bailey bowled, and was immediately hit straight over his head by Harvey. Not long before, Harvey had hooked Tyson hard to fine leg where Bailey, standing a few yards in, had gone forward only to find the ball clear him and bang the palings first bounce. Harvey's score moved from 64, when Johnston entered, into the eighties. The joke was turning a little sour. Australia required forty-six, which was little more than these two had already put on.

Tyson, almost at the end of his tether, was bowling with considerably lowered arm. Johnston stopped the straight balls with deceptive protestations of amazement; Harvey, beyond the reach of bowlers, had left fallibility trailing him.

The last ball of an over from Bailey, struck high on the rise by Harvey, slowly climbed the bank at mid-wicket, beckoned on by numerous small hands as it slackened pace.

Johnston therefore was faced with the prospect of a whole over. Hutton must have thought hard before offering it to Tyson, whose weariness was making him bowl helplessly down the leg side. He did so, however, though probably it would have been Tyson's last. Johnston picked one off his boot to get four to fine leg. He followed another past his hip, not able to reach it. To yet another wide of the leg stump he extended his bat, this time caught up with it, and Evans, standing back, safely took the ball.

Harvey, 92 not out, had reinstated himself amongst those who provide the legendary innings of cricket. For this was surely one such.

So England, on an afternoon of ignored time and weather, had won by 38 runs. Tyson became only the third fast bowler ever to take ten wickets in a Test match for England against Australia, Larwood having done so in 1932–33, and Farnes in 1934.

* * *

That night in Prince's we celebrated marvellously. Christmas was only two days off and we had, after all, received the best present anyone could have wished for. An American from Philadelphia, who had made a special trip to see the match, entertained the team: he had once played for the Gentlemen of England some decades ago in obscure circumstances, and his enthusiasm seemed only equalled by his generosity in the cause of English cricket. He had watched England draw the Second Test at Lords in 1953, when Bailey and Watson batted throughout a day of unbearable tension, and he had gone to West Indies in the following winter, when England were two down, and stayed to see the rubber squared.

It had been a memorable day, one fit to compete with any hauled out of the past by those who had witnessed the battles of 1902, or who had watched with innocent eye the achievements of Trumper and Hill, of Spofforth and Albert Trott, of Braund and Richardson. The bowling of Tyson and the batting of Harvey on December 22, 1954, was the contribution of a new generation to the classical repertory of cricketing drama. In one match Tyson had reimposed the menace of speed on Australian batsmen. At Brisbane it seemed that, as much by luck as by good judgment, Australia had inflicted psychological blows on England's speed attack from which immediate recovery could not possibly be hoped Hutton, too, had no feasible alternative to his fast bowlers: he was committed to them virtually in sickness as in health. Tyson's run, cut by over half, still showed the same shuffle and change of feet: but from three raking strides he managed to get his left shoulder quite as high as before and the increase in control was astonishing.

It had to be remembered that it was once again Bailey who started the fight-back on the second day, when Australia were scoring at a rate enough to put any bowler out of composure. He performed the duties that Bedser had so often done since the war on good wickets. He moved the ball consistently and sufficiently from a good length to reduce batsmen, hitherto scoring freely, to the defensive push that, like a virus, brings in its train a whole host of other symptoms.

Hutton, that evening at Prince's, was pointedly asked by an Australian journalist, 'Did you miss Bedser at all?' and, with the diplomatic twinkle that has become instinctive to him in public, he replied: 'We always miss Alec.'

It was not the least part of Hutton's triumph in this match that the decision to leave out Bedser, criticized almost without exception by correspondents of both countries, was honourably justified. Both Wardle and Appleyard, one of whom played in Bedser's place, made vital runs: and though Wardle bowled scarcely at all, the balance of the attack was improved as much by the fact that there were only three pace bowlers present, as through the performances of the two slower ones.

In a way this match was also a vindication of Hutton's predominantly defensive field-placing. Morris persisted with the close 'umbrella' field—5 slips, 2 leg slips—that does not permit of third man or long leg. England scored some 30 or 40 extra runs in this way, though possibly one extra wicket was taken by these two men being up close. Hutton, almost as soon as he could decently do so, dropped his third slip back to the boundary; long leg never came up at all. On several occasions Tyson, Bailey and Statham bowled only to one slip. I can't recollect a chance being missed on this account, and at least 40 runs were saved. Against this, Hutton provides his slow bowlers with a field so spreadeagled from the start that what little self-confidence he allows them anyway must soon evaporate.

Yet he captained England during these days with patience, skill and admirable control. He kept his bowlers as fresh as circumstances allowed, and, though he asked much of Bailey, Tyson and Statham in turn, he never failed to get a response. He attacked whenever possible, and he made the most of periods of enforced defence. He may not, off the field, draw his players out or encourage their confidences: still less, may he build them up as individuals. But he led them in this

Second Test match, in frequently trying conditions, with a most exemplary calm.

That night at Prince's, with the corks popping over plates of oysters, the band thudding behind the shuffle of dancers, was the most exciting of the tour. Later, coming out into Castlereagh Street, with the stars sparkling as though they were part of the Christmas decorations, one felt an elation altogether out of proportion. But, after all, we had been present at a rebirth, one situated so appositely in the year, that the sense of wonder, filling the streets like a vapour, communicated itself as in happiest childhood. Christmas may rightly belong to children: but it is still capable of surprising grown-ups.

* * *

Christmas in Sydney. Papier mâché sleighs and reindeer suspended across the ceiling of the foyer in the Hotel Australia: a toy Santa Claus pounding an organ over the entrance, and music mysteriously emerging from it. The streets were jammed with people up to see the decorations, made curiously nebulous by the sun. It was like being at an evening party in daylight. One's private euphoria vied with the unreality of women in summer dresses and men without coats. Hotel lounges trilled with the voices of meeting ladies, each hatted in a manner that made them seem to be just off to a fancy-dress ball. In Sydney, women hold large parties for women only: it is a city of Madame Bovarys condemned for large amounts of time to each other's company. They are to be seen in droves at lunch-time in Romano's or Prince's, posing their profiles to photographers, giving their names to the resident society editresses of local papers with as little show of satisfaction as prestige permits. They butt each other with crimson viziers or swing feathers at unwary waiters as they deposit the soup. Sometimes a party consists exclusively of buxom matrons; sometimes of young and pretty girls, primly formal, as though the convent wall had not long been leaped. Men play no part in this illusory debauchery of feminine spirit, and the women, frustrated, take it out on their hats.

THE SECOND TEST MATCH

Hats of Sydney: they need not poets, but massed choirs to do them justice. Hats like shovels and tea-cosies, like ice-chests and cabin-trunks; hats in the shape of aviaries and coal-scuttles, intimidatory as unicorns, receptive as soup-plates. Hats the size of shoes, the colour of elephants: hats with lives of their own, dominating the conversation. Hats with iron-wills and the effrontery of minor bureaucrats: hats bobbing or agreeing or expressing shock, to the strains of the Merry Widow Waltz and *La Vie en Rose*. Hats like aerodromes and sleeping-pills, hats like car-exhausts and crossword puzzles. Hats with haughty expressions at variance with their owners, hats coy as conjuring tricks on eagle-eyed domestics.

All afternoon, from my room on the fifth floor, I sat in the Christmas Eve sun and listened to the fire-engines racing across the city. Their bells were a perpetual incendiarist's carillon, as they flashed by on their scarlet errands. There were several large fires on this last day before Christmas, and the sound of engines and ambulances converging on the puffing flowers of smoke that dotted Sydney will remain part of my memory of it.

Christmas in Australia is essentially a time of beaches and barbecues. The weather in Sydney was not more than gently warm ('the climate is changing' the taxi-man said, as they always do), and sharp breezes ruffled the sea far out beyond the breakers. But on Christmas Day I drove with friends to Palm Beach, past the dozen half-moons of sand bracketed together for twenty miles northwards of Manly: Freshwater, Curl Curl, Dee Why and Collaroy; Newport, Bilgola, Avalon and Whale. Beyond them, a narrow spit of land reaches to Barranjoey at the entrance of Broken Bay, the white crumbling surf of Palm Beach separated by only a furrow of trees from the Pittwater.

They are not beautiful, these places, for the munificence of ocean and sand have made the people there careless of what they build inland of them. Each of these sea-faced suburbs is devoid of even the simplest dignities. Their houses are whimsical, their shopping-centres heavy with the stench of petrol and exhausts. But the bush, with its dragging smells of eucalyptus, is only a mile or two away, and these red, scraggy ribbons of development are of no consequence next to the pure, sweeping advances of the sea.

Palm Beach, not long ago, was the elegant and solitary preserve of the rich: now bungalows and snack-bars have sprung up all over it, and the transforming mutations of sunset are needed to restore the primary excellences of nature. But the Pittwater, one of the many lovely arms of the Hawkesbury River, lying against the back of Palm Beach, has survived. Wooded hillsides slope down to calm inlets, spreading comfortably at their foot into small bays or tightening into rocky creeks. Clean white villas hide amongst the pale stalking limbs of gum trees, off their boathouses yachts and launches circling with the tide. In late afternoon the sea turns silver, the trees blacken above the rockline. An island, blocking the entrance of the river like a lion, holds back the turbulence of the Pacific, and a feeling of serenity, rare in the Australian landscape, hangs over the sun-flushed water.

Probably, in time, the trees of the Hawkesbury River will be cut down to make room for new suburbs, and with it the Pittwater, glittering among its Norfolk Island pines and gums, be robbed of its quiet. But it will take some while, for the woods reach stubbornly over solid rock to the water, and building costs are fabulous. Until then, the Pittwater will endure as one of the most expressive, as well as arresting, coastal regions of Australia. Elsewhere the coasts have nervous energy; here there is perspective and depth.

12 Melbourne and the Third Test Match

I flew down to Melbourne on Boxing Day with Ian Peebles. It was a bumpy trip and we made a steep, awkward landing at Essendon in a strong cross-wind. We had left Melbourne in November in pelting rain. Now the sun shone out of a dull headachy sky, the heat on the aerodrome humid and exhausting.

By the time I had driven in to the city, checked in and showered at the Australia Hotel, and begun to walk up Collins Street to dine at the Melbourne Club, the heat was draining away as if through a leak. Within half an hour the plane trees in the club garden were rustling in a cool breeze, the sky, as the sun slipped off down the hill, turning a blotched gull's-egg grey. Soon it started to rain. The temperature had dropped thirty degrees since lunch.

That was typical of the weather we had in Melbourne. On some days the change was even more abrupt. On Sunday, January 2, between the second and third days of the Test, the temperature reached 105° in the afternoon, remaining at 95° at midnight, the highest ever recorded in Victoria. A burning north wind blew throughout the day, and bush fires, causing the loss of thousands of heads of cattle, as well as acres of crops, circled Melbourne on a sixty-mile front. Several people were trapped and burned to death. Yet the days subsequent to that were sunny and cool, and before the week was out all thoughts of surfing or lazing on the beach had been driven out by a fussy south wind that swept round corners and chased in huge airship-shaped clouds.

As the opening day of the Test approached, excitement steadily mounted. Australia had announced the same side as won the First Test at Brisbane, Ian Johnson returning as captain.

Keith Miller was fit to play, though still undergoing treatment for his knee. He was not expected to bowl more than an over or two. There was, however, a last-minute change, necessitated by injury. Maddocks, the Victorian wicket-keeper, came in for Langley, who was hit in the face over the week-end during a Sheffield Shield match. Maddocks had not yet played in a Test, but he would strengthen, rather than weaken, the Australian batting.

The only conceivable changes in the England side were Bedser for Wardle, and Compton for Graveney. Compton, who had scored 60 in an up-country game at Newcastle, was ready to resume his rightful place. Bedser has been always at his happiest at Melbourne and, though Wardle played one useful innings at Sydney, there seemed no real need for him as an extra bowler. Opinion generally favoured Bedser's return.

As it happened, Hutton once more announced twelve names, Bedser amongst them; Wilson was to be twelfth man. On the morning of the match he asked Bailey to take Bedser out with him to look at the wicket, which had been given a special preparation by an outside expert. The reason for this, presumably, was that it was financially important for the match to last the full six days. The wicket had cracks in it, which the Melbourne wicket often does, but they do not usually have much effect till the fourth or fifth days. In the Sheffield Shield match played on an adjacent pitch earlier in the week the side batting fourth had scored 360 runs.

Whatever Bedser's report on the wicket, he was omitted from the England side. Compton for Graveney proved to be the only change from Sydney.

THE THIRD TEST: December 31 — January 5

ENGLAND

L. Hutton, c. Hole, b. Miller	.. 12	l.b.w., b. Archer	..	42
W. J. Edrich, c. Lindwall, b. Miller	.. 4	b. Johnston	..	13
P. B. H. May, c. Benaud, b. Lindwall	0	b. Johnston	..	91
M. C. Cowdrey, b. Johnston	.. 102	b. Benaud	..	7
D. Compton, c. Harvey, b. Miller	.. 4	c. Maddocks, b. Archer		23
T. E. Bailey, c. Maddocks, b. Johnston	.. 30	not out	..	24
T. G. Evans, l.b.w., b. Archer	.. 20	c. Maddocks, b. Miller	..	22
J. H. Wardle, b. Archer	.. 0	b. Johnston	..	38
F. Tyson, b. Archer	.. 6	c. Harvey, b. Johnson	..	6
J. B. Statham, b. Archer	.. 3	c. Favell, b. Johnston	..	0
R. Appleyard, not out	.. 1	b. Johnston	..	6
Extras (b. 9)	.. 9	Extras (b. 2, l.b. 4, w. 1)	..	7
Total	.. 191	Total	..	279

FALL OF WICKETS. *First innings:* 1—14, 2—21, 3—29, 4—41, 5—115, 6—169, 7—181, 8—181, 9—190. *Second innings:* 1—40, 2—96, 3—128, 4—173, 5—185, 6—211, 7—257, 8—273, 9—273.

AUSTRALIA

L. Favell, l.b.w., b. Statham	.. 25	b. Appleyard	..	30
A. R. Morris, l.b.w., b. Tyson	.. 3	c. Cowdrey, b. Tyson	..	4
K. R. Miller, c. Evans, b. Statham	.. 7	c. Edrich, b. Tyson	..	6
R. N. Harvey, b. Appleyard	.. 31	c. Evans, b. Tyson	..	11
G. B. Hole, b. Tyson	.. 11	c. Evans, b. Statham	..	5
R. Benaud, c. sub., b. Appleyard	.. 15	b. Tyson	..	22
R. Archer, b. Wardle	.. 23	b. Statham	..	15
L. Maddocks, c. Evans, b. Statham	.. 47	b. Tyson	..	0
R. R. Lindwall, b. Statham	.. 13	l.b.w., b. Tyson	..	0
I. W. Johnson, not out	.. 33	not out	..	4
W. A. Johnston, b. Statham	.. 11	c. Evans, b. Tyson	..	0
Extras (b. 7, l.b. 3, n.b. 2)	.. 12	Extras (b. 1, l.b. 13)	..	14
Total	.. 231	Total	..	111

FALL OF WICKETS. *First innings:* 1—15, 2—38, 3—43, 4—65, 5—92, 6—115, 7—134, 8—151, 9—205. *Second innings:* 1—23, 2—57, 3—77, 4—86, 5—87, 6—97, 7—98, 8—98, 9—110.

Bowling Analysis

AUSTRALIA

	First Innings					Second Innings			
	O.	M.	R.	W.		O.	M.	R.	W.
Lindwall	10	0	59	1	Lindwall	18	3	52	0
Miller	11	8	14	3	Miller	18	6	35	1
Archer	13.6	4	33	4	Archer	24	7	50	2
Benaud	7	0	30	0	Johnston	24.5	2	85	5
Johnston	12	6	26	1	Johnson	8	2	25	1
Johnson	11	3	20	1	Benaud	8	2	25	1

ENGLAND

	First Innings					Second Innings			
	O.	M.	R.	W.		O.	M.	R.	W.
Tyson	21	2	68	2	Tyson	12.2	1	27	7
Statham	16.3	0	60	5	Statham	11	1	38	2
Bailey	9	1	33	0	Bailey	3	0	14	0
Appleyard	11	3	38	2	Appleyard	4	1	17	1
Wardle	6	0	20	1	Wardle	1	0	1	0

ENGLAND WON BY 128 RUNS

* * *

First Day: Blue sky, sparkling light, and Hutton, before 63,000 people, one up with the toss. It seemed for once that English batsmen might go into the New Year with something to celebrate. But, within an hour, Hutton, Edrich, May and Compton were out for 41 runs, Miller having taken three of the wickets for five. He bowled with magnificent disdain from an unmeasured and variable run, keeping a perfect length on the off-stump, and getting the ball to rear up and swing late. England's early batsmen lost their wickets on a cracked, spitting pitch mainly through reluctance to get their heads behind the ball. Cowdrey was not slow in putting these flaws of technique in perspective, and, assisted by Bailey and Evans in stands of 74 and 52, he took England to a final score of 191. His own century, his first in a Test, had the bloom of youth on it: but the soil from which it sprang had been tended lovingly and long.

Lindwall's opening over brought 11 runs: four byes past Maddocks, who had never kept wicket to either Lindwall or Miller before, three pushed towards extra cover by Hutton, a glanced boundary by Edrich. Miller, ordered by his physician to bowl in short spells only, began with a discreet maiden. Hutton twice slipped, which led one to suppose that either he was badly shod or that the pitch was of glassy hardness. It turned out to be the latter, for at moments the game resembled Cricket on Ice, a new form of entertainment. Hutton, playing back to a short ball on the off, all but shouldered it into Harvey's hands at gully: he no longer moves his right leg across the stumps, but relies on the quick withdrawal of his right hand from the bat if the ball should kick. Hobbs used to do this, already jogging off on his run as the ball slid down to third man, but I fancy his head was more over the ball than Hutton's. Edrich, playing forward to Miller, took a nasty jab on his deltoid muscle, the one above the elbow. Miller's eleventh ball swung in and Edrich glided it off the middle of the bat to Lindwall, the central of three leg-side slips. Lindwall clung to it as he fell, humpty-dumptyish. Edrich swished his bat in irritation: the first wicket had fallen at 14, about par for the tour. May, warm from two successive centuries, played discouraging strokes at his first two balls from Miller. Then, brought down to face Lindwall by a single from Hutton, he was unlucky to receive first ball one that kicked off a good length. He was no more behind the line of it than Hutton had been to a similar ball two overs earlier, and Benaud in the gully was offered a catch of insulting simplicity. England were 21 for two. Cowdrey, yet to come in to bat in a Test match with the drums beating anything but a dirge, immediately edged Lindwall past gully for four, deflecting him next ball for another to fine leg. Hutton, however, was not to observe affairs at such short range for long: in Miller's next over he played, in precise manner as at Brisbane, inside a good length ball swinging away from the off stump. He was caught low off the ground by Hole at first slip. Hutton now affects to play on the off past point, rather than mid-off, which widens the margin for error when the left foot is not across, and the ball still new. Miller had taken two wickets for nought: and Compton's push for three to extra cover in his fourth over were the first runs scored off him. That over cost him five, and no more were scored before lunch from him. At 41 Miller made one little short of a length on the off stand up, and Compton, his thumb jammed against the bat, succeeded only in gloving it gently to Harvey, one of two close gullies. An X-ray on Compton's hand showed it to be badly bruised: fortune is not these days part of his equipment.

At 41 for four, Lindwall and Miller bowling, and the ball as red as an apple, Bailey was virtually back in his discarded position of opening batsman. He turned Lindwall smoothly off his legs for four: causing, with this stroke, a change in the bowling, Lindwall retiring with thirty-five of the forty-eight runs scored having been made off him. Cowdrey pushed Archer through the short legs for three to make the score fifty. Bailey ran a single so imaginative that he was no more than half-way down the pitch when Archer, the bowler, dashing to silly mid-off, had the ball in his hand. His throw missed the stumps by less than a foot. Benaud bowled the last over before lunch, at which time Miller's figures were 9 overs, 8 maidens, 5 runs, 3 wickets, his doctor presumably not being present. S. F. Barnes, in the New Year Test of 1911–12 here, took 4 for 1 in seven six-ball overs.

Archer bowled for Miller subsequently, using an identical field of three men close in on the leg, two slips, and a pair of gullies. Lindwall bowled the other end, and Cowdrey once more hit two successive balls for four, a lazy-looking off drive, and a push off the legs that had to be run. The running at this period was encouragingly brisk: Bailey is quick to see a run, and Cowdrey makes up for lack of natural speed by backing up. Bailey's forward stroke was operating as rhythmically as a metronome. Cowdrey cut Archer square to the boundary, then chopped Benaud, on for Lindwall, for four past Hole at slip. Certainty had returned to the batting.

At 90, Cowdrey reached his second successive Test fifty, his own runs having been made out of sixty-nine. The applause for this had barely quietened, when Bailey swept Benaud for four to make their own partnership worth fifty. Not many balls later,

Cowdrey drove Benaud past mid-on to raise the hundred. Such a trio of achievements there had not been for many moons. Johnston bowled now to an off-side field numbering five from cover to mid-off, and Cowdrey, driving a series of floating half-volleys with lovely follow through, could not pierce them. Bailey found an easier route, twice cutting Johnston fine of slip, and then doing similarly to Benaud. At 114 Johnson had his first bowl of the match. One run later Bailey was out, swinging at a loping long-hop from Johnston and snicking it from his pads vertically to the wicket-keeper. A mean dismissal. Cowdrey now stuck on 56 for forty minutes: it is in this middle period that he tends to get becalmed, and then lose his wicket in a sudden squall. Suddenly he jumped out and smote Johnson through the outstretched fingertips of Archer at mid-on, placing a half-volley more safely to the mid-wicket fence in the same over. But he nearly went the first time, just as he did when 58 at Sydney. Johnston, who was festively indulgent in length, he then pulled violently to long leg. By tea-time England had mustered 130: Cowdrey 68, Evans 3.

Johnston dug away in the evening no more accurately, with Lindwall now at the pavilion end; Cowdrey, having leaned Lindwall heavily enough to beat cover point, moved in to Johnston, hitting him away square on the off, and then flicking him to fine leg.

At 155 Miller returned for Johnston, but Evans, unusually business-like, drove him high and straight for four, despatching him with a grin to the mid-wicket boundary in the same over. This time doctor's orders were obediently followed, and Miller forthwith retired to cover point. Evans, seeming at last to be on walking-out terms with the bowling, was quite surprisingly l.b.w. to Archer; he and Cowdrey had added 52. The ball had long since ceased to rap the knuckles of all and sundry. Cowdrey drove Archer straight to the sightscreen, a stroke of pure instinct, which took him to 97. The next ball he played away to the on for three, and all Melbourne seemed to shout the runs on. Such an innings set the mind searching for comparisons. But in fact it belonged only to Cowdrey, a blend of leisurely driving and secure back play, of power and propriety. The crowd cheered long and movingly. Cowdrey smiled with pure pleasure, a smile of disbelief. He made only two runs more. He padded up to Johnson and the ball, turning back a yard, spun off his buckles on to the wicket.

With Cowdrey's dismissal the innings fell crazily away. Archer, cutting the ball sharply off the seam, bowled Wardle, Statham and Tyson within the space of ten runs and ten minutes. The last wicket fell at five to six.

* * *

Second Day: After an absorbing day, too closely following the contours of Sydney for comfort, England have worked down to the very quick of Australia's tail. Australia, who lost their eighth wicket at 151, are now three runs behind with the same two wickets standing. Curiously, England did not bowl today anything like as well as in either innings at Sydney or as Australia yesterday. The fielding was of matronly slowness, yielding more than a score of runs to strokes not worth a farthing. Yet such is the threat and air of bustle about Statham and Tyson with the new ball that speed goes a long way to adjust discrepancies in length. Statham, in fact, bowled not at all badly: and Appleyard in mid-afternoon quite beautifully, till Hutton, for no evident reason, tired of him. But Tyson looked and bowled as one in need of rest; Bailey was less than himself; and Wardle, having skidded one along the ground to bowl Archer, emphasized depressingly that he is not at the present able to keep on a length. The pitch was of two paces, Favell and Morris both being out to balls that kept unfairly low. It began to take spin half-way through the day, and Appleyard turned one a whole lot to bowl Harvey when he was going nicely. England, therefore, are even better placed than at this stage at Sydney. A quick finish to Australia's innings and some runs from Hutton on Monday should put us on the way to winning. But England's batting is now beyond the realms of calculation, mathematical or poetic.

ON BOARD *ORSOVA*

T. W. Graveney
At the wicket, a golfer's swing
E. W. Swanton
At the microphone, a bedside manner

Frank Tyson
Wordsworth as well as wickets

Left arm round: J. Wardle
Right arm over: R. Appleyard

PERTH

A Captain's innings
L. Hutton, not out 100 at lunch, against Western Australia

F. R. Brown,
Geoffrey Howard,
Alex Bannister,
(*Daily Mail*)
Ian Peebles
Under the gum tree

L. Hutton
In the nets, the classical manner

ON SYDNEY HARBOUR

J. E. McConnon
(*in dark glasses*),
Keith Andrew,
Geoffrey Howard
For McConnon, an early return, for Andrew, a Test Match bonus, for Howard, smiles all round

George Duckworth
Scorer and baggage-man
This time, no appeals

On the slip machine
J. V. Wilson
L. Hutton
Practice makes perfect

MAN OF THE MOMENT

Colin Cowdrey
At Sydney, two separate centuries against New South Wales

CAPTAIN OF TOMORROW

Peter May
In the second innings, a match-winner

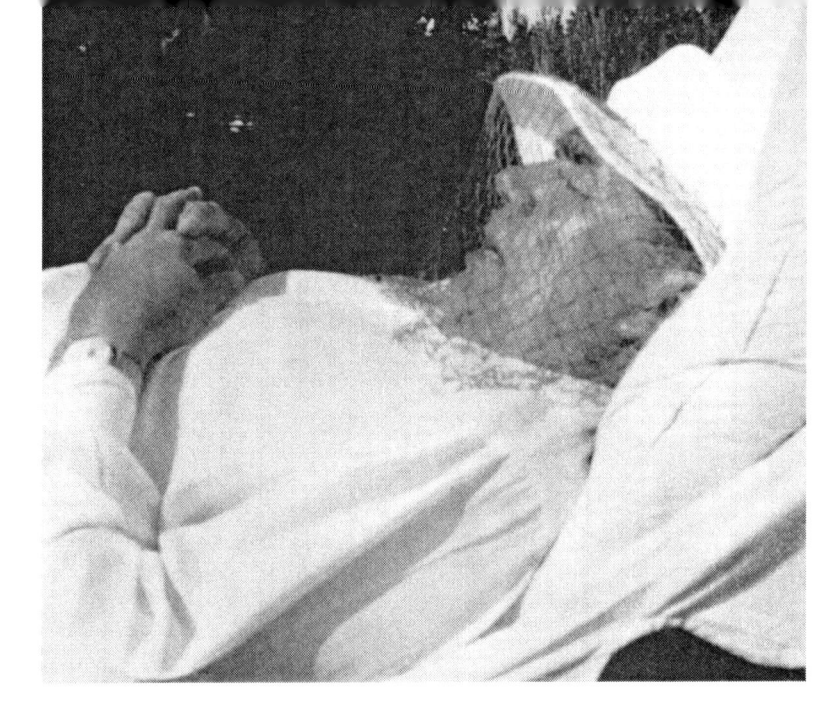

In the net: E. W. Swanton

On the beach: Alan Ross

Foreground: F. R. Brown
    I. A. R. Peebles
Background: J. B. Statham
    F. H. Tyson
Leg-breaks, antique but genuine

K. R. Miller, A. V. Bedser, A. R. Morris
Batting is not always fun

The Morning After
*Brian Statham and Frank Tyson at Glenelg Beach, Adelaide
The time: 10.30 a.m.
The date: February 3, 1955*
(*On the previous evening England won the Fourth Test, so retained the Ashes*)

Alec Bedser: *In decline, a great bowler, but still, to the young, a hero*

CORRESPONDENTS

top left: John Woodcock, *The Times*, on board *Orsova*
At sea, no copy

bottom left: F. R. Brown, *Adelaide Advertiser*, A. L. Hassett, *Melbourne Sun*, in Queen's Gardens, Perth
Tossing for drinks, not innings

top right: Norman Preston, Editor of *Wisden*, bass singer
On Sydney Harbour with oysters

bottom right: W. E. Bowes, *Yorkshire Evening News*, Denys Rowbotham, *Manchester Guardian*
On Bunbury Beach, baht 'aht

Tyson, accorded the first over in reward for Sydney, began as though intent on ignoring the lesson of that startling achievement. Also of Miller's bowling on Friday, when the ball was kept right up to the bat and cut sharply off the seam with the batsman already committed to his stroke. Tyson repeatedly pitched short, refusing the ball air in which to swing, and allowing Morris and Favell ample time to get back over their stumps. Statham, bowling from Miller's end of Friday, was immediately swung for three to long leg by Morris, though in the same over a ball found the edge of Favell's bat and shot over fourth slip's head to the boundary. Favell, a snick-craftsman of high authority, acquired eleven off the side, before he drove Tyson smoothly to the sightscreen and then amply square cut him. Morris, meanwhile, forced into thrusting three balls off his ribs, was beaten by one of fuller length that kept low and had him l.b.w. Hutton, after this second over of Tyson's, switched Statham, who had been slipping about on his run-up in the manner of an early tangoist, and brought Bailey on at the southern end. Miller, troubled by flies, paused from smacking them long enough to cut a long hop for four. Statham then had him feeling for his first ball from the other end and Evans threw himself in front of first slip to hold a tickle that would not have carried. Edrich stands some good way deeper than Evans, which allows him to take anything high that might otherwise clear him, but relies correspondingly on Evans' clairvoyance. With the score 43, Favell's streakiness was terminated by a fast creeper from Statham, who had deserved his wicket. Favell chirps his way regularly to the mid-twenties through a mixture of airy scoops and charming shots all round the field, then the equation of fortune seems to balance itself at his expense. Harvey made his now customary late and airy off-side stabs before hitting Statham firmly for four past cover, and then cutting him fine to leave third man puffing. Bailey was still dropping a shade short, and after forty-eight had been scored in an hour, he gave way to Appleyard. Appleyard also failed to keep the ball up, and Hole several times cut him wide of slip. It was fitting that the next wicket should fall in the last over before lunch to a full toss. Tyson, not long on for Statham, bowled it, and Hole, with habitual flourish, was adrift in steering it. At 65 for 4 Australia were only seven runs to the good of England's score at lunch yesterday. Neither Tyson nor Statham, however, had shown the probing accuracy of Miller, whose high action on this hard matting-coloured pitch gave the raised seam of the new ball a sharp dusting.

Archer, too, after tea on Friday, bounced the seam down in a way that no English bowler save Bedser has the height to manage. And Bedser, for reasons not honestly plain, is only watching this match, if the distracting memories of his last two Tests here are allowing him even that comfort. Wardle, presumably, was picked to bowl when Hutton was obliged to shut the game up, or in Australia's second innings if the pitch was wearing. But Bedser is much the better bowler for both these purposes: cutting the old ball at medium pace he is still beyond the resources of this generation of fledgling Australian batsmen.

Tyson and Statham bowled in the afternoon under a sky the same metallic grey as the corrugated-iron roofs of the stands. The air had lost its freshness, and it was in tank-like humidity that Harvey flicked both bowlers off his legs and swayed back to cut. When the hundred was only four runs away Appleyard had his second turn; a very much better one. Harvey played forward to find the ball move sufficiently from leg to beat his bat and hit the top of the off stump. Archer edged his first ball for four between Evans and Edrich, and had not the foggiest idea about the next two. Archer begins always with the fortune of one who must be one-third cat. He and Benaud then scampered singles with the effrontery of urchins outwitting an old, blindfolded aunt: it is no use pretending England are other than ripely game when they are put about in this way. Archer struck Appleyard high over his head to make a great segment of this 65,000 crowd crane in the hopes of a six: the effect was of the upper circle in a theatre being slowly tilted forward by invisible pressure. A single more to Archer, and then Benaud, misjudging the pace, politely pushed Appleyard into Wilson's huge hands at backward short leg. Compton, for whom Wilson substituted, would have been happy about that one. The last half-hour before tea produced only fifteen runs, Tyson bowling well short to Maddocks and Archer brought to fidgets by Appleyard's variations of flight.

Wardle then made to entertain: but not Australians, for going round the wicket he spun one low from leg to bowl Archer. Lindwall frolicked long enough to see the hundred and fifty up before Statham yorked him on the off stump. Lindwall is no great one for moving into the line of fast bowling. Maddocks batted in his first Test with honest application, encouraged by being able to run singles each time he pushed the ball to mid-off, mid-on or cover.

Hutton about now seemed rather more concerned about not having to bat than with getting the two remaining wickets. Appleyard, well tuned-up, was not bowled for over ninety minutes: nor Bailey since lunch. Also Hutton wasted more time in the field than was quite decent. The last hour saw Maddocks and Johnson take Australia doggedly towards the English score. The large assortment of ladies in the audience trilled excitedly: but it was impossible to avoid the feeling that this innings should long since have been neatly wrapped up.

* * *

Third Day: The resemblance to the Second Test continues. Sunday was the hottest day ever recorded in these parts, but the temperature slid down today from over the century to the comfort of the seventies. England took unduly long in polishing off Australia this morning but, starting their second innings 40 behind, they climbed to a lead of 119 with three wickets lost. At Sydney England, on the Monday night, were 130 ahead, with four wickets gone. May, 83 not out, drove even more commandingly than in his Sydney century. As then, the first hour of Tuesday's play should be the determining one: but these matches contain so many surprises, the balance veering from hour to hour, that any prophecy is folly.

The pitch, its cracks apparently healed, improved when play began. Australia batted on for an hour, adding 43 runs without great difficulty. England's fielders were again put to many indignities. Hutton began his bowling with Tyson and Appleyard, and it was not long before the Australian ninth wicket pair had, by the most formal methods, sent their side cantering ahead. The new ball was taken the moment it was due, but Maddocks, lifting his bat scarcely at all, demonstrated that the way to secure against any possible flightiness in the pitch was to get solidly behind the ball and slant the bat, French-cricketwise, at the last possible moment. These two, Johnson and Maddocks, had raised the first half-century partnership of the Australian innings, when Statham, who had taken two violent tumbles in the act of bowling, flipped one off Maddocks' bat to Evans. Johnston made many amiable passes at the ball, legs crossed like a pantomime horse, before straightening up to clout Statham high over cover point. He made a cut or two, inveigled several indiscreet overthrows, and was so hugely content that Hutton was obliged to have recourse to Bailey. It was an expensive move.

For Ian Johnson, without good reason, hit good-length balls for three spanking fours on the off-side in his first over, shots of a technical quality that only Cowdrey had so far exceeded in the match. Johnston, his laurel wreath knocked awry by this, aimed to set matters aright by hoisting Statham over the sightscreen; but, stamping his right foot a good yard to windward of the ball, lost, to his own great surprise, his off stump. Statham, taking the last two wickets, finished up with 5 for 60. He and Appleyard had been quite the best of the English bowlers. Had Appleyard been persevered with after tea on Saturday, Australia's lead of 40 might well have rested in England's favour. As it was, Australia's last two wickets added 80, a score usually worth the first three English batsmen.

The twenty-five minutes before lunch produced only six runs, but England did well to survive them without casualty. Hutton and Edrich both got off the mark in Lindwall's first over, which contained a rare and eccentric wide. Miller then beat Edrich several times with balls that climbed steeply away as Edrich pushed forward down the line of the off stump. It was an opening over, the intentions of which were as clearly expressed as a sonnet by Milton, its action as lovely.

The sun came out in the afternoon, training like a searchlight through low sultry clouds. Lindwall and Miller, as befitting veterans, were allowed to rest after an over apiece, and Archer, more of an age for immediate exertion, bore the heat with Johnston, who puffed, blew and depressed his elbows like a bagpipe player.

Hutton soon drove Johnston, bowling his spinners, almost in the happy manner through the covers, and Edrich glided Archer so fine and silently that it appeared a shot played out of mourning. But, though the wicket was playing easily, runs came incidentally rather than at the batsmen's behest. By degrees, however, England's previous best opening stand was doubled and Edrich became the first of Hutton's partners to reach double figures. The score was 40, and runs about to count positively when Edrich was bowled. Johnston pitched a ball on the leg stump, and Edrich, playing early and inside it, was beaten as it spun across the wicket. May soon set to forcing Johnston with sharp turn of wrists through the short legs, and, when Miller was recalled, brought the bowler to immediate applause for a straight drive that sped past him. Archer once found the edge of Hutton's bat, an achievement that cost him four runs between wicket-keeper and slip. Otherwise, as Ian Johnson, flighting the ball and maintaining perfect length, kept Hutton stretching exploratively forward for several overs, the runs ticked up in singles. England were fifty-six ahead and going much better, when Archer, who shared the bowling after tea with Lindwall, had Hutton l.b.w. The ball ducked in late on the middle and leg stumps and Hutton, hurried into playing across, missed. He looked nearer to an innings than he has yet done, but troubled by fibrositis and generally out of sorts, was content to push at balls which in other days left his bat without prospect of capture.

Hutton has batted since Brisbane rather as one who, long word-perfect in several languages, now seems increasingly to hanker for the dictionary. May's rendering of Lindwall on the contrary was free to the extent that subjunctives and conditional clauses were swept away in a series of lucid affirmatory statements. Twice he drove him with lovely swing on either side of mid-off and was only deprived of a whole series of off-side boundaries by the exceptional agility of Harvey. When Benaud came on soon after five o'clock, he moved out and hit him through mid-on to reach fifty. His play off the back foot, on either side of the wicket, was of exceptional power: and when Archer pitched up further he, too, was driven villainously low and straight. Johnson, who soon had eased the two longer spokes of third man and long leg out of Lindwall's and Miller's close umbrella field, was now obliged to denude the slips. Cowdrey defended quietly, not quite in touch and rather content to admire. Then, precisely as at Brisbane, he played on to Benaud, making so restricted a forward stroke that the ball spun hard back on to his leg stump.

Cowdrey, when he is resolved not to make mistakes, produces a feeling of uneasiness quite foreign to him at other times: but luck on these occasions has not been with him. Compton, though his bruised thumb might well have done with another night's rest, appeared next: an odd policy when there was scarcely half an hour left for play. Benaud was spinning his leg-breaks to an admirable length, able to keep Harvey and Favell squatting up on either side of the pitch within easy winking distance of Compton. Lindwall now came up to attack him ruthlessly at full pace at the other end. May, keeping as much of the strike as manners allowed, continued to place the ball away whenever length permitted. Compton, too, managed to pull Benaud to the long-leg boundary before the close, so possibly the earliness of his adventure was compensated for by the psychological value of his ten runs.

May's batting, which left him with 83 runs, was of the kind that the best amateur No. 3's used to display on seaside grounds in the 'twenties and 'thirties. Duleepsinhji or Melville would not have been displeased with the ease of it against county opposition. But May was faced by Lindwall bowling his fastest, and he attacked him to the extent that Lindwall eventually dared not pitch the ball up. Deep extra and deep mid-off were set for him, and repeatedly they were left standing. When an English batsman does this to the greatest fast bowler of his time, it registers, if nothing else, an exchange of dominations.

* * *

Fourth Day: The haunting Sydney pattern of this Test was emphasized even more strongly when Australia finished up the day needing 165 runs to beat England with eight wickets in hand. At the end of the fourth day at Sydney 151 runs were required, with Morris and Favell gone, as they are now. The pitch, whose improved aspect was widely stated in newspapers here to be the result of an illegal face-lift, due to week-end rolling and watering, was fairly predictable, though taking a fair measure of spin. The watering theory was officially denied by the Melbourne and Victorian cricket ground authorities, but, for whatever reason, the antics of the first two days have subsided very considerably. Australia, with Miller to come and Harvey newly in, appear this time to have the resources to win. But it has been a match of extraordinary fluctuations, and much will depend on Appleyard.

As at Sydney, the two overnight batsmen, in this instance May and Compton, on whom England's hopes seemed to lean largely, were both out for negligible additions within the first hour. Ian Johnson began his bowling with Lindwall and Bill Johnston, and though May once banged Lindwall to the sight-screen, the presence of a deep mid-off and mid-on, as well as extra-cover, made his progress rather slower than last night. Johnston was quick to strike a length, and May, after playing him quietly for an over or two, was beaten one ball and bowled the next. Johnston, spinning the ball sharply from leg to off, flicked May's pad as he came forward and hit his off stump. These first fourteen runs scored before May was out took thirty-five minutes: Compton lasted twenty-five minutes more before glancing Archer on the leg side to the wicket-keeper. He has been out like this so often that he did not even bother to look behind him. He made one square drive this morning, but, not properly able, because of his bruising, to fling his bat at the half-volley, was as Samson shorn of his hair. Evans was dropped by Lindwall at short leg as soon as he came in, but then steered Johnston for two fours past gully. That meant the two hundred, the new ball, and nine good runs later, lunch.

Quite certainly, the morning's play had gone to Australia. The pitch behaved with studious detachment, as if innocently unaware of any of the rumours being circulated about it. Johnston and Archer bowled persuasively and at skilfully contrasting lengths. Evans, who bustled twenty-two runs in half an hour before lunch, went immediately afterwards to Miller, feeling forward and edging the outward swing to Maddocks. At 211 for 6, the new ball shiny, England were again on the verge of capsizing. Wardle though, after being grotesquely at sea to Miller, set about Johnston, on in place of Lindwall, with such relish that he took sixteen runs in fours in one over—an assault that caused Johnston's swift retirement. Three times running he clouted him with the swing off the leg stump: a shorter ball he hit hard off the back foot through the covers. When Johnson, either hoping for an easy wicket or with a captain's self-sacrifice, offered his own brand of guile he was struck for three similar fours by means of well-timed circular sweeps to square leg. Thirty runs in two overs and the 250 up, advancing England's lead to 210, put the match in an agreeably different perspective. Wardle, however, could not, as he never can quite, contain himself, and when Johnson flighted one, dropping it short, in the next over, he fell hook, line and sinker. His leg-sweep was comfortably finished before the ball had got anywhere near him, and unfortunately it was straight.

As in the first innings at Sydney, Wardle had justified his presence. He no longer looks a batsman—which he once did— but he swung at the bowling as though he knew exactly what he was about. This was his most valuable ten minutes of the tour.

Bailey, meanwhile, was putting his bat with an air of noble martyrdom to some accurate overs from Archer, and, with Tyson in no obvious trouble, it looked as if Australia might yet be set the three hundred that seemed necessary, even if it took till doomsday. But at 273, Harvey at deep extra knocked up a hard drive from Tyson that appeared certain to clear him. Spinning round, he caught it as it fell, his back to the wicket. Statham was held by Favell at long-off in front of his face off an equally hard hit without scoring. Appleyard, after scoring six off the edge, was bowled by a shooter, leaving Bailey unconquered after nearly three hours' concentration, but with only 24 runs. He had, however, made the protraction of the innings possible, allowing Evans and Wardle to frisk under cover of his defensive smoke-screen. Bailey's batting in Test cricket is limited to three strokes, the forward defensive, the late cut and the swing to leg, with the ratio in favour of the first about a hundred to one. But he is firm in intent, unruffled by comment, and admirably devoted to the needs of his side.

Australia, needing 239, began their second innings immediately after tea. The sun shone, and a cool breeze flicked out of a clear sky at the trees curving below the girders of the new Olympic stand. Tyson, as in the first innings, pitched too short, and Favell was soon gathering runs with the busyness of a squirrel. Morris, however, was back on the shuffle once more, and Bailey, who took over from Statham after two overs, only lost a modest return catch to his left hand through lack of balance. Morris failed to profit by this for, in Tyson's next over, Cowdrey at forward short leg held a firm on-drive, his right arm thrust out at full extent just off the ground. Morris's contribution to the twenty-three runs scored was four, giving him a match aggregate of seven. Benaud, promoted presumably in the hope of quick runs without too much being at stake, flicked his second ball between Evans and Edrich for four, but then settled down to offer a fair imitation of Miller at the wicket. Round about now an exhibitionistic drunk, bored with the dreariness of the bar, held up the game for five minutes, circling the pitch and threading his way through the fielders in alternate samba and twenty-yard sprint. Satisfied with the release provided by this obscure performance, he consented to be escorted away. Favell cut several times deliciously late, as if put on his mettle by such competitive entertainment, and seemed on the point of extending his customary dismissal-range when, moving out to drive Appleyard, he was beaten by the late in-dip, lifted his head, and was bowled.

Miller being held back after a longish spell of bowling for a night's rest, Harvey now emerged, with rather less than half an hour to go. Appleyard offered him six runs in two opening long hops, and was then struck full pitch on to the pickets by Benaud. Tyson made several balls fly up over the batsman's head from a length, and Appleyard pushed one through very low. But, by and large, the whims of the pitch were not more than Harvey and Benaud could watchfully manage.

* * *

Fifth Day: At twenty minutes past one, that is to say after eighty minutes further play, the Third Test match, remaining faithful in essentials to its predecessor, even to the result, was all over. Bill Johnston snicked Tyson, and Evans, diving headlong, brought off his second fabulous catch of the morning. England had won by 128 runs. As the players left the field, the crowd broke over the palings and rushed to inspect the wicket. The pitch received during this extraordinary match about as much attention as the play, not altogether undeservedly, for its vagaries and sudden changes of mood persisted to the last. After England's chances had seemed on Tuesday evening to depend almost entirely on Appleyard—the wicket having apparently lost its pace for good and all—Tyson so resurrected its declining vitalities that the remaining eight Australian wickets fell in an hour and twenty minutes for thirty-six runs. There was no need for Appleyard to bowl a ball. It could not this time have been expected of Tyson that he would repeat his triumph of Sydney, for neither in Australia's first innings nor last night did he find the true length for his pace. Today, however, Hutton bowled him from the southern, instead of the Melbourne, end, hoping for the lift that Miller had occasionally managed to obtain. In fact, Tyson got Miller himself with a ball that kicked just enough to find the edge of the bat. For the first half-hour the pitch had definite ambiguities of pace and height, Miller receiving four in a row from Statham that squatted horribly. But once the sweat of night had evaporated in the warm sun the ball came through quite evenly. Suspicion lingered nevertheless, and once again Australian batsmen showed that they are as prone to mistakes of judgment as anybody when faced with bowling of real speed on a fast wicket. Today, they failed generally to play forward, the only honest form of defence when the ball is shooting; instead they preferred to glance, hook or cut, difficult enough strokes to control even on a plumb pitch, let alone on the fifth day, with the wicket not certain to play truly.

Harvey, Benaud and Hole lost their wickets exercising these strokes respectively. Benaud and Archer, on the occasions when they thrust out the left foot, met the ball safely in the middle of the bat, and Archer drove twice with a firmness that suggested the making of 165 runs need not have been unduly difficult. But by then it was too late: Tyson, who in 6.3 overs bowled not one bad ball, had already broken the Australian batting into splinters. He removed Harvey, England's main obstacle, in his first over, and at the end of an hour, during which six wickets fell for twenty-three runs, he had taken five of them for ten. He found his rhythm instantaneously, and length and direction followed.

Fifty thousand people chattering like magpies—the aggregate of 300,270 for the five days was a record for any cricket match in Australia—hushed suddenly as Tyson ran up to bowl the first over to Harvey. It was a morning of neither cloud nor humidity, the light golden. Harvey took two off the first ball to square leg. These had barely been recorded when he was out. His dismissal was so much against expectation that for some seconds no one seemed aware of it.

Tyson bowled a good-length ball going away outside the leg stump, Harvey flicked him blindly round the corner, and Evans, already on the move, dived to hold the ball wide and low to his right. It was a catch no less prescient and even more crucial than the one he took to send back Davidson at Sydney on the last day. Miller, with whom England had not to reckon at Sydney, was immediately made to stab and chop down in provincial manner; also, understandably, to scowl with lordly irritation at this early need to improvise. But he was seeing the ball late, and the pitch, though it gave him four off the edge past Evans, was doing the rest. Benaud looked to have made determined resolutions during the night; he was playing with unusual sobriety when, hooking at the first ball of Tyson's third over, short enough nominally but coming through lower than expected, he pulled it from a foot outside the off on to his leg stump. He departed very crestfallen, a bail in his pads, which he threw out disgustedly as he passed the jubilant slips. Miller went four balls, and one run, later, at 87. He lunged forward to a fast outswinger from Tyson, which, lifting from a good length, sped from his bat high to Hutton's left at second slip. Hutton could not hold it, but he took all the pace off the ball and Edrich, standing a good yard deeper at first slip, flung himself sideways and grasped it as it dropped. He threw the ball delightedly up, and once more the English fielders clustered round one another, scarcely able to believe it. Tyson had taken 3 for 3 in two overs, five balls. At twenty-five past twelve—play having begun at noon each day—Archer joined Hole. Hole made two cuts of customary finish; then Statham, testing his vulnerability to yorkers, bowled him three in succession. The following ball was much shorter, and Hole, finding the siege raised, flashed at it.

The flourish of his backlift delayed him, and Evans embraced the faintest of snicks off the lower edge. Maddocks, applauded with royal warmth as a local hero, received his first ball from Tyson. It was a fast yorker and Maddocks, almost stopping it, watched helplessly as it spun on just enough to knock off a bail. Lindwall, who has none of his usual fun batting to Tyson, was l.b.w. second ball. This meant that, in under an hour's play, Australia had shunted awkwardly from 75 for 2 to 98 for 8. The crowd sat silent for once, as if unable to relate what they saw to their understanding. The sun spilled down, its heat ignored in this sudden freezing of pleasurable anticipation. At ten-past one Archer square cut Tyson to the boundary, having driven Statham firmly for three to extra cover a moment before. He is a bold player, though much in need of early fortune, and the possibilities of revival were not extinct as long as he was still there. One remembered his second innings at the Oval in 1953, and at Sydney only a fortnight ago.

Five minutes later, with the score 110, Statham yorked him. That truly settled it, and Johnston was mercifully quick to perceive that the moment was ill-suited even for his genial powers of restorative comedy. Often Johnston arrives late in the fifth act with a tiny part so stuffed with opportunities that in next to no time he has buffooned the stars off the stage. This time his manner indicated a realization that he had been fobbed off with no lines at all. He swatted aimlessly at a yorker from Tyson, and Evans, leaping horizontally like a dolphin, caught him at full stretch with both gloves touching the grass. It was a catch to raise the roof in other circumstances; now it merely shook down the curtain, forgotten in the happy bustle of congratulations. Ian Johnson, undefeated a second time, walked over and shook hands with Hutton. The England team raced up to slap Tyson on the back and wring his hand. Tyson, for his part, put his arm round Statham, whose own contribution to victory was hardly less generous in endeavour. Together they walked off the field through the avenue made for them by their ecstatic colleagues. Tyson's figures were 7 for 27, the morning having brought him 6 wickets for 14 runs.

*   *   *

During the days following this extraordinary match there was much over which to reflect, as well as celebrate. For myself, there was little celebration in the material sense, for I had not been feeling well for a couple of weeks and, though the symptoms were not consistent, appendicitis was diagnosed. I decided to see the Test match through, although in some pain, and less able therefore to respond to the enthusiasm around me. However, around about the time when I felt free to have the operation, I began very slowly to feel better. Any definite decision about it was postponed, and in the meantime I roamed, or was driven, about Melbourne. I had planned to go to Tasmania, where two first-class, three-day matches were being played: and I hoped, if I continued to improve, to get over in time, at least for the second one.

The Melbourne newspapers at this time were agreeable reading. It was pleasant to find Australian cricket correspondents reduced to the straits that English writers had long accepted as their natural situation. Defeat is rarely easy to explain constructively: technical analysis nearly always leads to the conclusion that the better side won, which, satisfactory as that may be, is no comfort to the losers. A month earlier, this same Australian team had made over six hundred runs and defeated England by an innings and plenty. Now it had lost two Tests and failed to reach a score of 230 runs in four innings. England, it must be said, had made few runs more; but they had won their matches.

Most Australian critics had started out with the idea that the Australian team was the best available: a nice blend of experience and youth, magnificent in the field, batting down to No. 10, and with every kind of bowling imaginable. All of this was true. England, on the other hand, were slow in the field generally; they had insufficient close catchers, and even lacked a reputable cover-point. The batting ended at No. 6. Numbers 1, 2 and 5 had yet to reach 50 (only Hutton, among them, having once got beyond 30). The bowling depended to a frightening extent on the three pace bowlers who had been hit all over the field at Brisbane.

On the face of it, there should only have been one team in it. But during the last two Tests important changes had occurred. Firstly, Tyson, having cut his run, seemed to have become able under pressure to draw on a reserve source of power, rather as a motorist switches over to his emergency petrol supply. In both the Second and Third Tests Australia, when play began on the fifth mornings, was expected to win. In each match, she had led on the first innings and to a certain extent pegged the course of the play. That she did not in fact win was due solely to sudden bursts of inspired fast bowling by Tyson and Statham, who proved, what had not hitherto been suspected, that the all-rounders on whom the Australian team was based, were largely fair-weather players. Only Favell, with the aid of a fairy godmother, and Harvey looked to have the temperamental as well as technical resources to deal with fast bowlers who consistently pitched the ball up. The remainder were too slow in their reactions, too unreliable in their judgment of the proper stroke. The middle batting, in consequence, rarely averaged more than 15 runs a wicket. Morris, Benaud, Hole and Lindwall failed to reach 25 in four innings. Miller, in his two innings at Melbourne, scored 13 runs. Davidson, in his two at Sydney, 25.

The problem, debated urgently in the Australian press at this time, resolved itself into one that affects all winning teams which suddenly meet their match. Are you to persist with players regarded as the best and most promising, when they have proved themselves not good enough; or, ought you to replace them with inferior, less gifted cricketers, whose stolidity of temperament may make them, in certain circumstances, more successful? If Morris, Hole and Benaud were to be dropped, it would mean the virtual jettisoning of the two young players most likely to compete for the position of Australia's next captain. The replacements suggested were McDonald, McKay of Queensland, and Burke. McDonald failed completely in England and, though a heavy scorer in State games, appeared unlikely to develop into a Test-class batsman. McKay, a stubborn left-hander, vies with Walker of Hampshire and C. C. Case of Somerset in being among the most cramped and strokeless batsmen of all time. Burke, coming in for Miller at Sydney, showed a good defence. But none of these three could, in the pure sense of the term, be compared as cricketers with those they would have to replace. It was a pleasure for once to sit back, and watch others wrangling about it.

The Test wicket also came in for a good deal of discussion. Percy Beames, the cricket correspondent of the *Melbourne Age*, one of the soundest papers in Australia, stated, without qualification, in a front page article on the Tuesday of the match that the wicket had been illegally rolled and watered during the week-end, and the laws of Test cricket thereby violated. The same article included a vigorous denial by Melbourne and Victorian Cricket Association officials, who implied that there was conclusive evidence to the contrary. Other papers wrote in similar, scarcely less forthright terms. So much so that, eventually, an official denial was issued by the same authorities, on the basis of a thorough investigation.

Whatever the facts of the matter, many ingenious explanations were offered for the sudden binding together of the cracks on the Monday morning, the altered appearance and consistency of the turf, and the remarkably improved behaviour of the pitch. Arthur Mailey, cartoonist and painter, who once bowled Hobbs in a Test match with a full toss, dug up a waterdiviner, who expressed the view that a subterranean tributary of the Yarra must run under Melbourne cricket ground and that the abnormal heat of Sunday had drawn the water to the surface.

After the Test was over, two leading civil engineers, Mr G. D. Aitchison, senior research officer, division of soils, C.S.I.R.O., and Mr D. H. Trollope, senior lecturer in civil engineering,

Melbourne University, sent off a long and erudite letter, unsolicited, to the Victorian Cricket Association. They wrote:

> It can be concluded that the 'sweating' of the wicket was due to a natural phenomenon, the extent of which was aggravated by the abnormal climatic conditions which occurred in Melbourne on Sunday, and by the use of unventilated covers on the wicket.
>
> The abnormal temperature and hot north wind last Sunday would cause rapid drying of the surface of the pitch.
>
> When this drying-out had proceeded for a depth of say $\frac{1}{2}$ in. to 1 in., this layer became in effect a seal against further moisture loss.
>
> It is a well-known factor in soil studies, that as heavy clay soils dry out, they become more and more impermeable to the passage of water.
>
> In addition, with the high temperature during the day, the surface of the pitch would have been at a higher temperature than the soil at a depth of, say, 4 in. With these conditions the tendency of water to move as vapour would be towards the colder regions, that is downwards.
>
> After the first rapid drying-out of the surface, the tendency for evaporation through the thin crust was approximately balanced by the tendency for downward vapour movement, so that actually little moisture was lost during the day.
>
> Thus, if, as is most likely, there existed little or no grass showing above the surface (so that there could not be much loss of moisture due to transpiration through the leaves), the conditions of the pitch throughout Sunday were: a relatively thin, very hard, dry crust on the surface of the pitch; below this the clay soil, at, or near, the moisture content which existed before the rapid surface drying occurred.
>
> Then, early on Monday morning, when the cool change came, a reversal of the temperature conditions occurred, so that vapour movement was from the (warm) subsoil to the (cold) surface.
>
> With the covers over the wicket, moisture loss by evaporation would have been greatly restricted. Thus an accumulation of moisture in the soil surface would result, and the dry crust would disappear.
>
> The consequent swelling of the clay and closing of the cracks led to the recovery of the wicket.

The two engineers also suggested discussions with ground curators on the art of preparing pitches. They wrote:

> It appears that the advisability of rolling a pitch 'wet' or while it is drying out is primarily one of the desired density and structure of the soil.
>
> We feel again that accepted soil mechanics procedure, as applied to compaction problems in engineering works, would be of great value in determining the best rolling conditions.

Honour, therefore, seemed satisfied, though dissenters of integrity remained.

* * *

Perhaps the most important thing, from an English point of view, about these two great victories was the fact that, almost for the first time since the war, England had not relied exclusively on Hutton, Compton, Bedser, and, for the purposes of avoiding defeat, Bailey. Sydney and Melbourne were triumphs of youth, created by the same four players, May, Cowdrey, Tyson, Statham—all under twenty-five. Of the others, Hutton captained England with a mastery that defied, as well as exceeded, logic. Bailey played vital, but unobtrusive parts, in both matches. Wardle hit once in each Test with telling success. Appleyard took the vital wickets wanted of him. Evans held thrilling catches.

Cricket is, after all, a team game: and England showed that they were fitting together and acquiring a balance that a month earlier had seemed useless to expect. The batting had suddenly stiffened all the way down: a heartening discovery had been made by the bowlers that, provided sufficient will was there, runs could also be made. Not necessarily in startling quantities, but enough to make all the difference between disorder and respectability, defeat and victory.

Yet, all this apart, it was May's two innings and Cowdrey's two innings, Tyson's inspired passages of attack and Statham's perseverance, that brought England these Tests. The dispositions of strength were shifting within, as well as between, the two countries. Not since Hutton and Compton began to play Test cricket, the best part of twenty years ago, had England two such prospects as May and Cowdrey. And, in the last thirty years, only Larwood and Voce can have been as fast and feared an opening pair of bowlers as Tyson and Statham had, in the space of a month, become.

In a way, the most symbolic achievement of the Melbourne Test was the manner in which May set about Lindwall, driving him so hard and straight that he could not afford to attack the stumps. These were probably the truly revolutionary gestures of the match. Cowdrey has batted out here from the start with the responsible calm that marks the natural Test cricketer. He is a player of uncompromising intention. Defending, he comes forward, bat and pad as one, dropping the ball in front of him without thought of scoring; or else he is right back over his stumps, head outside the line of the ball, no attempt made to force. Because of this extra margin of safety, he plays the lifting ball better than any other English player.

Cowdrey does not score in ones and twos; when he moves into the ball to drive, it means four runs, not because he has hit it hard, but because he has timed it perfectly. He places the ball exquisitely off his legs, despatching the on-side half-volley or full toss with so correct a disposition of weight that the ball moves along the ground to the boundary as though of its own accord, inevitably. At the moment, he is almost exclusively a front-foot player.

May, when he hits the ball, cracks it; the air is split with the crispness of the impact. He plays forward defensively, not with the tolerance of Cowdrey, but with barely concealed impatience, as if only due necessity had forced him, reluctantly, and not for long, into such wearisome subservience. May is a player of the Renaissance, lean, hungry, adventurous. Cowdrey is a Georgian, discreet, handsome, and of substance.

Statham's bowling since he arrived in Australia has been no great surprise. He became a good bowler in the West Indies and he has steadily improved. On the fiery wickets of Perth he promised to hold the main threat to Australia. Tyson at that time was bowling everywhere except at the stumps, Bedser unfit, Loader generally unimpressive.

Statham, since then, has settled down into an attacking bowler of great stamina and accuracy, not perhaps quite as spectacular in achievement as those early matches suggested, but always dependable. He holds the seam upright to move the ball off the pitch rather than to swing it in the air. He keeps the ball up, relying on his whippety, double-jointed action to give him necessary lift. He bowls straighter than most opening bowlers, his pace and trajectory being of the sort that prevent him from being driven. His economy has been invaluable to Hutton, who looks to him at awkward moments more than to any other bowler.

Of Tyson's bowling it is still hardly possible to write with proportion. When the team was selected in England, he and Cowdrey seemed the two most debatable choices, their inclusion justifiable more for the value of Australian experience than because of any expectation that they would play in the Tests. Whatever faults of composition this party of eighteen players has shown, no praise can be too high for the selectors in these two instances. One tends to remember selectorial mistakes: Cowdrey and Tyson were brilliant examples of selectors backing their judgment against the facts.

Haunting images of Tyson's bowling in this match remain. He walks very loosely back to his bowling mark, chewing gum slowly. He has put on weight, making him less angular in movement, and is pleasantly tanned. He turns, moves back a pace, shuffles his feet as if wiping them on the doormat, lopes for three long strides, then quickens up for the climax of the delivery. As he runs he pushes his right hand, with the ball in it, twice from shoulder to waist, in the motions of an auctioneer knocking down an item. His left arm, as he approaches the umpire, is thrown up high and bent back near his right ear. His chest is turned inwards and fully expanded. The left foot, as he comes down on it, points nearer to first slip than long leg, but much less than it used. He has long arms and he brings the ball up from far back. When he is not bowling well, the initial shuffle is more pronounced, and his paces seem too close together for the distance of his run. After letting go the ball, he follows through, drops his shoulders and dangles his arms loosely in front of him, as though completely exhausted. His action is only striking at the moment of delivery; but for the few seconds that count he does most of the important things.

His advances in the control of length and direction can be put down partly to the shortening of his run; though that is more responsible for the great increase in the numbers of overs which he can now bowl at full pace. The sun has obviously helped considerably, for it has produced the looseness that he has rarely achieved in England. But the main causes seem to lie in the determined application that Tyson has brought to the problems of fast bowling. Intelligence has governed his attitude to them: and he is a man of sensibility, as well as heart.

* * *

It has been little warmer these last few days than during early May in England. The temperature remains steady in the lower sixties, though the sun shines continually. The light is quite lovely, soft and glowing, vastly different from Sydney. The sunsets last longer in Melbourne than further north, hanging up below the emptied lengths of Collins and Bourke Streets like melting strips of rouge and yellow wax. The night sky is midnight blue, not black, and in the triangular plantation off Spring Street palm trees thrust their still leaves and high *embonpoint* against white moonlit buildings. Though there is no river here, it is of the Quai Voltaire that one thinks. The conical spires of St Patrick's Cathedral sharpen into an electric sky, and a charming fountain, not in the style of Bernini, throws up its spray under a moon like a quartered orange.

Melbourne is a city of interlocking parks, of greenness curving like water and isolating the stone islands of commerce. The rectangular segment of shops, offices and hotels is a crazy *mélange* of architectural styles, but it is rarely dull. Above all, Melbourne has trees: you can walk about the streets with pleasure, which you cannot do in Sydney. The shops invite attention, their windows well dressed, like the women.

Two minutes walk from Collins Street the Yarra River curves in a wide, garden-flushed arc away from the city. From the far bank the towers and spires and tall modern blocks of Melbourne lean over skirting trees against the light. At lunch-time, on warm days, girls stream out of shops and offices to cross Princes Bridge and picnic in the sun along the grass verges of the river. Red, white and blue barges, awaiting afternoon travellers, lay their dulled reflections on the smooth, tree-shadowed water. Old, bearded men doze on benches in the shade, dreaming of gold or Macartney, the 'Governor-General,' heads sunk on their chests. Occasionally a boy bicycles along the towpath, scattering the gulls. The greenness expands and contracts, with changing strengths of light. The Yarra, limpid and peaceful, bears canoes and clouds on its still mirror. Placid family groups munching in front of the boat-houses might have come out of a painting by Seurat, a photograph by Cartier-Bresson. Yet a few hundred yards away the soot-covered domes of Flinders Street station bulge above grinding trams, and in nearby Collins Street solid lines of traffic hoot, past oyster-bars and pubs, down the stale, shop-soiled hill.

The suburbs of Melbourne, Toorak particularly, are miniature museums of modern architecture. Roy Grounds and Robin Boyd, partners in one of the most enlightened firms in Australia, are creating, amongst false Tudor and mock Georgian, an architectural style that obstinately owes nothing to any other country. Their refusal to build in what they consider a derivative manner, or in false contexts, has resulted in a fair start being made to the development of Melbourne as a modern Australian city—its houses not built out of the colonial's nostalgia for somewhere else, but relating Australians directly to their own environment, with understanding of its qualities of light and climate, its most suitable building materials.

Melbourne—I think of Cowdrey's sun-warmed century, of Tyson blasting his way through the Australian second innings, of May hammering Miller to the pickets and Miller turning to applaud him. I think of the ravioli and steaks in Molino's, the grilled butter-fish at the *Australia*, the torrid week-ends and cool weeks, the fresh evenings when, strolling past Captain Cook's cottage in the Treasury Gardens, the stars seemed to be perched on the plane trees and the trams rattled in the distance over the hooded banks of the Yarra. A city is, after all, only the sum of one's memories of it.

13 Notes in Tasmania

All the way from Melbourne a fleecy cloud-mattress separated us from Tasmania. There was no gradual approach, no preparation: the cloud was whipped away like a wrapping as we came down to land, and Hobart was suddenly revealed, like a surprise present.

It is a two and a half hours' flight. Of the Bass Strait we saw nothing, of Tasmania only a few scars of forest, a patch or two of dented plain. Breaking through the cloud in the Derwent Valley we bumped violently for twenty minutes, a circle of broken hills like the crust of a half-eaten Stilton narrowing ahead of us. Then we tilted over flat waters, silver in weak sunshine and bearing the impress of mountains.

Despite our sudden dive through cloud, the air approach to Hobart is not dramatic, for the airport is eleven miles away, and on the other side of the Derwent River. Landing there, the low mauve hills, with their trees and tangle of undergrowth, reminded me of Scotland. There was a smell of water, a sense of isolation: and the light nursed and drew the landscape close.

Hobart, which I had been told had the most beautiful harbour in the southern seas, is no disappointment, not to look at anyway. Possibly it is rather too far up-river for pictorial perfection, its seaward approach between long, muscled hills slowing down the visual impact and replacing the bracing energy of the open sea with a protective river-calm. But cargo ships and ocean liners make their way right up into the town, backing alongside metropolitan quays, and inserting their funnels into a skyline of domes and spires and cranes.

The town stretches up a steep hill, which flattens out before making a further sheer advance to the bouldered peaks of

Mount Wellington. Looking up from the port, I was struck most of all by the charm of the harbour buildings—the green cupolas of shipping offices and customs, the solid façades of warehouses and port authorities—the whole town leaning like a liqueur-bottle against the hill. Mount Wellington is the central top-heavy point of a wide curve of hills, its heaviness pushing the eye down to the thickening fall of houses that gather momentum beneath it, spilling from bottle-neck to bulge. There is no visible inland route out of Hobart except for the river itself: the whole setting is beautifully compact and tense, with no droop or tailing away of the taut, encircling outline.

Comparisons are not easy. I was reminded of two other ports in quite different ways: Copenhagen and Ajaccio. A photograph of Hobart from the sea, taken a little way out, would show the disposition of its buildings against the hills to be curiously like the view one gets of Ajaccio as one turns into the bay after rounding the Iles Sanguinaires on the west coast of Corsica. But Hobart lacks the vivid contrast of a Mediterranean port, its langour and heat. The light, the crisp air, the tones of brickwork are, essentially, to one's eye, 'northern.' Walking about the port, with its ships' chandlers, boat-building sheds, workshops and neat, scrubbed commercial hotels, I thought several times of Copenhagen—not of any particular area of it, but simply of its atmosphere and colour, its distilled, muted sounds and light.

Hobart is a view and a situation: the town itself is a fraud. Between the mountains and the lovely swing of quays and yacht-dotted anchorages, there is again the familiar conglomeration of corrugated-iron shacks, with here an odd admixture of Swiss-style chalets. On the upper slopes of Mount Wellington one expects to see edelweiss, and hear knobble-kneed men in Tyrolean hats and long white stockings yodelling across the valley. The port atmosphere does not survive fifty yards inland, where lines of jerry-built shops, interspersed with lady-like cafés, stretch dismally across, and up the hill. Ports get their flavour from noise, bars, fish-markets, restaurants, women, loafers, vice, foreigners, and bustle—not necessarily from these in themselves, but from the mysterious suggestion of them, the fact that they are there. Hobart, in these respects, is nearer to a seaside-resort than to a port. Its entertainments are of the nursery variety; its sailors and its women now only rarely come from the great cities of the imagination.

* * *

The National Gallery has a few objects of interest, principally the works of sailors. Their carvings on bone, their whalebone ornaments and decorated dolphin-jaws have the charm of good Sunday paintings. The numerous model sailing ships that sail through their glass cases, fully rigged and ready for sea, belong to the canvases of Alfred Wallis. Ships' figureheads, of noble countenance and divine breasts, lean purposefully into space, but salt seas no longer cool them.

The pictures are mostly timid affairs, by modest academic painters of the English third-rank. A painting of Venice by Sir Arthur Streeton compares badly with his earlier Australian pictures. I was captivated, however, by the landscapes and portraits of Benjamin Duterreau, who worked around the 1830's. He had two main styles: one, a lyrical, rather clumsy and primitive manner of painting landscapes, which, despite its technical inadequacy, succeeded in investing the country round Hobart with brightness and charm. It is amateur painting of natural genius, inconsequential and light. The other manner, painstaking and detailed, was devoted to portraits of aboriginals and to the depicting of local incidents of historical interest. These, in a completely different way, come off, mainly, perhaps, because of their honesty and strength of purpose. In both kinds of picture Duterreau succeeded in recording aspects of the life of his time. His portraits and dramatic reconstructions are real and crucial: his landscapes are pleasing fancies.

Wainewright, the poisoner and forger who was transported in 1837 for life, was the first art critic to reach Tasmanian shores. In Hobart, while still a convict (which status he retained till his death ten years later) he set up as a portrait painter, and the two best-known of his pictures, the delicately drawn studies of Mr and Mrs Wilson are, with a few others, in the Hobart Gallery.

* * *

Hobart is the second oldest city in Australia, and some of the first houses, principally those in a small circus on Battery Point, known as Arthur's Seat, have an unpretentious Georgian elegance. Most of the others have been, or are being, pulled down. The headstones in the original cemetery, many of which bear exotic testimony to the occupants, have been hauled out to make room for public gardens and a bandstand. They now lean their loving messages against the walls behind the flowerbeds. Two small hotels of honourable and decent appearance, the Lord Nelson and the Dr Syntax, might be in Rye or Portsmouth. But red-roofed villas converge on them from all directions, and probably they, too, will have to make way soon for some new row of bijou-residences.

* * *

Hobart cricket ground is on a high, spoon-shaped plateau half-way between town and mountain. Through the trees that ring it you can look down on the Derwent River and the suburb of Bellerive. Mount Wellington, immediately overhead, and the Mount Nelson range curve round to the west, dark and patched and blotchy.

M.C.C. play their week's cricket in Tasmania largely for the same reasons as warships show the flag in foreign ports. That is to say, out of courtesy, for relaxation, and as a polite indication of strength.

The first game, however, was very dull, an uneven pitch and short of a length medium-fast bowling restricting strokes and slowing down the scoring. The Combined XI, who included Harvey, Davidson, Favell and Benaud, batted all the first day for 221; M.C.C. batted throughout the second for 242 (of which Bailey made 53), and the final day, a scrappy affair, ended with

M.C.C. being offered ninety-five minutes to score 163 runs. They made no effort to do so. It seems a pity that, when good cricket so rarely comes to these small, isolated places, greater attempts are not made to please. The crowds at Hobart were a record for the island: but they saw only one innings, Harvey's on the first day, that was in any way notable. Batsmen on both sides find it hard enough at the moment to make runs at all, let alone make them well. Statham and Tyson were rested: Bedser toiled away as honestly as if it were in a Test match. But it is sad to see him reduced to unimportant matches like this. He has not failed, so much as, by a conspiracy of silence, found himself with lesser duties. By all accounts, Hutton has not been quite as forthright and open in this matter as he ought. Like Tate, Alec Bedser is finding that to succeed in a third tour requires more assistance from fate than any bowler has yet been afforded.

* * *

I went up by bus to Campbelltown, midway between Hobart and Launceston, to stay on a sheep station with Pauline and Henry Bentinck. One is constantly told that Tasmania is like England, but I could see no evidence of it. Pale, corn-coloured stubble stretched out to reddish hills, cars drew balloons of dust behind them along hedgeless roads, the trees were mostly gums. Tasmanians name their townships even more incongruously than Australians, whose settlements are generally named after explorers, English queens, English statesmen or English towns held in fond esteem. Near Hobart, the country towns of Brighton and Bridgewater are separated by Baghdad and Jericho.

Moving through the flat centre of Tasmania it grew hotter, the sheep chewing moodily in rare patches of shade, and rarely more than a shack or two in sight. Henry Bentinck met me at Epping, driving me out to Barton through thick gum forests that spattered the sun over us through an archway of branches.

Between Campbelltown and Launceston, the large sheep-stations, belonging to the old Tasmanian families of Taylor, Cameron, O'Connor and Archer, adjoin one another. The convict-built homesteads of the first settlers are less impressive than I had expected, and the country round them is dusty and featureless. The life on the stations seemed to me a terrible kind of internment, with few compensations, except variable profits, for a hard, lonely existence. There is no choice of friends, which seemed responsible for most graziers preferring their own company. Yet now and again, in a burst of sociability, they would drive a hundred miles along bad roads to a cocktail party. It is a life for ascetics, solitaries, or for those prepared to trade years of life for quick returns.

* * *

Launceston: a sprawling town, built on a series of hills forty miles from the mouth of a river. The shopping centre is gimcrack, crowded and narrow, with streets tilting out at all angles to rough slopes rashed with tomato-tiling. The heat gathers in the valleys, quivering above the corrugated-iron shacks, forming pockets of haze over the dusty undergrowth. The river elbows its way out of the suburbs, a few boats moored amongst its reedy banks.

The three-day match here against Tasmania has been better handled than the one in Hobart, M.C.C. winning by many runs, but with only twenty minutes to spare. The English batting worked better than usual, 427 runs being made for 7 wickets. Graveney, suited by the raffish, rodeo atmosphere, made his first hundred of the tour. Hutton and Compton and Wilson and Cowdrey also entertained in their several ways. Hutton allowed M.C.C. to bat on rather longer than necessary, both for the purposes of giving the lower-order batsmen practice and to prolong the match till the week-end. Tasmania, about the standard of Somerset, were shot out for 117 by Loader, somewhat too much in earnest for them, and then, a second time, after some kindly overs by Compton, for 200.

Hutton, with much self-denial, has played in both these matches. Apart from him and Compton, all the Test side have had at least one match off, Edrich and Evans both. In addition,

Loader and Wilson, who have had little serious cricket since Brisbane, have been able to disport themselves with a measure of success.

Launceston cricket ground, surrounded by predominantly English trees, bears some slight resemblance to Horsham, though the outfield is dusty and a white paddock fence runs the length of the boundary. Outside the ground, however, the sun beats, not on the green, swelling slopes, the single-track railway and church-spires of Horsham, but on steep dry hillsides, the scrub inflammable as tinder.

Hugh Ramsey, with whom I have been staying, drove me out to see some of the larger houses on neighbouring properties. The country round here, tobacco-coloured because of the present drought, is more akin to England, for the roads are hedged with hawthorn, and stretch away off the main roads to the houses themselves. One house, Panshanger, between Longford and Cressy, I like very much. Visiting them, however, is like moving back through time, for Tasmania, in atmosphere, bears much the same relationship to Australia as the remoter parts of Ireland do to England. The mustiness of the past, in-breeding, local power with its feudal overtones, contrive an unreality much more in keeping with the shuttered windows than with the unblinking sun.

* * *

I shall always feel a slight guilt about Tasmania, for I did few of the things the traveller is commonly supposed to do. I failed to visit the ruins of the penal settlement at Port Arthur, on the Tasmans peninsula, I never went to New Norfolk on the Derwent, or up Mount Wellington. I missed the hop-fields and orchards round Russell Falls, and took no boat cruise to the National Park. Nor did I go anywhere near the lakes, forests or mountains of the west coast. I omitted, also, to interview the gentleman in Hobart who holds the world record for propelling a bail the greatest distance after hitting the stumps.

Having confessed to all this, and having recorded my omissions, I can, tonight, retire to the Launceston Club for dinner, whisky and billiards with lightened conscience. I might add, in mitigation, that the area of Tasmania is 26,215 square miles, that it lies 150 miles off the south-east coast of Australia, and that, according to the Tourist Bureau brochures, the climate is 'cool, healthy and invigorating.'

* * *

We whirr northwards over streamers of cloud, a toy tanker embedded in the molten sea beneath us. Our wings carry the salmon-gold of the rising sun on their tips. Hutton, leaving his team for a rest in Adelaide, dozes in the plane behind me. He has looked pale and tired since Brisbane, though much better in spirits. M.C.C. fly later in the day to play a two-day match at Mount Gambier. Some of us are staying a few days in Melbourne, others go straight on to Adelaide, where the Fourth Test, preceded by a match against South Australia, begins in ten days time. The Australian papers are full of demands for a clear-out of the 'old gang' from their Test team. Hole seems certain to go; Morris, were it not for his record in Tests at Adelaide, is another probability; Maddocks may well prevent Langley's return, for it is the Australian middle batting that has been most consistently vulnerable. But there seem no obvious replacements for the other failures.

14 Adelaide and the Fourth Test Match

The match against South Australia was handsomely won by M.C.C. in three burning days. After a good opening spell by Bedser on the first morning, South Australia were put out for 180, of which Langley, whose dropping for the Test on his home ground has come near to causing a riot, ironically made 53. The second day, after three M.C.C. wickets had fallen for 70, Cowdrey 64, Compton 182, May 101 not out, scored much as they pleased. Of Cowdrey's runs, fifty must have come from on-drives or placings to leg. He batted with extraordinary ease from the moment he came in, until, tired by the great heat, he played a careless stroke and was bowled. Compton, as if determined to put fortune at least statistically straight, seemed bent on scoring first one hundred, then two: he took no chances, mopped his brow often, and was out in the last five minutes of the day. In his first Test at Adelaide in 1947 he made a century in each innings. He made a hundred here in November, straight off the plane, so patently Adelaide, with its palms, cathedral and mountains, has stimulus of one kind or another for him.

May, coming in at No. 7, drove all bowlers between mid-off and mid-on with a noise like gunshot. To see his shoulders at the moment when an over-pitched ball announces its length is akin to observing a tiger at the second its keeper thrusts raw meat between the bars. The body tenses, ripples into avid aggression. One can almost imagine the snarl, a sound depressingly absent from the lips of the tamed generations of post-war English batsmen.

On the Monday, South Australia showed little appetite or

aptitude for batting, and M.C.C. were saved a day's fielding in temperatures that had been around the hundred for a fortnight.

* * *

The Australian team for the Fourth Test showed several changes. Ian Johnson, despite doubts about his fitness and a bitter Press campaign against him, was retained as captain. The two South Australians, Hole and Langley, were dropped, being replaced by Burke and Maddocks. McDonald was chosen to partner Favell in place of Morris, a choice that was greeted with universal hostility. Davidson was announced as 12th man, the attack being unchanged.

Not long before the match, Lindwall pulled a muscle playing for Queensland and had to withdraw. Surprisingly, but to most people's satisfaction, Morris was reinstated in his place. The selectors then announced that the 12th man would be decided on the day, which meant, virtually, that Davidson would play, and either Favell or McDonald be omitted. In fact, it turned out to be Favell, so that all three South Australians who had played at Brisbane and Sydney were dropped on their own ground.

England, as expected, played the same team as at Melbourne. The only possible alternatives were Graveney for Edrich, Bedser for Wardle. Graveney was tried at No. 2 against South Australia, but, like Edrich, made only twenty, which was not enough to turn the scales. Bedser twice bowled excellently with the new ball, but both times unrecognizably when the shine was off. When he dropped a very easy catch, what chances he might have had of playing disappeared completely. The Adelaide wicket, which was expected to take spin by the third day, was, in any case, hardly the place for his return.

* * *

My account of the Fourth Test will be to a large extent second-hand, for though I heard a commentary of every ball on the radio, I saw only the English innings on the last day—

the innings that won us the rubber, and kept us the Ashes, only eight weeks after the drubbing of Brisbane. On January 24, four days before the Test began, I was operated on by Mr Ivan Jose for appendicitis. The next fortnight I spent in Calvary Hospital, admirably looked after both by the nuns and nurses who run the hospital, and by such friends as Ursula Hayward and Prue Holden, who came often to see me and made my life more than tolerable. If one has to be ill anywhere, I can, from all points of view, thoroughly recommend Adelaide.

My radio and newspaper impressions of the play were reinforced by several visits from Colin Cowdrey and Geoffrey Howard, from Arthur Gilligan and Alf Gover. At various other times Evelyn Wellings, Sidney Downer, Ronald Roberts, Norman Preston and Jim Swanton bolstered up my morale. Jim, in addition, lent me his admirable daily accounts of the play as an *aide-mémoire*. I was also especially happy to see Johnny Woodcock, whom I had last seen three weeks earlier propped up in a hospital bed in Hobart, where a duodenal ulcer had suddenly sprung on him.

For a week I was in no great comfort: the heat was such that I lay immobile in pools of water which, no matter how often I had been changed, resulted finally in excruciating backache. But by the last day of the Test, nine days after I had been operated on, I was able to walk, rather sedately, to a seat in the sun and watch England make the 94 runs needed to win the match.

THE FOURTH TEST: *January 28 — February 2*

AUSTRALIA

C. McDonald, c. May, b. Appleyard	48	b. Statham	29
A. R. Morris, c. Evans, b. Tyson	25	c. and b. Appleyard	16
J. Burke, c. May, b. Tyson	18	b. Appleyard	5
R. N. Harvey, c. Edrich, b. Bailey	25	b. Appleyard	7
K. R. Miller, c. Bailey, b. Appleyard	44	b. Statham	14
R. Benaud, c. May, b. Appleyard	15	l.b.w., b. Tyson	1
L. Maddocks, run out	69	l.b.w., b. Statham	2
R. Archer, c. May, b. Tyson	21	c. Evans, b. Tyson	3
A. Davidson, c. Evans, b. Bailey	5	l.b.w., b. Wardle	23
I. Johnson, c. Statham, b. Bailey	41	not out	3
W. Johnston, not out	0	c. Appleyard, b. Tyson	3
Extras (b. 3, l.b. 7, n.b. 2)	12	Extras (b. 4, l.b. 1)	5
Total	323	Total	111

FALL OF WICKETS. *First innings:* 1—59, 2—86, 3—115, 4—129, 5—175, 6—182, 7—212, 8—229, 9—321. *Second innings:* 1—24, 2—40, 3—54, 4—69, 5—76, 6—77, 7—79, 8—83, 9—101.

ENGLAND

L. Hutton, c. Davidson, b. Johnston	80	c. Davidson, b. Miller	5
W. J. Edrich, b. Johnson	21	b. Miller	0
P. B. H. May, c. Archer, b. Benaud	1	c. Miller, b. Johnston	26
M. C. Cowdrey, c. Maddocks, b. Davidson	79	c. Archer, b. Miller	4
D. Compton, l.b.w., b. Miller	44	not out	34
T. E. Bailey, c. Davidson, b. Johnston	38	l.b.w., b. Johnston	15
T. G. Evans, c. Maddocks, b. Benaud	37	not out	6
J. H. Wardle, c. and b. Johnston	23		
F. Tyson, c. Burke, b. Benaud	1		
R. Appleyard, not out	10		
B. Statham, c. Maddocks, b. Benaud	0		
Extras (b. 1, l.b. 2, n.b. 4)	7	Extras (b. 3, l.b. 4)	7
Total	341	Total (5 wkts.)	97

FALL OF WICKETS. *First innings:* 1—60, 2—63, 3—162, 4—232, 5—232, 6—283, 7—321, 8—323, 9—336. *Second innings:* 1—3, 2—10, 3—18, 4—49, 5—90.

Bowling Analysis
ENGLAND

First Innings	O.	M.	R.	W.	Second Innings	O.	M.	R.	W.
Tyson	26.1	4	85	3	Tyson	15	2	47	3
Statham	19	4	70	0	Statham	12	1	38	3
Bailey	12	3	39	3	Appleyard	12	7	13	3
Appleyard	23	7	58	3	Wardle	4.2	1	8	1
Wardle	19	5	59	0					

AUSTRALIA

	First Innings					Second Innings			
	O.	M.	R.	W.		O.	M.	R.	W.
Miller	11	4	34	1	Miller	11.4	3	40	3
Archer	3	0	12	0	Davidson	2	0	7	0
Johnson	36	17	46	2	Archer	4	0	13	0
Davidson	25	8	55	1	Benaud	6	2	10	0
Johnston	27	11	60	2	Johnston	8	2	20	2
Benaud	36.6	6	120	4					
Burke	2	0	7	0					

ENGLAND WON BY FIVE WICKETS

* * *

The Fourth Test was the only one of the series that was not won by the side batting first. When Ian Johnson won the toss for Australia, there seemed a fair chance that the rubber would not be decided till Sydney. The wicket was perfect, and the temperature, with a high degree of humidity, 90°. Huge scores have consistently been made at Adelaide, and since Australia, in similar conditions at Brisbane, had managed 600 runs, there seemed no reason why they should not score enough to make the difference between batting first and second a crucial one.

By lunch-time Australia were 59 for no wicket, the largest number of runs scored in any opening session of the series, beating the Brisbane total of 56 for one by three runs. From the outset the pitch admitted to no superfluous juices. So that, once Tyson and Statham had demonstrated their lift to be limited to the height of the stumps, and Morris and McDonald shown their mood to be possessive rather than expansive, Hutton's tactics were resolved. He used all his five bowlers in two and three over spells, set careful fields, and generally saw to it that, sooner or later, anxiety about the rate of scoring must penetrate the batsmen's consciousness. Morris and McDonald, except for an early boundary or two off the new ball, were content to score by deflections. Compared to Favell's habitual scurry, it was funereal; but the pace was correspondingly safer.

After lunch, things soon began to happen. Morris's meticulous and modest innings, during which his feet had not strayed from the front crease, ended when he failed to get over a good-length ball from Tyson and was caught by Evans. Burke started uncertainly against Statham; McDonald, however, batting better than in any of his previous encounters against M.C.C., went comfortably towards fifty. The thought of this seemed to unnerve him, for, on the verge of it, he gave two chances, the second of which was fatal. First, he mistimed a pull off Wardle, Compton dropping a simple catch at mid-on. In the next over, misjudging Appleyard's slower one, he drove too soon and was nicely caught by May, the first of four catches by him, at short leg. Harvey, entering at 82 for 2, was all but bowled by Appleyard, who had immediately dropped on, and maintained, an excellent length. He held the odd ball back, and, with his high, rhythmic action bounced it awkwardly when he quickened up. Just before tea Burke played Tyson firmly off the centre of the bat to May at backward short leg. Miller edged four runs past slip, and Australia went in at 119 for 3.

Harvey did not long survive Burke, slashing Bailey to Edrich at first slip. Bailey bowls very cleverly across Harvey's body; his oblique approach and natural movement away from the left-hander have frequently on this tour had Harvey playing inside the ball.

Benaud joined Miller, the pair of them scoring two runs in their first twenty-five minutes, and altogether thirty-two in the last hour and a quarter. Wardle bowled a good while from one end: the other four English bowlers in turn from the other. Both sides seemed content to disturb the scorers as little as possible, a matter that must have been considerably more satisfactory to Hutton than to Ian Johnson; 161 for 4 was a nervous total that could flower or close up: it was not, however you looked at it, an entertaining start.

The second day saw Australia collapse and then recover. From 161 for 4 they descended to 229 for 8. Johnson and Maddocks added 92 in 90 minutes for the ninth wicket, and finally Australia were all out for 323. From England's point of view it could have been much worse: it should, as things turned out, have been much better.

Statham and Tyson, with a breeze blowing straight up and down the pitch, bowled only two overs each. Hutton then brought on Appleyard and Wardle. Appleyard's hanging flight and changes of pace had accounted for Benaud at both Sydney and Melbourne, and it immediately did so again. In his first over, after Miller might have been stumped on the leg side, he induced Benaud to misjudge the length and push the ball gently to short leg. Miller was out a quarter of an hour later; he aimed to drive wide of mid-on but, playing too soon, miscued the ball to Bailey at mid-wicket. Bailey took it, as he does all catches away from the wicket, on bended knee. Harvey, a model for all catchers, habitually takes the ball over his left shoulder and in front of his face, where he can see the ball all the time without moving his head.

Maddocks, quixotically, after the fuss made about his selection, given the ovation of a returning war hero, was near to being caught by May at forward short leg off Appleyard before scoring. Surviving, he moved his bat vertically as little as decency permitted, while Archer, who hit his first ball, from Wardle, for six, showed customary defiance. Hutton took the new ball a few minutes before lunch, and it achieved Archer's wicket. May at third slip held a hard snick off Tyson, falling as he did so.

Bailey bowled with Tyson in the afternoon, Davidson soon snicking him to Evans. It was at this score, 229 for 8, that Ian Johnson arrived to put the Australian innings back on its pedestal—somewhat cracked and dusty, but an exhibit with recognizable features. Hutton, who rarely faces tail-enders with spin, gave Bailey only three overs, before calling up Wardle. Johnson immediately gave chase; Maddocks getting the hang of the thing too, they took 23 off Wardle's three overs. Appleyard was pulled and driven at unusual angles, and after a very short while Hutton was forced to rake Tyson and Statham in from their boundary meanderings. At 278 the partnership, which had grown fat on short singles, should have been broken by one. Maddocks pushed the ball to close mid-wicket and called. Johnson looked first to where Appleyard awaited the ball, then sent Maddocks back. With Maddocks hopelessly stranded up the pitch Appleyard took careful aim; then, with the unreality of nightmare, lobbed the ball high over Evans' head.

Tyson pitched repeatedly short when he came on, and both batsmen, getting firmly behind the ball, hooked him bravely and effectively. Bailey, dismissed at the beginning of this partnership, ended it in the last over before tea, Johnson driving him straight to Statham at mid-off. Maddocks had some time earlier reached fifty, which, together with Johnson's bold innings, doubtless settled some queasy selectorial stomachs. McDonald, the third much-resented selection, had succeeded also.

After Maddocks had been run out, scampering a second run to Wardle at long leg, England were left with ninety minutes batting. In this time Hutton and Edrich scored 54 runs, ten of which came in Benaud's one over, the last of the day. Miller beat both batsmen, bowling with the wind behind him, but runs were scored at a reasonable rate off Davidson, Archer and Johnston. Which was as well, for Ian Johnson, coming on at 21, bowled nine overs for 3 runs. Hutton and Edrich, their right feet anchored, stretched forward to drop the flighted, but not turning ball, as dead as a gull in front of them. It was finely-controlled bowling, determined batting; but it was a stalemate that, on such a wicket, batsmen of the experience of Hutton and Edrich ought not to have permitted. Johnson gives the batsman ample time to move his feet. But his skill in flight, his ability to float the ball in like a parachute before drifting it away, draws the stationary player to endless, and tortuous, thrusts.

Hardly an overnight batsman in this series, on either side, has benefited from his sleep. On Monday morning Johnson, in the first over, turned one in between Edrich's forward stroke and legs to bowl him without further score. Benaud, bowling at the other end, fizzed several from leg past May's bat, and, with only six runs scored, found one to touch the edge. Archer, at second slip, flung himself to hold it.

After this disastrous start Hutton and Cowdrey began patiently to wear the spin attack down. By lunch the total had reached 111, Cowdrey, once nearly bowled round his legs by Johnson, scoring slightly the faster of the two. In early afternoon Hutton went to his first fifty of the series. Soon afterwards he produced a cover drive that was made in the manner of a reformed reprobate indulging once more the vices of his youth. Cowdrey reached fifty with a hook off Benaud, the rhythm of the play having acquired a tranquil inevitability. Twenty minutes before tea Hutton was out. Usually the fall of Hutton's wicket seems an act of God, bestowed as divine favour on the bowler. It has not, till this innings, been so of late, for, since Brisbane, demons of temptation such as Saint Anthony would have recognized have appeared to be tugging at Hutton's flesh and dragging him pavilionwards.

This time, when he seemed safely beyond their reach, they struck unawares. Johnston bowled the first long hop of the day, Hutton hooked it, hard if a shade early, and Davidson, standing his ground at short leg, clutched the ball off his stomach, fortune coming to the aid of courage. Hutton's had been a monastic innings, for which he had prepared himself mentally through the same kind of contemplative discipline as a Cistercian exercises towards the refining of his soul. At tea England were 169 for 3, Cowdrey 61.

Like Australia on the first evening, England failed to hustle tiring bowlers. Cowdrey's stern and admirable concentration had left him, despite his own intentions to the contrary, almost strokeless. Compton, fortunately, in this, for him, crucial innings, settled in quickly, and his greater experience, as well as freshness, drew England out of her becalmed state into one in which the sails, if not actually billowing, were decently ruffled. The last hundred minutes produced 61 runs, Compton's share being 41. England, 230 for 3, were 93 behind.

Next morning Johnson gave the new ball to Miller and

Davidson. In a few moments, for the addition of two runs, Compton and Cowdrey were out. Compton went immediately, beaten and l.b.w. as he played back to an in-swinger from Miller. At the same score, 232, Cowdrey touched a ball moving diagonally across him from Davidson. The fall of these two wickets, disappointing after the arduous labours of the day before, was much in the pattern of the series, which followed a symmetry so predictable that batsmen seemed more than ever victims, rather than architects, of their fate.

There seemed small likelihood now of England leading Australia, the corollary to which was that Australia had acquired more than a slender chance of winning. Evans, however, since Christmas on much better terms with his bat, allowed this notion little time to develop. With Bailey watchful as Cerberus at the other end, he skirmished against Miller, Davidson and Benaud so successfully that the new ball was banged in the dust to the tune of 53 runs in 50 minutes. When he was out, caught at the wicket for 37, England were only 40 behind.

Wardle opened up with an enormous six to long-on but then, like a man threatened with the dangers of alcoholic indulgence, refused further enticements. In place of an orgy with an accompaniment of Wagner, the large, sun-blacked and sun-hatted crowd under the palms were treated, metaphorically, to buns and tea and chamber music. The Australian score was slowly, very slowly, overhauled. Johnson, coming on at 275, acted as an aphrodisiac. Wardle, dancing out to him, drove twice to the long, straight boundary. Attempting to do so a third time, he was caught and bowled. Tyson made no headway and was nicely caught at deep square leg. Eight wickets were down when Appleyard, joining Bailey, put England ahead, showing, for not the first time, a forward stroke of good family. England's lead finally was 18; not, by any means, what had once been hoped for, but acceptable as a small, unexpected remittance from an aunt is to a man whose capital has been lost overnight.

Morris and McDonald spent only a matter of minutes in flicking away this deficit, as if it were cigarette ash, from some fast overs by Tyson and Statham. Appleyard was quickly on, and Morris, full of strokes, cut him hard down in front of Cowdrey in the gully. The ball skidded up off the seam, and Cowdrey, unable to get his hands there in time, took a noisy crack on the bridge of the nose. He was carried off, the grass around him, if the impressionable radio commentators are to be believed, resembling the stage of *Hamlet* after the fall of the last curtain. Late that evening Cowdrey came in to Calvary Hospital for an X-ray, which showed a clean break of the bone. However, after the initial shock of the impact, he was very cheerful about it.

Morris repentently surrendered his wicket in the same over, playing back too early to Appleyard, and offering an easy return catch. After tea Appleyard, keeping a fine length and cutting the ball at varying speeds, pushed Australia into a state of siege from which they never broke free. At 40 Burke was bowled playing forward. Harvey failed for the second time, hooking at a ball pitched outside his leg stump which spun across his pads and bowled him. Miller saw out the day with McDonald. Appleyard had taken 3 wickets for 13.

As at Sydney and Melbourne, England's chances of victory seemed to rest on the fifth morning with Appleyard. Yet once again Hutton, either experimentally or out of conviction, began with Tyson and Statham. Appleyard, who had, as at Melbourne, opened the door to the interior of the Australian innings, was scarcely required. Statham, unlucky so far in this match, and further troubled with a sore toe, bowled McDonald with a full toss in his first over. He then raised Miller's leg bail with an in-swinger of great quickness in his second.

Once more, the symmetry had been preserved: this time, however, the Australian batting truly went to pieces, and there was no semblance of recovery. Benaud lasted only a minute, hitting across a half-volley from Tyson; Maddocks went back to Statham and was l.b.w. Archer, swishing on the off, was caught by Evans.

In half an hour five wickets had fallen for ten runs, a capitulation to speed no less hasty than that at Melbourne. It was not a matter for complicated explanation. With no time to consider their strokes, Australian batsmen had proved for the third Test in succession that instinct, uncorrected by technique, was insufficient defence against bowling of real speed and accuracy.

I had my first outing from Calvary during the luncheon interval, being driven down to the Adelaide Oval just in time to see the last Australian wicket fall. Appleyard bowled two maidens, then Wardle with his second ball had Davidson, sweeping across the line of the ball, l.b.w. Australia were all out for 111.

Ian Johnson, who had fallen on his elbow the day before, making his right arm virtually useless, led Australia out. Archer also was suffering from a pulled muscle and not expected to bowl. Hutton and Edrich were on their heels, as if wanting to waste no time over the 94 runs needed to win both Test and rubber. Edrich trotted like a terrier, and Hutton, on the edge of the unique achievement of having led England throughout two successive victorious Test series against Australia, seemed less preoccupied than usual.

Miller bowled, and Hutton was at once off the mark, taking three through the wounded Johnson at mid-off. Edrich played one ball back; his leg stump was rattled by the second, an in-swinging yorker. Davidson bowled at the other end. The loss of Edrich was, one felt, tiresome, but not disconcerting. Miller, in his second over, whipped one up and away from Hutton, who pushed forward, got an edge, and, for the third time in two Tests, found Davidson. Davidson this time was at second slip, and he held the ball low and left-handed. Cowdrey, not Compton as one had expected, came next; after once driving Miller to the cover boundary, he too played inside a beautiful ball that left him fast and late. Archer held him safely at first slip. 18 for 3 was no moment for imaginative conjecture, nor, with the crowd now thoroughly perky after having prepared for the worst, was it a moment one wished to prolong. May, fortunately, was of similar opinion; he is not often prepared to take his time, certainly not to wait for runs to come. It was essential now that the score be kept moving, and the task minimized as much as possible. May immediately set about the bowling, driving, placing to the on and cutting, so that the tension was kept within reasonable bounds. At 10 he had a narrow escape, Miller, following up, almost catching him off a ball that kicked brutishly. But, with Compton as partner, he saw Miller lose his initial pace and swing, bringing to an end an onslaught as fierce as any fast bowler can ever have made on so true a pitch. Within minutes, though, Miller was to give further proof of an all-round genius that seemed to have been roused to a new intensity by the sheer hopelessness of the position. It is at such times that the great player reveals the characteristics that separate him from his fellows. Miller was off, Johnston on, when May, 26, hit a half-volley with great force shin-high to extra cover. Miller, at grass somewhere in the region, dived to his left and held the ball as he rolled over and over.

At 49 for 4 the match was still not won. However, compared to some of the situations Bailey has faced over the years, the present one was child's play. From the start, he looked in no trouble at all, and, with Compton scoring steadily with chops and occasional sweeps, he even found time to hook twice for four. Miller came back when 20 more were needed but, though he looked fast and threatening, could now be contained. Sharp singles were scampered, the crowd, acknowledging the inevitable, began to drift away, and in clear, hot sun the Ashes were made safe by two cricketers who have many times served England well in adversity. Bailey lost his wicket with a few runs to go, Evans in fact making the winning hit, but Compton, as at the Oval in 1953, was there till the end. He had not, largely through ill-fortune, played a great part in this series, but his two innings in this match showed that, tuned up and fully fit, he is still a batsman to be reckoned with, even in Test matches against Australia.

I hobbled tenderly up the steps of Calvary that evening in high spirits, removing, on my way, the bottle of Veuve Clicquot which I had put on ice against my return.

* * *

For me this Fourth Test in Adelaide had been a strange experience. It is mingled in my mind with the endless repetitions of radio commentators, with the whirring of fans and the rustle of nuns' robes and, because my hospital room was in the same corridor as the operating theatre, with the smell of anæsthetic. If I look at the score-sheet, I see between the lines the dark vegetation on the Mount Lofty hills outside my window, and I hear the noonday rattle of trams. I was having my dressing done when Statham bowled Miller on the last morning, and I was woken from afternoon sleep by Charles Fortune's excitement at announcing that Hutton had been caught by Davidson.

All four Tests so far had ended with a day to spare. It was twenty-two years since England had won a Test series in Australia. Hutton, the first professional captain to lead England abroad in this century, had, despite much early criticism, proved that any inherent personal defects were outweighed by his perseverance, his patience, and his tactical skill. It is not in his nature to make the initial move in human relationships, for he is withdrawn and cautious in these as in much else, but gradually his team took shape round him, and this last match, especially, was a team victory. Australia, so confident and united at Brisbane, had long since been reduced to a party of individuals, hardly one of them, from the captain downwards, sure of his place. Hutton had persisted in his faith that speed was his key weapon, and with speed Australia had been routed on wickets more suited to spinners. That was the real paradox. Whether Appleyard, if given the job to complete at Sydney, Melbourne and Adelaide, would also have done it successfully, is an interesting question: on no occasion were there quite enough runs to play with, but, so well and accurately had he bowled since Christmas that, with reasonable help at the other end, he might have squeezed England home in the Third and Fourth Tests. As it was, he played a vital, if restricted part.

* * *

During my stay in Calvary my wife Jennifer, and my stepdaughter Victoria, arrived by boat from England. I had not timed my appendicitis very well, and they put into Port Melbourne unsuspecting of my absence, a cable having curiously gone astray. However, I was already convalescent, and as soon as I was allowed out Ursula Hayward lent us her pretty seaside house, a converted inn a hundred years old, at Port Willunga, thirty miles south of Adelaide.

We spent ten idyllic, peaceful days. The beach, one of the most curiously formed and unspoiled in Australia, was only two minutes walk away. On Sundays, a few striped awnings and umbrellas were dotted over it, but for the rest of the week we shared a curving mile of empty sand under steep, yellow cliffs, with some exceptionally sedentary seagulls and a solitary fisherman. The light was clear and soft, the sea calm and refreshing. At night we could see the orange glow of liners making their way down the Spencer Gulf. The gulls waddled all day in the sun, and took off at dusk with the smooth dipping colours of sunset on their feathers. Sometimes the hot north wind, blowing in over parched fields and red foothills, banged doors and shutters, filling the house with fine grains of dust. Sometimes it rained, the gulls sheltering in the grey cliff-caves that stored the fishing boats. But we had clear, warm days too, the sea sparkling and the waves uncurling on sand the colour of bronze. Then there seemed no lovelier place in the world.

15 Sydney Day by Day

A wet, steamy day, the rain falling hour after hour, with no hint of ever stopping. Last night we dined with Ralph and Barbara Oliphant at Hunters Hill, sitting out after dinner and drinking whiskies on the verandah, watching the lights flicker on the city side of the river, the prawn-boats move behind the great, dark palm trees that line this shore of the Parramatta. The sky was a pure indigo, the stars like pieces of crushed ice. The sun, sliding away down behind the Blue Mountains, had left behind it a pale yellow band over the western suburbs of Sydney. Against this, trees and buildings blackened, birds took wing, mosquitoes buzzed. Watching in civilized comfort this lovely cooling down of the day I felt one could easily become reconciled to the disadvantages of living on the underside of the world.

Today I am not so sure. To move is to break out in a sweat, a clammy sweat aggravated by alcohol, or tea. Clouds have come rolling in from the Pacific without a break, there has been neither sun nor light. The sky seems roof-high, every room like a Turkish bath. Now at dusk everything drips, the air itself a kind of pulpy substance, slowly dissolving. The frangipani are bowed, closed-up against streaming walls. Cicadas and bullfrogs belabour the sweating silence.

Sunday was grey, with brisk Pacific breezes. Bondi almost empty, a few dark heads rolling among the breakers like olives. A day for strong swimmers and practised surfers. In King's Cross, where we are staying, men strolled for their morning papers in pyjama-tops and shorts.

King's Cross has a reputation for vice and crime. In fact, it is convivial and informal, the houses mostly old with painted, cast-iron lacework on first-floor balconies, and frangipani in their gardens. The four commercial roads that form the 'cross' slope down to triangular patches of blue harbour. The tilted side-streets contain a varied cross-section of cosmopolitan life: there is something of Soho about them, and of Notting Hill Gate as well. The 'old colonial' dwellings can be seen here renovated, dilapidated, or completely derelict.

Woolloomooloo, another district of ancient romance, is five minutes walk. The hoot of tugs and the noise of ships' sirens announce voyages over the heads of the traffic. Rushcutters Bay (named after the convicts who once cut rushes there), possesses a cricket ground and an anchorage for yachts. I used to idle down there from our hotel on free days and watch both the cricket and the boats. For my next venture out I shall need frog-feet.

* * *

Twenty-four hours later, it is still pouring. The Test match is only a day off. M.C.C. (the second match against Victoria being, like the first, rained-off) were beaten this week by New South Wales. Each side made 172 in the first innings. New South Wales declared their second innings at 314 for 8, leaving M.C.C. to make the runs at almost a run a minute. May, Hutton, Cowdrey and Evans all played well for scores of between 35 and 60, partnerships being broken just when it seemed that the runs would be made. They were not, by 45. It is the first defeat of an M.C.C. side by a State since 1936. All the same, it was one of the best State matches we have had. Miller captained New South Wales so inspiringly and cleverly that he cannot surely be passed over as Australian Captain for the English tour in 1956. In the meantime, he has been appointed Vice-Captain to Ian Johnson in the West Indies. The New South Wales fielding was astonishing in its agility.

Bedser took 5 for 57 in the New South Wales first innings, opening the bowling on a damp, heavy day with a spell of 3 for 2. Bailey broke a finger at Melbourne, and is not yet certain to be fit tomorrow. Tyson, too, has strained a muscle: if either is not available, Bedser will play. It would make everybody very happy. This Test, interesting though it promises to be, will be the first England-Australia affair for twenty years that one will be able to contemplate without the nervous anxiety that takes away much of the pleasure. We have had too much sharp disappointment and opportunity for philosophic adjustment. I make no bones about the fact that, now the Ashes are safely guaranteed, I should like to see Hutton, Compton and May lash the Australian bowling all over Sydney. Australia will have to fight to win this match. England, with little to lose, has the chance of making this an exhibition, of tempering sternness with grace. Relieved of responsibility, Hutton, I hope, will show those who have begun to doubt it that he is still the greatest player in the world. Against New South Wales he made 48 and 59, top score in each innings, but he has not once on this tour dominated Test bowlers. Evans has recently returned to batting with the ardour of one long-estranged from a bride, and runs flow from him with happy ease.

Colin Cowdrey has a high temperature and influenza. His chances of playing tomorrow are small. It is bad luck, for he, more than anyone, deserves a Test innings in which the necessity for survival does not limit the exercise of art. Presumably Graveney, who has never quite come up to scratch, will take his place.

At the moment it looks like being a Test match on water-skis.

* * *

Too gloomy to write anything for three days, during which it has not stopped raining once. Already two days of the Test are gone: all the players are now fit, but not the ground. Though it is, in fact, the weather that is alone to blame: the pitch is still in perfect condition, and the water has been drawn off the wicket area by means of rubble drains that flank it at a depth of three feet. Despite the continuous rain, play could start within two hours of it stopping. The Second Test here produced

£8,000 in receipts on the first two days, so the loss already is a cruel one. Estimated expenses for the whole tour are £55,000. So far, the net profit made by M.C.C. is in the region of £20,000. At Melbourne M.C.C's share of the Third Test takings was £23,996, the largest ever received by a touring side. If it rains on Monday, it will be the first time that three days of a Test have ever been lost in Australia.

Today, Sunday, broke warm and sunny, the only morning free of rain and cloud since Tuesday. The harbour glinted under a heavy haze. Boats were being painted in Rushcutters Bay and Double Bay. The haze took the hardness out of the light, muting the red roofs. On such mornings of mauve sea, heat-hung palms, spires and boats, Sydney is a city of anticipation. At Bondi and Manly they come in, connoisseurs of timing, on the long Pacific rollers. Around the harbour coves and beaches they lie out on half-moons of sand under magnolia trees. The bays are full of small, scudding yachts beneath steep, house-indented headlands.

We bathed before lunch, eating salami and drinking white wine with Diana Phipps and George Molnar, brilliant cartoonist of the *Sydney Morning Herald;* then again the clouds mounted up from the west, the harbour waters blackened, and by dusk light rain began to fall. Now it is as though there had been no break at all.

* * *

Monday: it has been raining harder than ever, and there was not today the remotest possibility of play. Large areas of New South Wales are flooded, whole villages drowned. A month ago there was drought and persistent danger of bush-fire. The unkindness of landscape and the natural hazard in Australian life must be set against the usual lavishness of the sun (hard to credit at this moment), high wages and short hours. Last week a killer shark disposed of a young New Australian and a small boy in Sydney harbour. A tiger in Taronga Park Zoo has died today of a bite from a spider, one of the several deadly varieties that may be encountered at any time by the unlucky. In the flooded areas, where the number of floating corpses increases hourly, hundreds of snakes and scorpions seek refuge on rooftops, in buses, and on whatever protrudes above water. In urban Australia one tends to lose, from time to time, a sense of this antique relationship with death at the hands of Nature. I find it even hard to write the word Nature, so pious and temperate a phenomenon in one's own vocabulary, but here of sudden, incalculable brutality.

* * *

The weather cleared just enough for the Test match to begin half-way through its fourth day. The pitch, being covered, was dry, but with less grass on it than a Sydney wicket usually has. Considering the context, reasonable crowds turned up each day. It was a gentle kind of exhibition, not a Test match, except statistically. That probably accounts for Graveney's quite lovely batting. Graveney, in a match which Australia came astonishingly near to losing in two and a half days—and might in fact have lost except for an abominably pawky exhibition by Compton and Bailey on the fifth morning—played like the batsman one had always hoped he would become. He drove Miller and Lindwall with long flowing strokes, leaning into the ball and placing it away almost as it was bowled. For most of this tour he has, when playing defensively, pushed forward at the away-swinger with his left leg down the line of the middle or leg stumps, his bat aimed at mid-off and thereby moving diagonally across the ball. His left leg was there too early, his head correspondingly back. In this innings he got his head and legs further to the off, moving his bat full face within the same parallels as the ball. He drove the out-swinging ball between the bowler and mid-on or mid-off, which is where it should go. His 111, made in two and a half hours, was as exquisitely fashioned as an object by Fabergé. The Test match itself I shall write about separately.

* * *

No sooner was the Test over than the rains began again. In

addition, a cyclone of unexceeded intensity is reported moving towards the Queensland-New South Wales border.

In fine weather, King's Cross has a flavour not to be found anywhere else in Australia. The tenements, with their peeling woodwork, heavy, iron balconies, budgerigars and potted plants, smell of garlic and Italian cooking. At night, under the elms of Macleay Street, people wander slowly up and down as in Europe, stopping for coffee or beer, looking in at the shops, or buying fruit from the great, banked stalls that are illuminated like altars. The harbour, with its lights and water-bug ferries, winks under the curve of the hill. There is a fragrance of coffee, the generation of that warm geniality which is produced only by people for whom the street is as much a place of assignation as the home.

From King's Cross the tram loops round a succession of bays to the harbour entrance, the Heads, eight miles away: Rushcutters Bay, Double Bay, both with neat greens, Georgian-style terraces and a sprinkle of sailing-boats. On fine, glassy days the headlands of Darling Point and Point Piper, their expensive houses collared with trees, are mirrored in water. Further out, Rose Bay spreads more widely between less defined promontories. Sometimes, driving by, you see the skim and splash of a flying boat coming cleanly to rest. Watson's Bay, next along, is almost free in feeling of the city—a small fishing village, its painted boats used for commerce, not pleasure. The water begins to work off its harbour staleness, to acquire an ocean cleanliness. Further out still, below and beyond the red roofs of Vaucluse, waves crash and hiss on the cracked, sheer cliffs of the Gap (where a hundred years ago the clipper *Dunbar* foundered, with the loss of all hands but one). Near here, the Macquarie Lighthouse, a tall, white cone, the original of which was designed by Greenway, swings its steady beam over the Pacific.

* * *

More rain, the floods in Maitland, Singleton and Dobbo the worst in Australian history. The room-maid says the world will end, not with an atom bomb, but with a flood. She may be right. At a wine lunch given the other day by Leo Buring in his cellars, Trevor Bailey reminded me that on the 1951 tour at this period it rained for ten consecutive days. In dry moments, I have driven about Woolloomooloo, King's Cross and Macquarie Road, taking photographs. Sydney will appear a city of grey light, dripping foliage and shadowed waters. Trams, ships, cranes, derricks, lighthouses, gleam palely against the blackness of sky and landscape. From Mrs Macquarie's 'chair,' a vantage-point on the rocks above Woolloomooloo, Sydney Bridge curves behind a heavy fringe of fig trees and palms—an illusion of the exotic that the Australian temperament does nothing to sustain.

Suddenly, after occluded stars and a watery moon, a perfect day. M.C.C. left early this morning by air for New Zealand, and we, too, were due to sail today, March 5. The wharf strikes of a few weeks back, however, have resulted in a queue of ships waiting to be loaded. *Oceania's* sailing has been postponed by forty-eight hours. King's Cross is refracted with light shining off tiled roofs at oblique angles. Honey-brown girls, their coloured blouses thickly belted into darker skirts, patrol leafy, summer-heavy streets. The loops of bays crinkle under splintering sun. The siege is raised.

Bondi, this afternoon, at last as postcards show it. A dazzling arc of sand plunging to two house-hung headlands, the whiteness almost obliterated by brown flesh. The breakers come in long and foaming, arching up out of a sulky, silken sea. The sky blue, devoid of cloud, and coloured umbrellas speckling the beach. Bondi is brazen, vulgar, vivid and marvellous in its contrasts. The open Pacific, sea of explorers, for whom this coast was the mirage realized, stirs at the feet of a packed half-moon of settlers, airing bodies and minds, craving the ocean.

The ocean is the moving axis of Australian happiness. In the dry, exhausting, empty interior, Australians find a historic pride of conquest; in the raising of cattle, a reason for existence. But in the surf they come to terms with beauty in their unique context. At Bondi the timid majority wallow and splash safely between flags of safety, whistled out of rips and undertows by pedagogic beach inspectors. But these are, as it were, only the necessary chorus of Greek drama, affording the crowd-movement, violent but circumscribed, against which the heroes and heroines, the surfers, perform their exploits.

For, far beyond the noisy huddle cavorting in the shallows, the surfers swim out to the first line of breakers, perhaps three hundred yards from the shore. That initial swim, through waves half a house high, is the essential prologue. To reach the point of departure for the surf-journey, that final green, remorseless and motionless flight to rest, requires that you are not merely an excellent swimmer, but a strong, enduring one.

Around where the impulse of the ocean begins to shape itself visibly, the swimmers turn, creating an imaginary, calculated line. Beyond them, the shark-boat, manned by half a dozen capped and mahogany oarsmen, idles on the last strip of patient sea. The heads of the surfers bob over several ignored undulations. Then, expert eyes having read and approved a particular wave's physique as skilfully as breeders size up the prowess of horses, the line strikes out for the shore, making a score of frenzied strokes before the wave arches. Someone may lose the impetus, having estimated wrongly, and have to turn back. The others, acquiring one by one the final motive force of the Pacific airs, stop swimming: and, the fifteen-foot wave suspended like a banner from their breasts, they take the current as motionlessly as the albatross, the sea hollowing under them, a hollow into which they look far down, and, doing no more than lean on their springs of foam, glide proudly in. This last surge up the beach is compounded of the elements of flight and diving— man becoming a sea-bird.

The essential art of surfing is timing, instinct developed by knowledge of when to turn, of when to start swimming, of friendly and cruel waves. There are kinds of seas, species of waves and current, the distinguishing of which requires years of apprenticeship. The technique is simple in expression, elaborate in its subtle harnessing of the body to racing air. For, of course, it is only the air behind the wave, not the water itself, that moves. And it is propelled by the air, and supported by the wave, that the surfer comes in to his long, clean climax.

The bad wave, which the novice fails usually to discern, is the 'dumper,' an ugly curling wave that, not coming to a perceptible head, throws the swimmer under it and batters him repeatedly. Being 'dumped' is as necessary a part of the surfer's experience as being thrown is of the jockey's. Only it is more disagreeable, the sea seeming to take on a personal vindictiveness, its violent assault on the human body appearing to emphasize the frailty of man and the indulgence of the sea.

Surfing, as we saw this afternoon at Bondi, when teams from the neighbouring clubs of Bronte, Maroubra, and Manly competed with Bondi in a surf carnival, has several forms of expression. Boards are used, beautiful to watch when the rider stands up straight, arched against sea and sky, appearing to be motionless, but in fact readjusting his balance with neat dancer's steps. In carnivals, boat teams race out to coloured floats on the water, rowing their boats in on the surf against one another and beaching them. The afternoon begins with the parade, when the pageantry of life-saving, which is the graver corollary to use of the surf, is demonstrated in a march-past. The teams, wearing costumes and bathing caps striped with club colours, parade round a marked area of beach, carrying their equipment of belts and reels, and stepping out high and robustly on the sand. There is, to the casual eye, an element of absurdity about this solemn-faced stamping in antique costumes; but in fact, once one has got used to the startling sight of so many men the size and colour of wardrobes, all marching in rhythmic procession, one takes the presence of the uniformed life-saver on the beach for granted. Which is what should not be done, for these men, who pay 10s. 6d. a year for the privilege of risking their lives, as well as devoting hundreds of hours to training and practice, on an average rescue over a thousand people a summer. It is not uncommon, on a Sunday of sudden sweeps and bad rips, for life-savers on one beach to go in after, and save, a hundred people, with great danger to themselves.

Surfing or, at its simplest equivalent, sea-bathing is, curiously, still not legal in Australia. Section 77 of the Police Force Act No. 5 of 1901, still in force, reads: 'Whosoever bathes in any part of Sydney Cove, or in any waters exposed to view from any wharf, street, public place, or dwelling-house in or near the said city or towns between the hours of six o'clock in the morning and eight in the evening shall be liable to a penalty not exceeding one pound.'

Nevertheless, a gentleman by the name of Mr W. H. Gocher, of Manly, is generally honoured as the pioneering spirit who made Australians free of the surf. The truth behind the various versions of what Mr Gocher accomplished, and the manner in which he did so, is not easy to find. In Mr Gocher's own account the issue first arose in November, 1902. Some young boys who had been yachting were arrested and taken to gaol after 'a joyous plunge in the cool Pacific.'

'My ire was aroused at the absurdity and injustice,' Mr Gocher wrote, 'so I rose up on my hind legs and informed the police that they would have to arrest me on the following Sunday as well, for I meant to test the matter. At that time I was proprietor and editor of the *Manly and North Sydney News*, so my next issue blazoned forth my intentions, to the effect that we would bound in for a bathe at noon on the morrow and the police would therefore be expected to do their duty and likewise arrest us. Three of us, I might explain, had made up our minds to test the Act, they being Arthur Edwards, Percy Oldman and myself. The proprietor of the Steyne Hotel, Mr Rosenthall (who was better known in those days as Old Rosie), entered fairly into the spirit of the joke, and granted us a room to change our costumes.

'The time arrived, but only two of us materialized, and, to make matters worse, my old friend Percy Oldman had forgotten his costume. Nevertheless, he stood most loyally by me and even ventured to go right with me on to the sands to hold my mackintosh whilst I cut loose amongst the hissing breakers. It was the most enjoyable bathe of my lifetime. But nothing happened. Very few people were about. No posse of police came flying down with drawn batons to the waters edge to yell out to me to come forth and be arrested. There was no mighty concourse of citizens to cheer me as I came shooting in on No. 4 breaker, breathing salt spray and defiance. Outside my few bosom pals present on the sands the passing pedestrians took but a tired sort of interest in my plunge for public liberty and the popularity of the great old sport on all beaches.

'The next issue of my paper was flavoured with cayenne pepper for the police for not doing their duty. I announced my intention of going in for a bathe at precisely the same time and at the same place. . . . Certainly more people rolled up to watch events—still, no police.

'On the occasion of my third dip matters commenced to be merrier. The law swooped on me and I was trotted along to the limbo. Frank Donovan bailed me out.'

Mr Gocher, after his arrest, interviewed the Inspector-General of Police, who, in Mr Gocher's words, 'stated that no magistrate would convict me: but that men would have to wear neck to knee costumes and that the ladies would have to take care not to expose their bosoms.'

Mr Gocher's testimony, since he was both the man principally concerned and a journalist as well, should hardly be in question. However, Mr J. S. Jones, of Lane Cove, Sydney, one of the policemen on duty at Manly beach at the material time, recorded the facts quite differently. 'Mr Gocher went in wearing a three-quarter-length frock-coat, striped trousers and a hard hat, and he had an umbrella under his left arm. I can see it all quite clearly.'

In other material details, Mr Jones differs considerably. Mr Gocher denied the presence of police, admitted few spectators, and described himself 'bounding in among hissing breakers.' Mr Jones comments dryly: 'He waded in up to his armpits, made two strokes, and then came out and walked up to us expecting to be arrested. There were 200 or 300 people watching. They opened up to make a way for him. We took no notice.'

On the matter of Mr Gocher's 'third dip,' Mr Jones is flatly contradictory. 'He was never arrested.'

Half a century after Mr Gocher's walk in the sea, he is acknowledged as the spiritual father of surfing. Yet the law against which he 'bounded in for a bathe' or 'waded in up to his armpits' in frock-coat and hard hat—according to whether you put more faith in Mr Gocher's confident, unpunctuated prose, or Mr Jones' constabulary memory—remains unchanged.

* * *

The beach empties, a tanker scrawling a firm, black signature against the sky. The light, harsh and focusing at high noon, forms a kind of soft luminous screen between sand, sea and houses. The ugly roof-red turns rose, the chipped-blue sea a watered green, the glaring white sand a dull bronze.

At Bondi, night falling, the trams unhooked, the twin headlands pricked with lit windows. On the sand, the ephemeral impress of women's bodies, of the feet of children. The warm air is full of salt, of the subsidence of surf.

16 The Fifth Test Match

February 25 — March 3

ENGLAND

L. Hutton, c. Burge, b. Lindwall	6
T. W. Graveney, c. and b. Johnson	111
P. B. H. May, c. Davidson, b. Benaud	79
M. C. Cowdrey, c. Maddocks, b. Johnson	0
D. C. S. Compton, c. and b. Johnson	84
T. E. Bailey, b. Lindwall	72
T. G. Evans, c. McDonald, b. Lindwall	10
J. H. Wardle, not out	5
Extras (b. 1, l.b. 3)	4
Total (7 wkts. dec.)	371

FALL OF WICKETS. 1—6, 2—188, 3—188, 4—196, 5—330, 6—359, 7—371.
Did not bat: J. B. Statham, R. Appleyard, F. Tyson.

AUSTRALIA

W. Watson, b. Wardle	18	c. Graveney, b. Statham	3
C. McDonald, c. May, b. Appleyard	72	c. Evans, b. Graveney	37
L. Favell, b. Tyson	1	c. Graveney, b. Wardle	9
R. N. Harvey, c. and b. Tyson	13	c. and b. Wardle	1
K. R. Miller, run out	19	b. Wardle	28
P. Burge, c. Appleyard, b. Wardle	17	not out	18
R. Benaud, b. Wardle	7	b. Hutton	22
L. Maddocks, c. Appleyard, b. Wardle	32		
A. Davidson, c. Evans, b. Wardle	18		
I. W. Johnson, run out	11		
R. R. Lindwall, not out	2		
Extras (b. 10, l.b. 1)	11		
Total	221	Total (6 wkts.)	118

FALL OF WICKETS. *First innings:* 1—52, 2—53, 3—85, 4—129, 5—138, 6—147, 7—157, 8—202, 9—217. *Second innings:* 1—14, 2—27, 3—29, 4—67, 5—87, 6—118. Did not bat: I. Johnson, A. Davidson, R. Lindwall, L. Maddocks.

Bowling Analysis
AUSTRALIA

	O.	M.	R.	W.
Lindwall	19.6	5	77	3
Miller	15	1	71	0
Davidson	19	3	72	0
Johnson	20	5	68	3
Benaud	20	4	79	1

ENGLAND

First Innings

	O.	M.	R.	W.
Tyson	11	1	46	2
Statham	9	1	31	0
Appleyard	16	2	54	1
Wardle	24.4	6	79	5

Second Innings

	O.	M.	R.	W.
Tyson	5	1	20	0
Statham	5	0	11	1
Wardle	12	1	51	3
Graveney	6	0	34	1
Hutton	0.6	0	2	1

MATCH DRAWN

* * *

First, Second and Third Days

NO PLAY

Fourth Day: England, sent in to bat by Ian Johnson when play began here at two o'clock, disported themselves in the manner of conquerors. Since this match appears now to have only statistical interest, it is agreeable to record that it was played in the nicest way. Hutton was out for six to Lindwall off the fourth ball of the game, but from then on Graveney, who had replaced Edrich, and May drove the bowlers of both speed and spin with that freedom of follow-through which is particular to themselves. They have two of the highest back-lifts in cricket, and they showed today that even when the ball is kept well up at a good pace this need not be the disadvantage that is commonly supposed. Their partnership of 182 runs made at over a run a minute contained the finest driving of the tour. The nerveless context of their innings' must, however, be remembered: their value was not commensurate with their pleasure.

Graveney made up for many disappointments this afternoon: the sadness of it is that this beautiful first hundred against Australia, over which he took only two and a half hours, should not convince one any the more of his ability to make runs when they are of true importance. It emphasized merely that a gifted batsman has too often either through defect of temperament or some looseness of technique frittered away his chances. Seven thousand five hundred people turned up in steamy, sunless weather to watch the play, and they could be pardoned if they left the ground thinking Graveney one of the most considerable players in the world. But they would be mistaking the potential for the achievement.

May, after a quieter start than usual, batted no less strikingly than Graveney. May had hitherto not reached double figures in the first innings of any of the previous four tests: each second innings he has hammered the bowling without trace of apprehension and today, perhaps because the match was so long getting under way, he batted as if it was the second innings.

The pitch, when play began, was a pale, grassless grey in the centre of a dark, mud-brown area. Lindwall and Miller were once again united in bowling partnership, Australia strangely leaving out Archer and including Watson and Burge, each for the first time. England omitted Edrich, and once more Bedser, from the chosen thirteen. Cowdrey and Bailey proclaimed themselves fit.

Burge was not long in getting the feel of things, for Hutton, after playing Lindwall's in-swinger twice rather casually off his legs for four and two, sent the next ball knee-high, a few feet finer, for Burge to catch. Lindwall bowled for three-quarters of an hour in his opening spell, Miller for an hour. At the end of that time, Graveney, batting as if at Bristol, and May, had taken England to 51 for 1. Davidson and Johnson took over the attack, and Graveney, who had driven Miller straight for fours in his first two overs, jumped out to pull Johnson for four to mid-wicket. This stroke gave him 50 in 75 minutes; and, for good measure, he hit Johnson's next ball for four more.

At 80 Benaud bowled for Davidson, and immediately got some quickish spin from the anæmic wicket. May twice hit Johnson as high as the clock-tower over mid-on's head, and prettily late cut Benaud, who once might easily have had Graveney's wicket, his turn from leg beating the forward stroke.

The hundred went up in 96 minutes and May drove Davidson, who shared the bowling after tea with Benaud, for successive fours straight and past extra cover. The batsmen took turns in dominating the strike, each one scoring in spurts while the other rested. Nearly every hit of any consequence was a drive, between mid-wicket and extra cover: the Australian bowlers kept the ball fully up, and all of them, Miller especially, were generous in acknowledging the excellence of the batting. Graveney when 80 might have been caught and bowled by Benaud, but he hit the ball so hard back that by the time the bowler had seen it the ball was half-way to the fence.

Graveney went to his hundred with four boundaries in an over off Miller. Two were firm drives past the bowler, one was an off drive that Harvey could not reach at extra cover, and the fourth, a full pitch on the leg, Miller gave him without trouble.

At five o'clock, Graveney's gorgeous innings ended, Johnson clutching a juicy drive off his own bowling to his stomach. In the last 25 minutes two more wickets were lost, only 8 runs scored. Cowdrey, looking pale after his few days in bed, was out to Johnson first ball, playing as if he had lost sight of it. In Benaud's last over May was snapped up at slip, a wicket Benaud thoroughly deserved. Altogether England batted three hours for 196 runs, a scoring rate pleasing in any circumstances, and one which provides its own comment. The bowling was made to look not quite at full stretch: but when the sniff of wickets is not in the air, bowlers, like tortoises, do not overreach themselves gratuitously. They keep their reserves protectively encased.

* * *

Fifth Day: The weather, though humid as well as sunny, was an improvement on yesterday: the cricket was not. England, batting on till tea-time, carried their overnight score of 196 for 4 to 371 for 6 declared. For all but twenty minutes of this time Compton and Bailey were together: both are players who have little to lose even when the exercise of imagination entails some small element of risk. In the hundred minutes before lunch 51 runs were scored, Bailey contributing 29, Compton 22. For half an hour after lunch there was no improvement. Finally, after even Hutton had been stirred to signal from the dressing-room his wish for greater activity, Compton began to give some inkling that England were not in grave danger. Bailey proceeded stoically to his fifty, which monumental achievement took him three hours, all but five minutes. However, when one is most irritated by Bailey, one does well to remember those many times when his forward defensive stroke and unwavering concentration have saved England from ignominy. Having satisfied himself, if few others, with the numerals five nought against his name, Bailey then played a stream of lofted drives off all the bowlers, Lindwall especially. It was as though the bat had been suddenly fitted with a hydraulic lift. Lindwall, in what might just be his last over against England, required one wicket only to become the first fast bowler to achieve 100 wickets in Anglo-Australian Tests. Bailey, in the nicest way possible, surrendered his wicket to him when it seemed unlikely to come by direct methods. Lindwall, with Bedser, has dominated the bowling of these contests since the war, and, since weather has robbed him of greater scope these last days, it was not really too indulgent. The crowd was very reasonable considering the circumstances. The public stands were almost full, the Hill liberally sprinkled. Although no result could ordinarily be expected from this match, and bearing in mind also that

England have suffered much at Australian hands during Hutton's career, it still seems a pity more effort was not made to entertain, let alone show a readiness to contemplate victory. Intention, morally speaking, is everything. The general dreariness of the morning's play was broken only by an astonishing over from Davidson, in which five times the ball swung in like a boomerang from outside the off stump and came near to completing the circle back to the bowler. Compton, legs spreadeagled, made nothing of it at all. Lindwall, Miller and Johnson, the other bowlers, showed no such capacities to intrigue.

In the first over after lunch Johnson dropped Compton at mid-on off Lindwall, a comfortable chance which Johnson, rather avuncular in the field, seemed scarcely to see.

Benaud beat Compton twice in successive balls and was snicked by both batsmen fine of slip. He has bowled well this last month. Compton in desperation threw his cap to the square leg umpire, but not his caution to the winds. He passed fifty after two hours. Some time later, as if remembering that this would be his last innings in Australia, he made some agreeable strokes to the off, and one or two distinguishing sweeps to leg. Generally, he has seldom timed the ball worse. However, he was moment by moment growing more recognizable when he hit Johnson hard back and was caught. Evans batted busily. Bailey finally swung his bat, and on the stroke of the declaration Lindwall claimed his desirable century of English wickets. Australia, left with 100 minutes to bat in an evening of spilling gold light, made an honourable start. McDonald and Watson played Tyson with fine assurance, scoring readily in many directions. Statham once nearly bowled the small, eager and lobster-pink Watson, and he several times brought the ball back sharply. Appleyard and Wardle were soon in action, but 52 were up in an hour before Wardle bowled Watson with his off-break. Watson, who has a severe late cut, looked impressively equable. Favell, flimsy as a puppet these days, took a single off Wardle, and then was too far across to Tyson's first ball to him from the other end. It hustled back from the off

SYDNEY

*Through the trees, a
new city*

*Sydney Bridge
Arrival and
Departure*

Woolloomooloo
*Old Colonial, and the
New Look*

SYDNEY

Macquarie Street
*Doctors to starboard,
lawyers to port*

Double Bay
Residential area

King's Cross
Rooms to let

BONDI BEACH

Life-savers

On Parade

At Ease

Rushcutters Bay
On Sunday, boat races and bookmakers

SYDNEY

St. James's Church
Architect: Francis Greenw
Status: Convict

SYDNEY

Boathouse

Bathing-pool
(*sharkproof*)

Central Quay
Pierstakes like bunches of asparagus

TASMANIA

Hobart
In the distance, Mount Wellington

Sheep-station, Ross

Landscape, Launceston

top left: Colonel Light's Statue
To posterity, a legacy
top right: The Torrens River
Trial eights at tea-time

ADELAIDE

From the Press Box
Cricket, to the music of typewriters

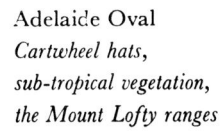

Adelaide Oval
Cartwheel hats, sub-tropical vegetation, the Mount Lofty ranges

Queensland-New South Wales Border
Dead eucalypts, hard light, colourless sky

VIEWS FROM THE TRAIN

The town of Casino
Level-crossing, corrugated iron, Jacaranda, sheep

and bowled him. Wardle beat Harvey well and truly with his chinaman, and bowled several excellent overs. McDonald showed once more how real has been his improvement since his melancholy trip to England. He should come again with happier results.

* * *

Sixth Day: England, on this last day of their tour, bowled Australia out on a pitch of easy pace for 221 runs, a total exactly low enough to oblige Australia to follow-on. Batting a second time with two hours left for play, Australia were again made to look a shabby side. With 75 minutes still to go, Watson, Favell and Harvey were out, the last two to Wardle, who, spinning the ball constantly out of the back of his hand, looked a better bowler than at any other time in these Tests. In fact, Australia, batting all told for only one and one-third days, came uncomfortably close to being beaten. Ian Johnson, who sent England in on Tuesday afternoon, came nearer than he can have enjoyed to the unenviable achievement of his side being defeated by an innings after he had won the toss. England, therefore, despite their drab performance yesterday morning, leave for New Zealand tonight in the highest spirits. A record that is morally four Tests to one should please the most exacting conscience: at the same time, nobody should know better than Hutton how slight a push of fortune the other way would have been needed to produce a reverse result.

This morning, with another generous crowd sweating under a straining, metallic sky, Australia quickly lost wickets. Harvey, a cardboard replica of himself two months ago, hit Tyson's first ball to him fiercely back and was caught and bowled at digestive level. Miller played pleasantly for some while until McDonald impolitely called him for an unlikely run to Cowdrey. McDonald, stolidly inelegant but purposefully acquisitive, then used even more right hand than usual in sweeping across the line of Appleyard and was safely held by May at mid-wicket. Benaud faced Wardle as one uncertain of whether a rabbit or clock was coming out of the conjuror's hat. The former it was, and Benaud departed, chewing ruminatively. Burge, in his first innings for Australia, was beefily to the point, but his experience of long hops seemed limited for, offered one by Wardle, he hit it straight to Appleyard at mid-wicket. Davidson and Maddocks appeared to be taking Australia gently out of the regions of humiliation when Wardle spun one from leg to get Davidson caught at the wicket. Wardle was doing a lot at this period, but Maddocks, though frequently stabbing like a bamboozled marionette, survived to reveal a pretty off-drive. He went the way of Burge, however, this time reaching Appleyard at mid-wicket off a half-volley. When Lindwall—surely the only man who has scored a century in a Test to bat at number eleven—joined Johnson, five runs were needed to avoid the follow-on. Four were made; then Lindwall, striking Wardle to Compton at cover, started to run, changed his mind, and Johnson, well-lost, found his batting average, over a hundred a minute earlier, abruptly lowered.

The Australian second innings should have been quiet formality; in fact it was enjoyable calamity. Watson was beautifully taken off Statham by Graveney at slip, Favell limply steered Wardle's natural spinner from leg to Graveney, and Harvey, for the second time in the day, was caught by the bowler, 'driving without due care,' as the police like to term it. McDonald was thorough till Graveney, rewarded with a bowl, had him caught at the wicket cutting at a leg-break. Miller batted long enough to satisfy honour. Finally Hutton, bowling the last over, trimmed Benaud's bails with one that swung from leg, corkscrewed, and blandly straightened out. England's captain, stoically denying himself the luxury of a smile, took his cap, and walked from the field with the air of one who could have taken wickets as easily as that at any time he chose. An inquisitive jostle of people swarmed over the pickets on to the pitch and the England team strolled deprecatingly into the pavilion. The tour was over.

* * *

THE FIFTH TEST MATCH

Strictly speaking, this last Test had at no time the tension of one likely to produce a definite result. That Australia were not far off losing it was in a sense accidental: their failures were inscribed mostly in the margin, that area in which Graveney, for one, made such enjoyable decorations. But Test cricket is not generally played in the margins, and the scores of this match can be taken with a pinch of salt.

Two days later, I sent my final cable from Australia to the *Observer:*

'In the early hours of yesterday morning M.C.C. flew from Mascot Airport to New Zealand for a brief epilogue to their Australian tour. It is almost exactly five months since *Orsova* docked alongside the corrugated-iron shanties of Fremantle, and during that period of heat, rain and travel, 17 first-class matches have been played, 8 won, 7 drawn, 2 lost. That is a better record than any English side has had in Australia since Jardine's body-line tour of 1932–33. Yet the statistics of Hutton's team, impressive as they are, convey little of the dramatic revolution that has taken place within the English party, as well as in cricketing relations with Australia. The October revolution of 1917 was no less final in its implications than the overthrow of maturity by youth in this Australian summer of 1954–55.

When, in the crude, steamy surroundings of Brisbane, the First Test match was begun, England relied, as they had done for nearly ten years, on Hutton, Compton and Bedser. In the Australian side were Miller, Lindwall, Harvey, Morris and Ian Johnson, all of whom had been members of Bradman's touring side of 1948. At Brisbane, England, whose attack was founded on pace, allowed, through a series of appalling fielding errors, the sharpness of their main weapon to be blunted beyond apparent recovery. Morris, Harvey and Miller took runs at their ease, as did Hole, Lindwall and Benaud. Lindwall and Miller once again made deep inroads into the England batting, which was as evidently insecure as we have long known it to be. The vastness of Australia's victory and the manner of it offered little prospect of remedy. In the Victoria match immediately before the Second Test at Sydney, Tyson quite suddenly showed new control over length and direction. His form in that game was responsible for the subsequent omission of Bedser, a policy that puzzled, and was strenuously opposed by, nearly every correspondent of both countries, and which ultimately proved justified. Tyson was initially a selectors' gamble: they owe it to Hutton's dogged faith that it succeeded beyond anybody's dreams. In Sydney, in dull heavy weather, England's batting was quite inadequate on the first day. Australia were galloping away with the match when some superbly concentrated bowling of late swing and perfect length by Bailey halted them. After he had taken the first 3 wickets, Tyson achieved his first breakthrough of the series. His left foot was still well wider from the stumps than his right at the moment of delivery, but it was much less so than previously: his run, almost halved, seemed to increase the abruptness of his break-back, he discovered the whereabouts of the wicket, and at great speed he made the ball lift sharply from a good length.

Only once after this, in the first innings at Melbourne, did he revert to his old habits of bowling short and wide in an effort to achieve speed. Otherwise speed came to him of its own accord. His endurance became phenomenal. He put on weight, got the sun into his back, and even if his action still achieved beauty and rhythm from sideways on only, he brought his arm from well back and caught an unprepared generation of Australian batsmen with their bats horizontal. The Australian habit is to crouch and to face the bat at the left instep. By the time they had straightened both themselves and their bats, Tyson was past them.

In the English second innings at Sydney, May and Cowdrey set the pattern for the next two Tests. It was not till the Fifth Test that May managed double figures in the first innings, but his second innings at Sydney, Melbourne and Adelaide won England the match. For May at Sydney and Melbourne destroyed the legend of Lindwall. Lindwall may yet come to England in 1956 as a medium pace bowler of formidable arts, but May dominated him to such an extent that he no longer dared to bowl his most deadly ball—the fast swinging half-volley. Where English batsmen from Hutton downwards had pushed infirmly and fatally out at these balls of a full curving length, May put his left leg down the wicket and thrashed them to the sight-screen. Under this treatment, Lindwall aged noticeably.

Cowdrey, not so destructive as May, did no less than take over Hutton's role in the English batting. Except for this Fifth Test, for which he was not fit and in which he ought not to have been asked to play, he came in each time with England well on the way to collapse. With the first ball he played, the moral recovery began. His defensive technique was of unassailable soundness, he got firmly behind the pace bowlers, and he placed and drove the ball to the on with a distribution of balance that would have delighted Michelangelo. It was Cowdrey who rendered the Australian bowling human: May domesticated it and taught it tricks. The relative value of their performances can be assessed in those simple terms.

On the fifth day of the Second Test the English team went to the ground resigned to the fact that they would leave it two matches down. Tyson and Statham that day bowled as few pairs of English fast bowlers can have done in this century. At Perth, amongst the soaring gulls of the Swan River, Statham seemed to have established himself as the spearhead of the English bowling. He never again got such fast wickets nor looked so physically intimidating, but, unexpectedly finding himself the second string, he bowled with unflagging life and accuracy in support of Tyson, very often necessarily into the wind. He was the unluckier bowler of the two, and without his sustained pace and onslaught on the stumps, which allowed the batsmen no rest, Tyson's success would have been greatly reduced. Tyson was the first to recognize this, and the friendship and collaboration of the two was as charming as it was efficient.

Bailey, whose all-round tenacity throughout the series, was little less invaluable than in 1953, as a bowler largely ignored the stumps, but he moved the ball in the air more than any bowler on either side and his skill in floating his slower ball across the wicket in both directions got him important wickets, particularly Harvey's. Appleyard, once Hutton used him with any frequency, and he had himself adjusted his pace and direction, fitted perfectly into the general pattern. His ability to make the ball hang and then quickly dip, found the Australians consistently pushing out too soon, and the shade he was able to move the ball off the seam from the left-hander's leg to off twice accounted for Harvey at vital stages. Only in the Fifth Test, when he consented to spin the ball out of the back of his hand, was Wardle effective as a bowler. On Thursday he spun both ways and the Australians were as perplexed as if he were Cinquevalli. Fortunately, he was not much required as a bowler in the other Tests, and as a batsman he came off when most necessary. His rural comedy was a simple, effective job of public relations.

The problem of a partner for Hutton was never satisfactorily solved. That will be the first need this coming season. Graveney's wonderful innings on Tuesday convinced one only that he is a rare player when it doesn't truly matter. His values are calculable æsthetically: he failed crucially when character was tested before technique. Going in first, when concentration is forced on him from the start, with no easy way out, might be the making of him.

Hutton, apart from a few early innings of fantasy and fortune, was mostly a struggling batsman. The disasters of Brisbane increased his inhibitions, and the solid concentration of captaining the side in the field drained his imaginative resources to the degree that he had few reserves for batting. As a captain he did much to create Tyson and Statham as dominating fast bowlers and as the general accuracy of the bowlers improved, so did Hutton's placing of the field, and the fielding itself. Twice Hutton won Tests by using his fast attack against reasonable supposition on spinners' wickets. He was exceptionally popular with Australians until the Tests, but he made one or two needless errors of taste right at the very end, and amongst his own team his tact over major issues of selection was not marked. However, he had a long complex task, and in essentials he proved a master of strategy. He is a strange compound of personal charm and great diffidence.

There are, of course, failures on any Tour: none, fortunately, this time upset the balance of the party. Bedser alone seemed to get less than his due, a shrinking shadow of a great bowler whose greatness evaporated, or was robbed from him, in a single night—the night it was first decided to drop him.

Five months is a long tour, and few were not mentally as well as physically tired at the end. It was certainly a greatly exciting series, one filled quite unexpectedly with promise for English cricket. For Australia, beset with inter-state jealousies, the problems of ageing genius, and newly-discovered defects of technique, it looked like the end of an era.'

Further to this a few random comments.

I made no mention of Compton, whose luck was truly abominable, but who showed at Adelaide in the Fourth Test that his experience, if not exuberance, remained of great value. Many other times he batted charmingly, though more soberly than once he used. He daydreamed often when fielding, which if not excusable is understandable. It is hard for the particular brand of enchantingness with which Compton grew up to survive maturity. He has managed very creditably to persuade the innocence of his character to accept the experience of the flesh.

Edrich, whose inclusion in the side I had long championed, despite the professed amazement of many friends, just about broke even. He concentrated with visible determination on the field, but too often seemed to have to shake himself into focus. He batted magnificently at Brisbane, disappointingly everywhere else. After an appalling start, when his bat seemed to have not only edges but holes, he began to show an off-drive, in addition to his usual hook and cut, that from him was as surprisingly exotic as a newly-invented rose. He did not quite fail in any Test: Hutton played him presumably because he felt he could depend on him, and to a degree he could. He was worth his place, I still think, because there was no genuine alternative. Had Graveney recovered his pose and technique earlier, it would have been another matter. Simpson played one lovely innings, against Queensland, was unfortunate in the First Test, and never got going again.

Evans started the tour indifferently, and it was not till the Third Test that he looked as if he had ever been instructed in the use of a bat. 'There is no secret so close as that between a rider and his horse,' Robert Surtees wrote in *Mr Sponge's Sporting Tour*. Evans' bat had many secrets from him. At Melbourne, however, in the Third Test, he twice batted with a jauntiness altogether more effective, and thereafter appeared to remember that he had, after all, made Test centuries and that the pleasures of batting amply repaid any additional trouble. As a wicket-keeper Evans was as great as he has ever been. He must rank with the first three or four wicket-keepers of all time, and he gave a series of brilliant displays. Throughout the tour he was as fizzy as a bottle of soda.

Andrew, Evans' understudy, was quietly efficient, his manner striking many people as resembling Oldfield's. It took him some while to get the pace of the wickets and gather the ball cleanly, but all the same he missed few chances. He moves his hands very little, getting his feet quickly into position, but he has not the inspiring qualities of Evans, and is not probably above county class. His batting was as unassuming as his character. It is likely, though, that a different successor to Evans will eventually have to be developed.

Loader bowled fairly well in the unimportant matches. Again, this tour showed him to be rather below Test class and his temperament not really ideal. He is a hostile bowler, of a type always uncomfortable to bat against, for he gets a nasty lift from an awkward length. His slower ball often took wickets, but Test batsmen seemed to dispose of him with no great difficulty, and on any wicket not of exceptional pace he just did not do enough.

Wilson, a splendidly comforting sight in the field—great in stature, red-faced, huge-handed, equable—early on looked as if he might make the Test side. But, once away from Perth, he moved his feet less and less, failed to drive the fast bowlers as he can do in England, and was hopelessly at sea to the most domestically-inclined spinners.

Throughout the tour, the fielding steadily improved. It could hardly have done otherwise, for it began at rock bottom. Hutton himself was not basically responsible for this improvement; generally, he was as unexacting in his requirements of his players as he was spare in his comments on them. His attitude was that any player good enough to be a member of the party should need little advice from him. That may be partly true; but more purposive practices, greater attention to fitness, and private discussions on individual problems of technique would have insured against the bad periods of the tour, and created a greater urgency. Hutton is not by nature explicit: he inhabits a world of hints, allusions, smiles and obscure ironies. He is perfectly able to time his own fitness and to judge what amount of practice he needs. But in expecting others considerably less mature in character to be able to do the same he expected too much. In this respect, he was a civilized, adult and uninterfering captain. But once the Second Test had been unexpectedly won, the separate needs of the various members of the side seemed to coalesce. Those previously weak in the field, like Appleyard, improved out of recognition. Cowdrey proved himself a safe and agile catcher. The throwing-in, a safe matter for jest at one time, tightened up visibly under the shrewd, appreciative scrutiny of Australian crowds. On Australian grounds a good throw earns as much applause as a good stroke: the music of it eventually became pleasant to the ears of English fieldsmen.

Hutton had greater difficulty in fitting his players to suitable positions in the field than he ever had over problems of field setting. There were, first of all, no natural slip-fielders. Edrich made of first slip a position akin to that of short third-man, though Evans' mobility compensated for much of the difference. Graveney later took some lovely slip catches, but, at Sydney in the Second Test, dropped alternate chances. May, like Graveney, was a converted slip-fielder and was really needed to do the running about. Hutton, of late so unreliable close to the wicket in England, in fact proved the most assured catcher at slip or short leg of them all. The outfielders were no more happily disposed: there was no cover point at all, the fast bowlers were obliged to make long walks to the boundary, patrolling large areas, and there was an embarrassing cluster of those more properly suited to mid-on.

By taking his time about it, however, Hutton eventually worked out successful compromises. England never caught the eye as a fielding side; but they increasingly caught their catches, and the bowlers inspired them into unusual efforts.

Tactically, Hutton seemed occasionally cautious, sometimes surprised one, but was thoroughly effective. He appeared reluctant to give his own batsmen any instructions, which more than once proved to be outstandingly necessary. Yet, when all is said and done, he handled his bowlers with a conviction and understanding of their powers that made victory possible. He calculated exactly when to attack and when to slow down the Australian rate of scoring. Having made his decisions, he used bowlers and fields accordingly. Nothing was given away. If the genius of captaincy lies in the precise husbanding of resources, then Hutton on this tour frequently demonstrated it. He deserved all the praise in the world for England's success: that one criticizes him at all is because it would be insulting to judge such a great player by any but the highest standards. Over a long period—a decade almost—he has been technically the most perfect model of contemporary batsmanship. He seems no longer that, for he has contracted, rather than grown expansive, in his last period. There may, of course, be an Indian (preferably an Australian) summer to come. But whether it does or not, Hutton's place in history is secure. He proved that the important thing about a captain is not whether he is amateur or professional, but what kind of man he is. I have mentioned what seem to me Hutton's inherent defects. If he lacked an imposing presence, an encouraging manner, he possessed a curious magnetism of his own. His smile, emerging from lips and eyes with the freshness of sun suddenly dispelling clouds, is worth a fortune. Because of what he is, he will always be entitled to, and get, respect. He is, in some ways, a typical Yorkshireman. In other ways, he is the very antithesis. But, whatever one's views about the Yorkshire character, it is impossible to be in Hutton's company without liking him immensely.

I thought the side very well, and unobtrusively, managed by Geoffrey Howard. There were varying views about his appointment: that an experienced Test cricketer would have been more appropriate, or else someone whose nature approximated more nearly to an old-fashioned company commander's. As it happened, tact and willingness were Geoffrey Howard's main assets: and his willingness extended not only to interesting himself in the minor problems of his charges, but to doing all he could to ensure that the side's relationship with the Press was a happy one. He succeeded admirably. He and Hutton took an evident liking to each other; there was a complete absence of managerial formality, at the same time a tacit insistence on the proper deference being paid by the players to the manager. Few managers can have made a point of being so readily available at all times as did Geoffrey Howard.

George Duckworth, scorer and baggage man, could not help being a great deal more than either of those capacities might suggest. His experience, robust common sense and native wit, combined to make of him a solid bulwark against pettiness and folly.

In the matter of injuries, the players were fairly fortunate. Bedser's early attack of shingles may have affected him more than was estimated: he never quite reached his peak afterwards, bowling steadily without the final nip from the pitch which used to bring him wickets. But he is as greatly honest a character as he ever was a bowler, and his sturdy, homely philosophy, his amused fatalism, was an enviable defence against evident disappointments.

Compton's injury at Brisbane against the pickets was wretchedly disappointing, and it was only in the last two Tests that he went to the wicket completely fit. Of the others, Evans and Graveney missed the first Test through a brand of influenza. But, once out of Queensland, the luck seemed to change, and thereafter it was really only McConnon who suffered. Shortly before the Fourth Test, McConnon, for the second successive winter, was obliged to return home. He was hurt first in the Queensland match at Brisbane, taking a hard hit at short leg in the groin, and then in Hobart he broke a finger. Altogether he travelled some 25,000 miles to bowl 83 first-class overs and take 8 wickets. Patently, the gods were not on his side.

Responsible for massage, and for the treatment of minor injuries was Harold Dalton, who, his victims alleged, 'blinded them with science.' His worried, greatly-bespectacled countenance suggested a mind at perpetual grips with problems of alarming abstruseness.

About its own team, the Australian press was persistently critical. Few writers cared for Ian Johnson as captain: at one stage a campaign for Keith Miller as captain was conducted as fervently as if it had been for Premier. Possibly Miller, judging by the results of the two New South Wales games, would have been the more inspiring choice. Johnson, nevertheless, was perfectly competent. He is not a naturally gifted batsman, but on several occasions he batted with a determination that should have been an example to his team. His Test average was 58, the highest on either side: moreover, he earned his runs. As a bowler, his action is altogether too doubtful for my taste, but he flicked in his off-spinners with an accuracy and control over flight that frequently brought the rate of scoring to a halt. He is, unfortunately, a poor fielder. By and large, there seemed no genuine reason for the outcry against him. He handled his bowling intelligently, and, despite an excessive fussiness in offering advice to his bowlers each time a run was scored off them, he seemed a capable, agreeable captain.

Various reasons were responsible for Australia's defeat. Johnson's captaincy was not among them. Individual preference must determine which causes can be accounted most important. The fielding, it must be said at the outset, was superb. Thrilling catches were taken close to the wicket, by Davidson especially, also by Hole and Archer; the throwing-in, with Harvey at cover and Favell in the deep outstanding, was of a uniform excellence. Both these two are baseball stars, and there is no doubt that their fast, flicked throws, without the laborious wind-up usual to English fielders, owes much to baseball training.

The Australian bowling, as far as figures are concerned, compares favourably with England's. No Australian bowler produced any sustained devastating spells like Tyson's at Sydney and Melbourne, but otherwise the speed attack of Lindwall, Miller and Archer was little inferior to Tyson, Statham and Bailey. Lindwall demonstrated the beautiful art of fast bowling no less variously than in previous series: he was generally a shade slower, though on occasions bowled very fast indeed. That he was less effective was due largely to the fact that he was more familiar. May, Cowdrey, and finally Graveney, treated him with the respect one shows to a thoroughbred Alsatian rather than to a jungle tiger. Miller at Brisbane, Melbourne and Adelaide bowled as well as he has ever done. Hutton expressed the opinion that he was still the greatest new-ball bowler in the world, and he should know. Archer, who headed the averages, was extremely accurate, difficult to get away always, and, at similar pace to Loader, lively off a length six inches or so shorter than one would like to see.

With Johnston left-arm at varying paces, Johnson off-spin, and Benaud leg-break, it is obvious that Australia possessed an exceptionally well-balanced attack. Johnston, who took more wickets in the series than Statham, did not happen on his customary nagging, spinning length so reliably as once, but when it was found he kept it. Benaud improved steadily: he often spun the ball when no one else could, and he was admirably persistent with little luck. Now and again he seemed to be using too monotonously low a trajectory, and, like most of his kind, at moments he was buffeted about.

There remains the Australian batting, and it was, of course, here that the weakness lay. It was a weakness, moreover, in performance rather than potential. Morris and Favell are batsmen with a hunger for runs quite indecent among openers. Morris, after his uneven hundred and a half at Brisbane, got completely out of control. He batted subsequently with the frenzied impatience of a man who hears the telephone ringing for him in the dressing-room, a call long-awaited, and wonders whether he can get there in time. Perhaps it was. Favell, too, a brisk, squat player, seemed infected by Morris' anxiety. His history has always been that of a brilliant player who habitually ruined his innings with off-side slashes. But at Adelaide in November, when he made a hundred against M.C.C., he was alleged to be a reformed character. For some while, indeed, he kept his eyes averted from anything pitched outside the off stump with the modest concentration of a cleric about to encounter a street-walker. But, like Oscar Wilde's famous character, he found the only thing he could not resist was temptation. He gave in to it more and more as the tour progressed, and by the Fifth Test his batting was a pitiable sight. McDonald, a pedestrian player in comparison, provided in the last two Tests the kind of solidity that could have won Australia the Ashes. Not only was there no dependable opening pair, but No. 3 altered from Test to Test. Miller was succeeded by

Burke, who gave way to Miller, who was replaced by Burke, who was dropped for Favell. In the circumstances it was not surprising that all of them failed. Miller, for two matches in November, was as Cæsar before Cassius made the rounds. He missed the Sydney Test, and at Melbourne was faced by Statham and Tyson on a flying pitch. He made 6 and 7, and thereafter was not a recognizable improvement on the lunging, strained Miller whom we saw in 1953 in England. Majestic batsman that he is, he can disconcertingly easily be put out of good humour.

Harvey, in the second innings of the Sydney Test, played one of the memorable innings of a lifetime. That apart, he looked more fallible against speed than ever before. Against Tyson and Statham he played and missed by a hair's-breadth with unswerving regularity. Made fretful by this, he then found Appleyard's changes of pace and cut from leg more than he could manage for long stretches at a time. It was this persistent tightness of the English attack, reinforced by Hutton's placing of the field, that did most to induce the Australians to folly. They are not, like the generation of Woodfull, Ponsford, and Fingleton, used to wearing an attack down: they grew up accustomed to the unnatural ease of Bradman's stroke-play and, following in the wake of Lindwall's and Miller's bowling, could bat with detachment. Though the English bowling might be said to lack variety, it was probably harder to score off than any English Test attack since Larwood, Voce and Allen.

The middle Australian batsmen failed, the First Test excepted, repeatedly and completely. Hole once or twice flashed out a late cut of exquisite sharpness, but his bent stance, his facing of the left shoulder to wide mid-on and slow back-lift, made him quite unequal to playing bowling at Tyson's pace. He was dropped for the Fourth and Fifth Tests, was not chosen for the Australian tour of the West Indies, and, after being the most promising young Australian batsman in 1953, must now be regarded as extremely doubtful for further Tests.

The trouble with the Australian batting order, though this

had hitherto been regarded as an advantage, was that from Numbers 6 to 10 it was interchangeable, and that, of these, only the wicket-keeper was not a regular bowler. Archer, Benaud, Davidson, Lindwall and Johnson are bowlers primarily, all-rounders second, batsmen third. They were called upon in four successive Tests to do the job of batsmen, each in turn following on the defection of his predecessor. For half an hour or so all were capable of looking the part. At Sydney, however, in the Second Test, Lindwall's distaste for fast bowling was properly laid bare, for the first time, and he was no trouble subsequently. Archer was no player at all when not hitting, and hitting carries the seeds of its own destruction. Benaud, such a magnificent driver on lesser occasions, fought against temptation in the Tests, but his powers of concentration were not adequate against the testing length of Appleyard or the speed of Tyson. Both took his wicket three times.

Davidson was in and out of the side, and looked a poor relation to the batsman who played so beautifully at Lords in 1953. One came to realize how essential a solid start to the innings was to players of these types. Without it, it became evident that all-rounders were a liability, their energies dissipated too variously and the responsibility for making runs spread too shallow.

Whatever else one might feel about this series, there can be no doubt that it was amongst the most exciting, and level, of the century. Moderate scoring always provides a more enjoyable spectacle than the mammoth totals of one's youth. Neither of these two sides were reliable in batting, and the extra grass on the wickets, with the consequent variation in the height at which the ball came through, also contributed to the low scoring.

But with the view that the less bad of two bad sides won, I cannot agree. Top-class fast bowling, systematically applied, can upset all batting sides, even of exceptional strength. It would not be surprising if this same Australian side were to make huge scores in the West Indies, or England do so this summer against South Africa. That they did not do so in

Australia was because neither side was allowed to settle down: the fast bowlers carried out their duties precisely. You cannot have it both ways; and if one must choose between complacent batsmen and a successful fast attack, then surely the latter is the rarer, and lovelier, sight.

It ought not to be necessary to praise umpires, yet it is. The Australians who stood in this series were most excellent, their errors hardly accountable. They had much to contend with, particularly from their own younger players whose accusatory optimism in appealing, regardless of probability, was not endearing. Arthur Gilligan, I believe, has suggested that the whole procedure of appealing could be abolished. I'm not sure he isn't right. After all, the umpire must judge for himself whether a man is out or not, and he ought not to require interested advocacy.

17 At Sea

Probably, this last chapter should attempt some general conclusions about my stay in Australia. I had intended that it should. Now I know that it will not; for we are once more at sea, the dolphins flinging themselves happily from one medium of blue into another, and, with the sun flooding the calm water each evening, demoralization has again set in.

In fact, it has taken me over a fortnight to get as far as writing the paragraph above. Cape Guardafui, the eastern tip of Africa, is off the port bow, beyond it Ras al Fil, that grey lonely hump of rock known as the Elephant. We have left behind us the tropic seas, Ceylon, Java, the islands of the Sunda Strait. A swallow joined us unexpectedly this morning, taking passage on a masthead to the spring, which it seemed to have wind of ahead of us. I hope it is a bird with a good sense of timing. We crossed the Equator seven months ago into one spring and now have recrossed it into another. There is, in that alone, something of goodness and promise.

From Sydney to Fremantle, it took us nine days. The swell in the Bight was long and uncomfortable, accompanied, as it was, by cold, flicking winds. Huge albatrosses swooped and glided magnanimously over us. We turned northwards to Perth, and a temperature of 110°, a rowdy wind loading the desert heats of Central Australia on to the sinuous curves of the Swan River. We were back in the regions of bush fires and burning corrugated-iron. Australia is not a country easily disposed of.

But now we have trailed steadily through several thousand miles of simmering, scarcely interrupted, blue seas, the nights full of close, choking stars, shooting fancifully for the gratification of wishes, and the days lazy, sleep-ridden, salt-swept. The

Southern Cross, most unobtrusive of constellations, has long since dropped anchor.

We have no news, only memories and hopes. This being an Italian ship, cricket scores are not scooped out of the air by the radio. I fancy none the less that New Zealand have been by now given a trouncing. A fleeting image comes to me of how Hutton, at moments of crisis, would raise and resettle his cap with affirmatory tugs. I smile with affection.

The ice clinks in cocktail-shakers; shapely, and some less shapely, bodies splash in and out of the swimming pool. Officers emerge from the engine-room to take the scarcely less humid airs of the upper deck. There is a smell of sun-tan oil, of distant cooking. It is also time for Raffaele to concoct that delicious and decorative Singapore cocktail, of which I have, for some minutes now, been dreaming.

Scorebook

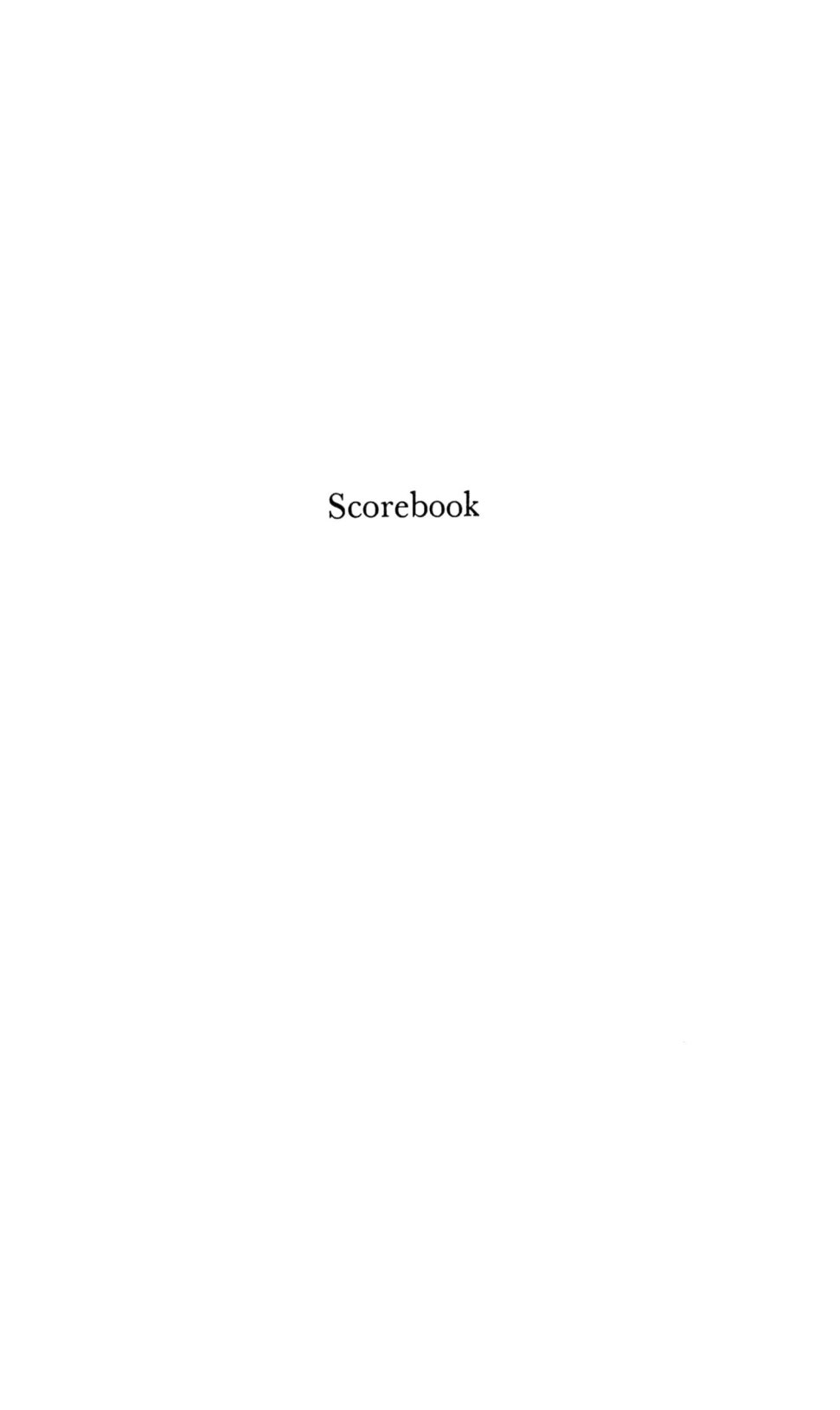

TEST MATCH AVERAGES

ENGLAND—BATTING

	Innings	Times not out	Runs	Highest score	Average
T. W. Graveney	3	0	132	111	44.00
P. B. H. May	9	0	351	104	39.00
D. C. S. Compton	7	2	191	84	38.20
T. E. Bailey	9	1	296	88	37.00
M. C. Cowdrey	9	0	319	102	35.44
L. Hutton	9	0	220	80	24.44
W. J. Edrich	8	0	180	88	22.50
R. Appleyard	5	3	44	19*	22.00
J. H. Wardle	6	1	109	38	21.80
T. G. Evans	7	1	102	37	17.00
J. B. Statham	7	1	67	25	11.16
F. Tyson	7	1	66	37*	11.00
R. T. Simpson	2	0	11	9	5.50
K. Andrew	2	0	11	6	5.50
A. V. Bedser	2	0	10	5	5.00

ENGLAND—BOWLING

	Overs	Maidens	Runs	Wickets	Average
R. Appleyard	79	22	224	11	20.36
F. Tyson	151	16	583	28	20.82
J. H. Wardle	70.6	15	229	10	22.90
J. B. Statham	143.3	16	499	18	27.72
T. E. Bailey	73.4	8	306	10	30.60
A. V. Bedser	37	4	131	1	131.00

Also bowled: W. J. Edrich 3-0-28-0; T. W. Graveney 6-0-34-1; L. Hutton 0.6-0-2-1.

WICKET-KEEPING

	Byes	Catches	Stumpings
T. G. Evans (4 Tests)	30	13	0
K. Andrew (1 Test)	11	0	0

AUSTRALIA—BATTING

	Innings	Times not out	Runs	Highest score	Average
I. W. Johnson	6	4	116	41	58.00
C. C. McDonald	4	0	186	72	46.50
R. N. Harvey	9	1	354	162	44.25
P. Burge	2	1	35	18*	35.00
A. R. Morris	7	0	223	153	31.85
L. Maddocks	5	0	150	69	30.00
R. R. Lindwall	6	2	106	64*	26.50
K. R. Miller	7	0	167	49	23.85
J. Burke	4	0	81	44	20.25
L. Favell	7	0	130	30	18.57
G. B. Hole	5	0	85	57	17.00
R. G. Archer	7	0	117	49	16.71
R. Benaud	9	0	148	34	16.44
A. K. Davidson	5	0	71	23	14.20
W. Watson	2	0	21	18	10.50
G. R. Langley	3	0	21	16	7.00
W. A. Johnston	6	2	25	11	6.25

AUSTRALIA—BOWLING

	Overs	Maidens	Runs	Wickets	Average
R. G. Archer	97.6	32	215	13	16.53
I. W. Johnson	111	37	243	12	20.25
W. A. Johnston	141.4	37	423	19	22.26
K. R. Miller	88.4	28	243	10	24.30
R. R. Lindwall	130.6	28	381	14	27.21
R. Benaud	116.7	23	377	10	37.70
A. K. Davidson	71	16	220	3	73.33

Also bowled: J. Burke 2-0-7-0.

WICKET-KEEPING

	Byes	Catches	Stumpings
G. R. Langley (2 Tests)	10	9	0
L. Maddocks (3 Tests)	16	7	0

FIRST-CLASS AVERAGES

BATTING

	Innings	Times not out	Runs	Highest score	Average
D. C. S. Compton	16	2	799	182	57.07
L. Hutton	21	2	959	145*	50.47
P. B. H. May	23	3	931	129	46.55
M. C. Cowdrey	24	0	890	110	37.08
T. W. Graveney	15	1	519	134	37.07
T. E. Bailey	17	2	508	88	33.86
R. T. Simpson	21	2	518	136	27.26
V. Wilson	15	2	271	72	20.84
J. H. Wardle	18	2	291	63	18.18
T. G. Evans	16	2	243	40	17.35
W. J. Edrich	16	0	274	88	17.12
J. McConnon	7	1	85	22	14.16
R. Appleyard	13	7	74	19*	12.33
J. B. Statham	12	4	98	25	12.25
F. Tyson	17	2	181	37*	12.06
A. V. Bedser	11	2	85	30	9.44
K. Andrew	9	2	63	28*	9.00
P. Loader	10	1	70	22	7.77

BOWLING

	Overs	Maidens	Runs	Wickets	Average
F. Tyson	296	44	1,002	51	19.64
R. Appleyard	187.1	50	519	26	19.96
J. G. Statham	244.4	40	778	38	20.47
T. E. Bailey	201	32	689	33	20.87
P. Loader	203.2	30	721	34	21.20
J. H. Wardle	269.7	61	832	37	22.48
A. V. Bedser	206.7	33	659	24	27.45
J. McConnon	75.1	18	267	8	33.37

Also bowled: L. Hutton 0.6-0-2-1; V. Wilson 19.1-0-90-4; T. W. Graveney 6-0-34-1; D. C. S. Compton 16-1-101-2; M. C. Cowdrey 7-1-63-1; W. J. Edrich 8-2-53-0; R. T. Simpson 3.4-1-5-2.

WESTERN AUSTRALIA COUNTRY XI
Played at Banbury, October 11th and 12th

M.C.C.

L. Hutton, b. Outridge	59
W. J. Edrich, c. McCormack, b. Snell	129
V. Wilson, c. Snell, b. Herbert	17
T. W. Graveney, c. Slattery, b. Sheppard	58
M. C. Cowdrey, not out	48
T. E. Bailey, b. Herbert	12
J. McConnon, not out	18
Extras (b. 2, w. 1)	3
Total (5 wkts. dec.)	344

FALL OF WICKETS. 1—79, 2—134, 3—249, 4—267, 5—300.

WESTERN AUSTRALIA COUNTRY XI

J. Hutchinson, b. Tyson	37	c. and b. Wardle	9	
E. Stephen, c. Hutton, b. Loader	13	b. Cowdrey	40	
A. Sampson, b. Loader	2	not out	10	
T. Outridge, c. Loader, b. McConnon	5	c. Bailey, b. Cowdrey	21	
M. Herbert, c. Tyson, b. McConnon	14	c. Graveney, b. Cowdrey	29	
B. Sheppard, c. Tyson, b. McConnon	27	c. and b. McConnon	14	
G. McCormack, c. Bailey, b. McConnon	0	st. Andrew, b. Cowdrey	4	
M. Slattery, st. Andrew, b. McConnon	7			
J. Morris, b. Loader	10			
E. James, b. Loader	0			
H. Snell, not out	0			
Extras (w. 1)	1	Extras (n.b. 1)	1	
Total	116	Total (6 wkts.)	128	

FALL OF WICKETS. *First innings*: 1—51, 2—53, 3—58, 4—60, 5—87, 6—87, 7—95, 8—112, 9—112. *Second innings*: 1—24, 2—45, 3—83, 4—110, 5—116, 6—128.

Bowling Analysis
WESTERN AUSTRALIA COUNTRY XI

	O.	M.	R.	W.
Snell	12	0	28	1
Slattery	6	1	33	0
James	11	0	75	0
Outridge	21	0	110	1
Herbert	15	0	64	2
Sheppard	4	1	31	1

M.C.C.

First Innings

	O.	M.	R.	W.
Tyson	11	3	32	1
Loader	14	3	35	4
Bailey	3	0	9	0
Wardle	2	0	9	0
McConnon	12	3	30	5

Second Innings

	O.	M.	R.	W.
Tyson	4	1	12	0
Loader	6	1	11	0
Bailey	2	0	11	0
Wardle	17	8	31	1
McConnon	6	1	27	1
Cowdrey	5.5	0	35	4

MATCH DRAWN

WESTERN AUSTRALIA
Played at Perth, October 15th, 16th, 18th, 19th

WESTERN AUSTRALIA

J. Rutherford, b. Statham	0	b. Loader	9
R. Sarre, c. Evans, b. Bailey	0	b. Statham	5
P. McCarthy, b. Statham	3	c. May, b. Wardle	13
K. Meuleman, c. Evans, b. Loader	23	c. Evans, b. Statham	109
D. K. Carmody, b. Loader	25	c. Statham, b. McConnon	75
L. Pavy, c. May, b. Statham	20	c. Evans, b. Loader	0
M. Herbert, b. Statham	0	run out	0
R. Strauss, c. Loader, b. Bailey	10	lbw. b. McConnon	4
J. Munro, b. Statham	15	c. Evans, b. Bailey	6
H. R. Gorringe, b. Statham	0	c. May, b. Statham	4
R. H. Price, not out	0	not out	21
Extras (l.b. 5, n.b. 2)	7	Extras (l.b. 6, n.b. 3)	9
Total	103	Total	255

FALL OF WICKETS. *First innings:* 1—0, 2—0, 3—7, 4—38, 5—38, 6—57, 7—57, 8—101, 9—101. *Second innings:* 1—7, 2—25, 3—32, 4—160, 5—163, 6—171, 7—178, 8—197, 9—236.

M.C.C.

L. Hutton, retired hurt	145		
R. T. Simpson, c. Munro, b. Gorringe	7	b. Price	4
V. Wilson, c. Munro, b. Gorringe	38	c. Rutherford, b. Sarre	9
P. B. H. May, c. Rutherford, b. Herbert	8	not out	3
M. C. Cowdrey, c. Gorringe, b. Strauss	41	c. Pavy, b. Sarre	6
T. E. Bailey, c. Munro, b. Gorringe	0		
J. McConnon, run out	12	not out	13
J. H. Wardle, c. Munro, b. Strauss	5		
P. Loader, c. Strauss, b. Herbert	22		
T. G. Evans, b. Gorringe	18		
J. G. Statham, not out	5		
Extras (b. 9, l.b. 5, w. 3, n.b. 3)	20	(b. 4, w. 1)	5
Total	321	Total (3 wkts.)	40

FALL OF WICKETS. *First innings:* 1—23, 2—94, 3—125, 4—252, 5—252, 6—266, 7—297, 8—297, 9—321. *Second innings:* 1—11, 2—24, 3—25.

Bowling Analysis
M.C.C.

	First Innings					Second Innings			
	O.	M.	R.	W.		O.	M.	R.	W.
Statham	10	4	23	6	Statham	23.3	6	68	3
Bailey	11	2	36	2	Bailey	21	6	51	1
Loader	9.2	4	26	2	Loader	22	5	56	2
Wardle	5	2	11	0	Wardle	10	1	29	1
					McConnon	19	7	42	2

WESTERN AUSTRALIA

	First Innings					Second Innings			
	O.	M.	R.	W.		O.	M.	R.	W.
Price	20	0	72	0	Price	4	0	9	1
Gorringe	27.5	4	102	4	Gorringe	1	0	6	0
Meuleman	7	0	23	0	Herbert	5	2	9	0
Strauss	12	1	57	2	Sarre	2.5	0	11	2
Herbert	16	4	47	2					

M.C.C. WON BY 7 WICKETS

WESTERN AUSTRALIA COMBINED XI
Played at Perth, October 22nd, 23rd, 25th, 26th

WESTERN AUSTRALIA COMBINED XI

J. Rutherford, c. and b. Wardle	39	c. Wilson, b. Tyson	0
L. Sawle, c. Evans, b. Bailey	7	c. Bailey, b. Wardle	25
N. Harvey, c. Evans, b. Bailey	3	c. Evans, b. Bailey	8
G. Hole, c. Evans, b. Tyson	4	c. Graveney, b. Appleyard	33
D. K. Carmody, c. Statham, b. Tyson	8	c. Wilson, b. Bailey	38
L. Pavy, st. Evans, b. Wardle	9	not out	36
I. Johnson, lbw., b. Statham	2	c. Tyson, b. Appleyard	10
J. Munro, not out	5	c. and b. Appleyard	5
R. H. Price, c. Evans, b. Statham	4	c. Appleyard, b. Wardle	0
E. James, b. Statham	0	b. Wardle	0
H. Gorringe, run out	0	c. Wilson, b. Wardle	4
Extras (l.b. 4, n.b. 1)	5	Extras (b. 1, l.b. 3)	4
Total	86	Total	163

M.C.C.

W. J. Edrich, b. Price	0
R. T. Simpson, c. Rutherford, b. Johnson	28
P. B. H. May, c. Rutherford, b. Price	129
T. W. Graveney, c. Munro, b. Johnson	0
V. Wilson, c. Hole, b. Gorringe	72
T. E. Bailey, c. Sawle, b. Johnson	35
T. G. Evans, c. Pavy, b. Price	0
J. H. Wardle, st. Munro, b. James	6
F. Tyson, c. Sawle, b. Gorringe	21
R. Appleyard, c. Harvey, b. James	0
J. B. Statham, not out	12
Extras (b. 3, w. 3, n.b. 2)	8
Total	311

FALL OF WICKETS. *First innings:* 1—1, 2—42, 3—42, 4—221, 5—236, 6—243, 7—252, 8—289, 9—294.

Bowling Analysis
M.C.C.

First Innings	O.	M.	R.	W.	Second Innings	O.	M.	R.	W.
Statham	8.6	3	21	3	Statham	12	3	41	0
Tyson	9	3	14	2	Tyson	11	6	13	1
Bailey	11	4	16	2	Bailey	13	3	35	2
Appleyard	10	5	19	0	Appleyard	17	4	36	3
Wardle	4	0	11	2	Wardle	11.6	2	34	4

WESTERN AUSTRALIA COMBINED XI

	O.	M.	R.	W.
Price	25	7	73	3
Gorringe	12	4	61	2
James	32	6	92	2
Johnson	22.6	7	44	3
Harvey	1	0	8	0
Hole	6	0	25	0

FALL OF WICKETS. *First innings:* 1—19, 2—25, 3—35, 4—48, 5—75, 6—78, 7—78, 8—86, 9—86. *Second innings:* 1—4, 2—22, 3—61, 4—76, 5—117, 6—144, 7—154, 8—159, 9—163.

M.C.C. WON BY AN INNINGS AND 62 RUNS

SOUTH AUSTRALIA
Played at Adelaide, October 29th, 30th, November 1st, 2nd

M.C.C.

L. Hutton, c. Roxby, b. Wilson	37	c. Hole, b. Roxby		98
W. J. Edrich, c. and b. Horsnell	0	c. Langley, b. Drennan		2
R. T. Simpson, c. sub., b. Wilson	26	b. Drennan		16
D. C. S. Compton, st. Langley, b. Wilson	113	b. Drennan		2
T. W. Graveney, b. Drennan	20	c. Langley, b. Hole		34
M. C. Cowdrey, st. Langley, b. Roxby	20	c. Hole, b. Wilson		7
J. McConnon, st. Langley, b. Roxby	4	l.b.w., b. Wilson		12
F. Tyson, c. Wilson, b. Roxby	8	not out		4
P. Loader, c. Ridings, b. Wilson	6	c. Pinch, b. Wilson		4
K. Andrew, c. Favell, b. Wilson	2	c. Hole, b. Wilson		0
R. Appleyard, not out	5	b. Roxby		0
Extras (b. 4, l.b. 1)	5	Extras (b. 1, l.b. 1)		2
Total	246	Total		181

FALL OF WICKETS. *First innings:* 1—4, 2—42, 3—92, 4—162, 5—211, 6—225, 7—227, 8—234, 9—236. *Second innings:* 1—5, 2—29, 3—31, 4—96, 5—111, 6—173, 7—173, 8—173, 9—181.

SOUTH AUSTRALIA

L. Favell, c. Hutton, b. Tyson	84	b. Tyson		47
D. Harris, b. Tyson	43	c. and b. Loader		0
G. Hole, c. Simpson, b. Loader	12	c. McConnon, b. Appleyard		10
C. Pinch, b. McConnon	12	c. Andrew, b. Appleyard		9
P. Ridings, c. Andrew, b. Loader	19	c. Graveney, b. McConnon		27
N. Dansie, c. Hutton, b. Tyson	11	l.b.w., b. Appleyard		18
G. Langley, not out	36	b. McConnon		23
R. Roxby, l.b.w., b. McConnon	28	not out		6
J. Drennan, b. Tyson	2	c. Simpson, b. Appleyard		1
K. Horsnell, b. Tyson	0	b. Appleyard		2
J. Wilson, run out	0	b. Loader		2
Extras (b. 3, l.b. 3, n.b. 1)	7	Extras (b. 5, l.b. 1, n.b. 1)		7
Total	254	Total		152

FALL OF WICKETS. *First innings:* 1—119, 2—136, 3—146, 4—167, 5—182, 6—186, 7—246, 8—249, 9—253. *Second innings:* 1—2, 2—42, 3—95, 4—102, 5—127, 6—142, 7—142, 8—144, 9—147.

Bowling Analysis

SOUTH AUSTRALIA

	First Innings					Second Innings			
	O.	M.	R.	W.		O.	M.	R.	W.
Drennan	7	0	16	1	Drennan	16	3	32	3
Horsnell	13	2	38	1	Horsnell	8	0	34	0
Roxby	23.6	4	82	3	Roxby	16.5	3	59	2
Wilson	24	4	81	5	Wilson	16	5	32	4
Hole	1	0	1	0	Hole	10	3	14	1
Dansie	5	0	23	0	Dansie	5	1	8	0

M.C.C.

	First Innings					Second Innings			
	O.	M.	R.	W.		O.	M.	R.	W.
Tyson	19	3	62	5	Tyson	12	3	37	1
Loader	17	0	73	2	Loader	8.6	2	25	2
Edrich	5	2	25	0	Appleyard	11	1	46	5
Appleyard	9	2	31	0	McConnon	8	0	37	2
McConnon	11.1	1	56	2					

M.C.C. WON BY 21 RUNS

AN AUSTRALIAN XI

Played at Melbourne, November 5th, 6th, 8th, 9th

M.C.C.

R. T. Simpson, c. and b. Benaud	74
W. J. Edrich, c. Harvey, b. Johnson	11
P. B. H. May, c. Drennan, b. Archer	45
D. C. S. Compton, c. Maddocks, b. Benaud	16
V. Wilson, c. Archer, b. Benaud	6
T. W. Graveney, not out	22
T. E. Bailey, c. McDonald, b. Johnson	4
T. G. Evans, b. Johnson	1
J. H. Wardle, b. Johnson	8
A. V. Bedser, b. Johnson	3
J. B. Statham, c. Harvey, b. Johnson	13
Extras (w. 1, n.b. 1)	2
Total	205

FALL OF WICKETS. 1—48, 2—111, 3—135, 4—153, 5—159, 6—166, 7—168, 8—181, 9—185.

AN AUSTRALIAN XI

C. McDonald, l.b.w., b. Statham	4
R. Briggs, b. Bailey	48
N. Harvey, c. Evans, b. Statham	4
R. Harvey, c. Edrich, b. Bailey	7
J. de Courcy, l.b.w., b. Bailey	0
R. Benaud, c. Evans, b. Bedser	47
R. Archer, b. Bailey	23
L. Maddocks, not out	24
I. Johnson, not out	5
Extras (b. 4, n.b. 1)	5
Total (7 wkts.)	167

FALL OF WICKETS. 1—12, 2—18, 3—44, 4—44, 5—110, 6—115, 7—156. Did not bat: J. Drennan and W. Johnston.

Bowling Analysis

AUSTRALIAN XI

	O.	M.	R.	W.
Drennan	8	1	27	0
Archer	12	4	22	1
Johnston	11	2	30	0
Johnson	17.6	2	66	6
Benaud	19	4	58	3

M.C.C.

	O.	M.	R.	W.
Statham	14	3	29	2
Bedser	16	2	39	1
Bailey	17.1	3	53	4
Wardle	21	9	41	0

MATCH DRAWN

NEW SOUTH WALES

Played at Sydney, November 12th, 13th, 15th, 16th

M.C.C.

L. Hutton, c. Davidson, b. Treanor	102	c. Simpson, b. Treanor	87
W. J. Edrich, c. Watson, b. Crawford	7	c. Burke, b. Davidson	37
R. T. Simpson, c. Simpson, b. Crawford	0	b. Crawford	21
P. B. H. May, c. Lambert, b. Treanor	1	c. de Courcy, b. Treanor	16
V. Wilson, c. Simpson, b. Miller	9	b. Crawford	0
M. C. Cowdrey, c. and b. Davidson	110	l.b.w., b. Crawford	103
T. G. Evans, c. Watson, b. Crawford	11	c. Simpson, b. Davidson	7
F. Tyson, c. Simpson, b. Treanor	7	b. Crawford	15
A. V. Bedser, c. Lambert, b. Davidson	0	c. Simpson, b. Treanor	5
P. Loader, c. and b. Davidson	0	c. Burke, b. Treanor	16
R. Appleyard, not out	0	not out	9
Extras (l.b. 2, w. 1, n.b. 2)	5	Extras (l.b. 5, n.b. 5, w. 1)	11
Total	252	Total	327

FALL OF WICKETS. *First innings:* 1—24, 2—24, 3—25, 4—38, 5—201, 6—245, 7—249, 8—252, 9—252. *Second innings:* 1—0, 2—39, 3—69, 4—158, 5—226, 6—253, 7—292, 8—298, 9—312.

NEW SOUTH WALES

A. Morris, c. Simpson, b. Bedser	26		
W. Watson, l.b.w., b. Tyson	155	c. May, b. Loader	8
R. Benaud, c. May, b. Tyson	2		
K. Miller, c. Wilson, b. Bedser	86		
J. Burke, l.b.w., b. Bedser	6	not out	34
J. de Courcy, b. Appleyard	20		
R. Simpson, c. Evans, b. Tyson	22	b. Loader	4
A. Davidson, c. Loader, b. Bedser	30	not out	27
O. Lambert, c. Wilson, b. Loader	6		
J. Treanor, c. Wilson, b. Tyson	12		
P. Crawford, not out	0		
Extras (b. 8, l.b. 4, n.b. 5)	17	Extras (l.b. 2, n.b. 3)	5
Total	382	Total (2 wkts.)	78

FALL OF WICKETS. *First innings:* 1—48, 2—51, 3—212, 4—253, 5—294, 6—328, 7—335, 8—343, 9—374. *Second innings:* 1—16, 2—29.

Bowling Analysis

NEW SOUTH WALES

	First Innings					Second Innings			
	O.	M.	R.	W.		O.	M.	R.	W.
Crawford	17	6	51	3	Crawford	19	1	80	4
Davidson	19.2	3	41	3	Davidson	27	18	63	2
Treanor	16	3	64	3	Treanor	25.5	6	96	4
Miller	8	0	31	1	Miller	6	1	8	0
Benaud	15	2	50	0	Benaud	29	17	52	0
Burke	3	0	6	0	Burke..	1	1	0	0
Simpson	2	0	4	0	Simpson	3	1	17	0

M.C.C.

	First Innings					Second Innings			
	O.	M.	R.	W.		O.	M.	R.	W.
Bedser	24.5	3	117	4	Bedser	4	0	13	0
Tyson	25	2	98	4	Tyson	2	1	1	0
Loader	18	2	92	1	Loader	4	0	14	2
Appleyard	21	3	58	1	Appleyard	3	1	7	0
					Cowdrey	3	0	38	0

MATCH DRAWN

QUEENSLAND

Played at Brisbane, November 19th, 20th, 22nd, 23rd

M.C.C.

R. T. Simpson, c. Grout, b. Walmsley	136	c. Bratchford, b. Raymer	38
M. C. Cowdrey, c. Grout, b. Lindwall	4	b. R. Archer	0
T. E. Bailey, b. Lindwall	0	not out	51
P. B. H. May, c. Bratchford, b. R. Archer	0	l.b.w., b. Mackay	77
D. C. S. Compton, c. Grout, b. Mackay	110	c. Bratchford, b. Flynn	69
V. Wilson, c. and b. Lindwall	4	b. Flynn	0
J. McConnon, b. Lindwall	1	absent hurt	0
J. H. Wardle, c. Harvey, b. R. Archer	1	l.b.w., b. R. Archer	27
A. V. Bedser, c. Burge, b. Mackay	30	c. K. Archer, b. Walmsley	16
K. Andrew, b. Bratchford	15	b. Bratchford	0
J. B. Statham, not out	1	b. Walmlsey	0
Extras (l.b. 1, n.b. 1)	2	Extras (b. 9, l.b. 1)	10
Total	304	Total	288

FALL OF WICKETS. *First Innings:* 1—17, 2—17, 3—18, 4—252, 5—252, 6—253, 7—258, 8—258, 9—302. *Second innings:* 1—1, 2—8, 3—60, 4—72, 5—156, 6—205, 7—245, 8—288, 9—288.

QUEENSLAND

K. Archer, c. Andrew, b. Bedser	23	c. Bedser, b. Simpson	9
C. Harvey, c. Andrew, b. Bedser	49	b. Simpson	9
K. Mackay, b. Bailey	33	not out	3
P. Burge, b. Wilson	26		
R. Archer, c. Andrew, b. Bailey	22		
J. Bratchford, c. Andrew, b. Statham	21		
W. Walmsley, c. Cowdrey, b. Statham	34		
N. V. Raymer, c. Cowdrey, b. Statham	11		
W. Grout, not out	32		
B. Flynn, b. Bailey	26		
R. Lindwall, absent ill	0		
Extras (b. 7, l.b. 3, n.b. 1)	11	Extras (b. 4)	4
Total	288	Total (2 wkts.)	25

FALL OF WICKETS. *First innings:* 1—41, 2—111, 3—115, 4—150, 5—177, 6—209, 7—225, 8—234, 9—288. *Second innings:* 1—20, 2—25.

Bowling Analysis

QUEENSLAND

	First Innings					Second Innings			
	O.	M.	R.	W.		O.	M.	R.	W.
Lindwall	15	0	66	4	R. Archer	15	1	34	2
R. Archer	15	4	37	2	Bratchford	8	2	22	1
Bratchford	10	1	27	1	Flynn	15	1	80	2
Flynn	11	1	73	0	Walmsley	20	1	90	2
Walmsley	10	1	54	1	Raymer	13	1	39	1
Raymer	8	1	40	0	Mackay	9	3	13	1
Mackay	3.2	1	5	2					

M.C.C.

	First Innings					Second Innings			
	O.	M.	R.	W.		O.	M.	R.	W.
Statham	23	4	74	3	Wilson	4	0	16	0
Bedser	31	9	56	2	Simpson	3.4	1	5	2
Bailey	20.3	2	74	3					
Wardle	19	7	57	0					
Compton	1	0	5	0					
Wilson	4	0	11	1					

MATCH DRAWN

QUEENSLAND COUNTRY XI
Played at Rockhampton, December 4th and 6th

M.C.C.

L. Hutton, c. Duckham, b. Watt	40
W. J. Edrich, c. Brown, b. Greenough	74
P. B. H. May, c. Johnson, b. Watt	69
T. W. Graveney, st. Thorpe, b. Watt	29
M. C. Cowdrey, c. Bichel, b. Greenough	19
V. Wilson, c. Johnson, b. Jenkins	61
J. H. Wardle, c. Greenough, b. Jenkins	7
R. Appleyard, not out	6
P. Loader, c. Duckham, b. Watt	1
K. Andrew, b. Jenkins	2
A. V. Bedser, c. Sippel, b. Watt	3
Extras (b. 2, l.b. 4)	6
Total	317

FALL OF WICKETS. 1—112, 2—117, 3—191, 4—242, 5—291, 6—305, 7—305, 8—308, 9—312.

QUEENSLAND COUNTRY XI

W. Brown, run out	22	b. Graveney	78
L. Westaway, c. Graveney, b. Loader	0	b. Bedser	1
R. Sippel, b. Wardle	17	b. Appleyard	45
D. Watt, c. Graveney, b. Appleyard	4	c. Wilson, b. Appleyard	29
L. Thorpe, b. Appleyard	0	c. Andrew, b. Graveney	22
F. Greenough, b. Wardle	10	st. Andrew, b. Appleyard	0
K. Jenkins, c. and b. Loader	4	b. Appleyard	8
L. Johnson, b. Loader	4	b. Appleyard	2
D. Bichel, not out	15	b. Appleyard	1
D. Duckham, st. Andrew, b. Graveney	9	not out	4
J. Sneddon, c. Wilson, b. Graveney	0	b. Appleyard	0
Extras (b. 5, n.b. 5)	10	Extras (b. 10, l.b. 5, n.b. 5)	20
Total	95	Total	210

FALL OF WICKETS. *First innings:* 1—10, 2—48, 3—49, 4—49, 5—60, 6—67, 7—71, 8—71, 9—95. *Second innings:* 1—9, 2—117, 3—153, 4—183, 5—183, 6—203, 7—203, 8—208, 9—208.

Bowling Analysis

QUEENSLAND

	O.	M.	R.	W.
Johnson	11	0	39	0
Greenough	12	0	75	2
Sneddon	5	1	11	0
Bichel	12	0	70	0
Watt	18.2	0	56	5
Jenkins	8	0	44	3
Duckham	2	0	16	0

M.C.C.

	First Innings				Second Innings			
	O.	M.	R.	W.	O.	M.	R.	W.
Bedser	4	0	15	0	14	1	38	1
Loader	6	1	22	3	4	1	19	0
Wardle	19	9	22	2	11	1	33	0
Appleyard	11	4	18	2	14.7	4	51	7
Graveney	2.1	0	8	2	12	0	49	2

M.C.C. WON BY AN INNINGS AND 12 RUNS

PRIME MINISTER'S XI
Played at Canberra, December 8th

M.C.C.

L. Hutton, c. Miller, b. Backen	15
W. J. Edrich, b. Robin	0
P. B. H. May, c. Harvey, b. O'Reilly	101
V. Wilson, st. Gibb, b. Johnson	29
T. W. Graveney, st. Gibb, b. Benaud	56
M. C. Cowdrey, l.b.w., b. Hassett	8
T. G. Evans, b. Hassett	14
J. H. Wardle, not out	37
J. McConnon, not out	14
Extras	4
Total (7 wkts. dec.)	278

PRIME MINISTER'S XI

I. Johnson, l.b.w., b. Edrich	4
R. Benaud, c. Wilson, b. Wardle	113
S. Loxton, st. Evans, b. McConnon	47
K. Miller, c. Wilson, b. Wardle	38
Bellchambers, b. Edrich	4
N. Harvey, c. Wilson, b. Wardle	8
L. Hassett, c. Tyson, b. Hutton	11
J. O'Reilly, b. Wardle	4
J. Backen, c. Edrich, b. Hutton	11
K. Gibb, st. Evans, b. Hutton	0
B. Robin, not out	0
Extras	7
Total	247

Bowling Analysis

PRIME MINISTER'S XI

	O.	M.	R.	W.
Robin	5	0	29	1
Backen	6	0	35	1
O'Reilly	8	0	41	1
Hassett	5	0	34	2
Benaud	6	0	55	1
Johnson	5	0	20	1
Miller	2	0	15	0
Bellchambers	1	0	11	0
Loxton	2	0	34	0

M.C.C.

	O.	M.	R.	W.
Bedser	2	0	17	0
Edrich	5	0	41	2
Tyson	3	0	16	0
Graveney	3	0	26	0
McConnon	7	0	52	1
Wardle	9	0	73	4
Hutton	1.3	0	15	3

M.C.C. WON BY 31 RUNS

VICTORIA

Played at Melbourne, December 10th, 11th, 13th, 14th

M.C.C.

L. Hutton, l.b.w., b. Loxton	.. ..	41
T. E. Bailey, c. Maddocks, b. Loxton ..		60
P. B. H. May, c. Maddocks, b. Johnston		4
T. W. Graveney, c. Power, b. Johnston		48
M. C. Cowdrey, run out	.. ..	79
R. T. Simpson, c. and b. Hill ..	..	3
T. G. Evans, c. Maddocks, b. Hill	..	14
J. H. Wardle, b. Power ..	..	16
F. Tyson, c. Hill, b. Power	.. ..	15
J. McConnon, c. Loxton, b. Johnston ..		21
P. Loader, not out	.. .. ..	3
Extras (b. 5, l.b. 1, w. 1, n.b. 1)	..	8
Total	.. ..	312

c. Maddocks, b. Loxton	..	25
b. Power	.. .. ..	9
not out	.. .. ..	105
c. Maddocks, b. Loxton	..	12
c. McDonald, b. Johnson		54
c. Chambers, b. Hill	..	4
not out	.. .. ..	11
Extras (b. 12, l.b. 1, w. 1, n.b. 2)		16
Total (5 wkts. dec.)	..	236

FALL OF WICKETS. *First innings:* 1—97, 2—104, 3—126, 4—192, 5—196, 6—213, 7—233, 8—253, 9—306. *Second innings:* 1—26, 2—52, 3—69, 4—189, 5—199.

VICTORIA

C. McDonald, c. Evans, b. Tyson	..	24
J. Hallebone, b. Tyson ..	.. ..	17
R. Harvey, b. Tyson	.. .. ..	11
N. Harvey, b. Tyson	.. .. ..	59
J. Chambers, run out	.. .. ..	42
S. Loxton, b. Bailey	.. .. ..	26
L. Maddocks, c. Cowdrey, b. Loader ..		35
I. Johnson, b. Tyson	.. .. ..	5
J. Hill, not out ..	.. .. ..	34
J. Power, b. Tyson	.. .. ..	5
W. Johnston, c. Loader, b. Wardle	..	4
Extras (b. 8, l.b. 5, n.b. 2) ..	..	15
Total	.. ..	277

retired hurt..	.. ..	0
l.b.w., b. Loader	.. ..	7
c. Hutton, b. McConnon ..		38
not out	.. .. ..	34
l.b.w., b. Wardle	..	1
not out	.. ..	6
Extras (b. 1, l.b. 1)	..	2
Total (3 wkts.)	..	88

FALL OF WICKETS. *First innings:* 1—37, 2—54, 3—59, 4—159, 5—160, 6—225, 7—225, 8—248, 9—258. *Second innings:* 1—29, 2—53, 3—68.

Bowling Analysis

VICTORIA

	First Innings					Second Innings			
	O.	M.	R.	W.		O.	M.	R.	W.
Power	14	1	67	2	Power	10	0	63	1
Loxton	15	2	54	2	Loxton	14	2	67	2
Johnston	23	6	60	2	Johnston	10	4	37	0
Hill ..	22	1	71	2	Hill ..	12	3	30	1
Johnson	15.6	1	52	1	Johnson	7	2	23	1

M.C.C.

	First Innings					Second Innings			
	O.	M.	R.	W.		O.	M.	R.	W.
Tyson	21	3	68	6	Tyson	6	0	33	0
Bailey	10	0	48	1	Loader	5	0	16	1
Loader	15	2	60	1	Wardle	4	0	14	1
Wardle	12.5	2	41	1	McConnon	11	5	23	1
McConnon	11	2	45	0					

MATCH DRAWN

NEW SOUTH WALES COUNTRY XI
Played at Newcastle, December 27th, 28th, 29th

N.S.W. NORTHERN DISTRICTS

A. Dews, c. Bedser, b. Loader	21	run out	27
K. Hill, c. Evans, b. Loader	6	b. Appleyard	28
R. Harvey, c. McConnon, b. Bedser	41	b. Bedser	36
R. Wotton, b. Appleyard	13	b. Bedser	52
R. McDonald, c. Evans, b. Wardle	63	l.b.w., b. Appleyard	10
C. Stephenson, c. Evans, b. Wardle	30	b. Appleyard	3
J. Bull, b. Wardle	22	c. Graveney, b. Bedser	4
D. O'Connor, b. Wardle	0	b. Wardle	24
W. Welham, c. Evans, b. Wardle	6	c. Loader, b. Appleyard	33
L. Fowler, b. Wardle	0	b. Appleyard	0
B. O'Sullivan, not out	0	not out	4
Extras (b. 1, l.b. 2, n.b. 6)	9	Extras (b. 10, l.b. 11, n.b. 4)	25
Total	211	Total	246

FALL OF WICKETS. *First innings:* 1—7, 2—51, 3—85, 4—85, 5—171, 6—192, 7—192, 8—200, 9—200. *Second innings:* 1—57, 2—73, 3—145, 4—161, 5—166, 6—171, 7—177, 8—228, 9—237.

M.C.C.

W. J. Edrich, c. O'Connor, b. Bull	3		
J. McConnon, c. Fowler, b. O'Sullivan	43	not out	4
T. W. Graveney, b. Bull	2		
D. C. S. Compton, st. O'Connor, b. O'Sullivan	60		
V. Wilson, c. and b. O'Sullivan	3	not out	14
P. B. H. May, c. Bull, b. McDonald	157		
T. G. Evans, b. Bull	69	b. Fowler	2
J. H. Wardle, b. Bull	29		
A. V. Bedser, c. Stephenson, b. Bull	33		
R. Appleyard, not out	9		
P. Loader, c. Harvey, b. O'Sullivan	21		
Extras (b. 5, l.b. 2, n.b. 2)	9		
Total	438	Total (1 wkt.)	20

FALL OF WICKETS. *First innings:* 1—4, 2—16, 3—101, 4—104, 5—125, 6—243, 7—290, 8—392, 9—409. *Second innings:* 1—4.

Bowling Analysis

M.C.C.

	First Innings					Second Innings			
	O.	M.	R.	W.		O.	M.	R.	W.
Bedser	10	0	37	1	Bedser	13	1	49	3
Loader	12	0	56	2	Loader	5	0	18	0
Appleyard	12	2	44	1	Appleyard	19.2	2	59	5
Wardle	10.2	1	36	6	Wardle	14	1	73	1
McConnon	5	0	29	0	McConnon	3	0	22	0

N.S.W. NORTHERN DISTRICTS

	First Innings					Second Innings			
	O.	M.	R.	W.		O.	M.	R.	W.
Bull	21	5	80	5	Fowler	2.5	0	16	1
Welham	15	1	90	0	Dews	2	0	4	0
O'Sullivan	20.4	4	107	4					
Hill	5	0	44	0					
Fowler	13	0	81	0					
McDonald	3	0	27	1					

M.C.C. WON BY 9 WICKETS

TASMANIAN COMBINED XI

Played at Hobart, January 8th, 10th, 11th

TASMANIAN COMBINED XI

L. Favell, c. McConnon, b. Bedser	..	0
L. Smith, c. Andrew, b. Loader	..	21
M. Thomas, c. Graveney, b. Loader	..	6
R. N. Harvey, b. Bailey	..	82
R. Benaud, c. Hutton, b. Bedser	..	13
E. Rodwell, c. Bailey, b. Bedser	..	70
A. Davidson, c. Graveney, b. Bailey	..	5
B. Brownlow, c. Andrew, b. Bailey	..	0
T. Cowley, c. Wardle, b. Loader	..	12
W. Hird, not out	..	4
B. Considine, c. Wilson, b. Loader	..	5
Extras	..	3
Total	..	**221**

b. Loader	..	9
c. Bedser, b. McConnon	..	17
b. Loader	..	6
b. Bedser	..	47
not out	..	68
b. Bailey	..	17
c. Simpson, b. Bailey	..	7
not out	..	0
Extras (b. 10, l.b. 2, n.b. 1)		13
Total (6 wkts. dec.)	..	**184**

M.C.C.

L. Hutton, c. Hird, b. Cowley	..	15
R. T. Simpson, c. Smith, b. Cowley	..	28
T. W. Graveney, c. Brownlow, b. Davidson	..	7
D. C. S. Compton, c. Favell, b. Davidson		46
V. Wilson, c. Favell, b. Considine	..	3
T. E. Bailey, c. Benaud, b. Davidson	..	53
J. McConnon, c. Davidson, b. Benaud		22
J. H. Wardle, l.b.w., b. Hird	..	9
K. Andrew, not out	..	28
A. V. Bedser, b. Hird	..	19
P. Loader, b. Davidson	..	1
Extras (b. 5, l.b. 1, n.b. 5)	..	11
Total	..	**242**

not out	..	37
l.b.w., b. Hird	..	26
not out	..	33
b. Cowley	..	1
Extras (l.b. 2)	..	2
Total (2 wkts.)	..	**99**

Bowling Analysis

M.C.C.

First Innings

	O.	M.	R.	W.
Bedser	15	3	56	3
Loader	16.2	1	81	4
Wardle	9	3	26	0
Bailey	8	0	29	3
McConnon	7	2	26	0

Second Innings

	O.	M.	R.	W.
Bedser	13	0	42	1
Loader	8	2	21	2
Wardle	11	3	38	0
Bailey	6	0	19	2
McConnon	8	1	38	1
Wilson	2	0	13	0

TASMANIAN COMBINED XI

First Innings

	O.	M.	R.	W.
Considine	19	1	54	1
Cowley	17	5	36	2
Davidson	18.5	2	45	4
Benaud	19	0	79	1
Hird	8	2	17	2

Second Innings

	O.	M.	R.	W.
Considine	4	1	12	0
Cowley	5	0	25	1
Davidson	5	0	10	0
Hird	7	1	31	1
Favell	2	0	14	0
Rodwell	1	0	5	0

MATCH DRAWN

TASMANIA

Played at Launceston, January 13th, 14th, 15th

M.C.C.

L. Hutton, l.b.w., b. Considine..	61	not out	21
R. T. Simpson, c. Cowley, b. Considine	4	c. and b. Cowley	18
T. W. Graveney, c. Smith, b. Diprose..	134		
D. C. S. Compton, c. Rodwell, b. Considine	50	b. Diprose	20
M. C. Cowdrey, b. Diprose	27	c. Richardson, b. Cowley..	11
V. Wilson, not out	62	b. Cowley	9
J. H. Wardle, c. Brownlow, b. Diprose..	63	not out	12
F. Tyson, c. Brownlow, b. Diprose	15	c. Hyland, b. Cowley	27
R. Appleyard, not out	1	c. Richardson, b. Diprose..	14
Extras (b. 5, l.b. 3, n.b. 2)	10	Extras (b. 1)	1
Total (7 wkts. dec.)	427	Total (6 wkts. dec.)	133

FALL OF WICKETS. *First innings:* 1—11, 2—138, 3—242, 4—276, 5—281, 6—393, 7—413. *Second innings:* 1—21, 2—57, 3—69, 4—70, 5—93, 6—114. Did not bat: Andrew and Loader.

TASMANIA

M. Thomas, c. Andrew, b. Loader	17	st. Andrew, b. Wilson	10
L. Smith, l.b.w., b. Loader	6	c. Andrew, b. Cowdrey	18
M. Hyland, l.b.w., b. Appleyard	18	c. Wilson, b. Loader	49
J. Maddox, b. Wardle	19	not out	62
E. Rodwell, b. Loader	11	b. Tyson	13
B. Richardson, b. Wardle	22	c. Appleyard, b. Tyson	0
R. Brownlow, b. Compton	3	c. Compton, b. Wardle	11
T. Cowley, c. Simpson, b. Loader	12	c. and b. Wardle	10
W. Hird, not out..	6	b. Wardle	19
N. Diprose, b. Loader	0	b. Compton	5
B. Considine, c. and b. Loader	1	b. Wardle	1
Extras (b. 1, l.b. 1)	2	Extras (l.b. 2)	2
Total	117	Total	200

FALL OF WICKETS. *First innings:* 1—19, 2—24, 3—52, 4—71, 5—78, 6—100, 7—106, 8—111, 9—115. *Second innings:* 1—13, 2—42, 3—102, 4—126, 5—126, 6—147, 7—161, 8—192, 9—199.

Bowling Analysis

TASMANIA

	First Innings					Second Innings			
	O.	M.	R.	W.		O.	M.	R.	W.
Considine	20	0	93	3	Cowley	15	2	53	4
Cowley	19	1	84	0	Hird ..	9	0	34	0
Hird ..	22	1	94	0	Diprose	13	1	45	2
Diprose	27	2	107	4					
Richardson ..	6	0	39	0					

M.C.C.

	First Innings					Second Innings			
	O.	M.	R.	W.		O.	M.	R.	W.
Tyson	9	0	22	0	Tyson	6	1	20	2
Loader	12	3	22	6	Loader	10	1	34	1
Wardle	9	2	29	2	Wardle	13.1	2	37	4
Wilson	3	0	6	0	Wilson	1	0	1	1
Appleyard	6	0	15	1	Appleyard	4	2	6	0
Compton	4	0	21	1	Compton	11	1	75	1
					Cowdrey	4	1	25	1

M.C.C. WON BY 243 RUNS

SOUTH AUSTRALIA COUNTRY XI

Played at Mount Gambier, January 18th and 19th

M.C.C.

W. J. Edrich, c. Eaton, b. Gwynne	22
R. T. Simpson, c. Gross, b. Pengilley	68
P. B. H. May, c. Gwynne, b. Beare	62
T. W. Graveney, c. Darling, b. Beare	44
D. C. S. Compton, b. Darling	53
T. E. Bailey, l.b.w., b. Gross	0
T. G. Evans, b. Gross	15
F. Tyson, b. Gross	0
A. V. Bedser, not out	18
J. G. Statham, b. Darling	23
R. Appleyard, b. Darling	5
Extras (b. 12, l.b. 6)	18
Total	328

FALL OF WICKETS. 1—60, 2—119, 3—197, 4—214, 5—215, 6—234, 7—234, 8—280, 9—322.

SOUTH AUSTRALIA COUNTRY XI

G. Fuller, b. Statham	5	b. Bedser	0
H. Bennett, b. Bailey	25	not out	14
K. Hanna, l.b.w., b. Bedser	34	l.b.w., b. Bedser	2
J. Milnes, b. Statham	1	b. Bedser	0
P. Eaton, c. Evans, b. Appleyard	2	b. Statham	15
J. Gwynne, b. Appleyard	1	b. Statham	0
L. Curtis, not out	20	b. Statham	0
M. Darling, l.b.w., b. Appleyard	0	b. Statham	0
L. Beare, c. Statham, b. Appleyard	4	b. Statham	0
W. Pengilley, c. Evans, b. Appleyard	0	b. Statham	0
G. Gross, c. Graveney, b. Appleyard	6	l.b.w., b. Bailey	14
Extras (b. 7, l.b. 1)	8		
Total	106	Total	45

FALL OF WICKETS. *First innings:* 1—8, 2—52, 3—59, 4—70, 5—75, 6—78, 7—80, 8—88, 9—88. *Second innings:* 1—0, 2—2, 3—3, 4—27, 5—27, 6—27, 7—27, 8—31, 9—31.

Bowling Analysis

SOUTH AUSTRALIA

	O.	M.	R.	W.
Beare	9	0	64	2
Gross	8	0	31	3
Curtis	7	1	44	0
Gwynne	10	0	47	1
Darling	13.4	0	55	3
Pengilley	11	0	69	1

M.C.C.

	First Innings				Second Innings			
	O.	M.	R.	W.		O.	M.	R.	W.
Tyson	3	0	10	0	Tyson	6	1	16	0
Statham	8	3	16	2	Statham	4	3	3	6
Bedser	11	1	22	1	Bedser	6	1	11	3
Appleyard	12.2	4	26	6	Appleyard	7	4	8	0
Compton	1	0	9	0	Bailey	1.3	0	7	1
Bailey	8	2	15	1					

M.C.C. WON BY AN INNINGS AND 177 RUNS

SOUTH AUSTRALIA

Played at Adelaide, January 21st, 22nd, 24th, 25th

SOUTH AUSTRALIA

L. Favell, c. Andrew, b. Bedser	1	c. Cowdrey, b. Bedser	11
N. Dansie, b. Appleyard	29	c. Appleyard, b. Bedser	2
C. Pinch, c. Edrich, b. Bedser	1	run out	4
G. Hole, c. Wilson, b. Loader	2	c. Graveney, b. Loader	1
P. Ridings, c. May, b. Loader	40	not out	40
D. Trowse, l.b.w., b. Appleyard	21	l.b.w., b. Loader	32
G. Langley, b. Wardle	53	c. Andrew, b. Bedser	5
J. Osborne, c. Compton, b. Loader	1	b. Loader	0
K. Horsnell, b. Wardle	23	b. Wardle	1
J. Wilson, b. Wardle	6	l.b.w., b. Wardle	2
D. Gregg, not out	2	b. Loader	4
Extras (b. 1, l.b. 2, n.b. 3)	6	Extras (b. 5, l.b. 7, w.1, n.b. 8)	21
Total	185	Total	123

FALL OF WICKETS. *First innings:* 1—4, 2—13, 3—18, 4—38, 5—80, 6—117, 7—120, 8—160, 9—172. *Second innings:* 1—3, 2—17, 3—18, 4—22, 5—29, 6—96, 7—96, 8—108, 9—118.

M.C.C.

W. J. Edrich, b. Gregg	14
T. W. Graveney, c. Favell, b. Gregg	21
V. Wilson, l.b.w., b. Wilson	22
J. H. Wardle, c. Langley, b. Gregg	7
M. C. Cowdrey, b. Wilson	64
D. C. S. Compton, c. Favell, b. Wilson	182
P. B. H. May, b. Horsnell	114
A. V. Bedser, c. Langley, b. Horsnell	0
K. Andrew, not out	6
R. Appleyard, c. Langley, b. Horsnell	1
P. Loader, c. Pinch, b. Gregg	10
Extras (b. 1, l.b. 4, w. 3, n.b. 2)	10
Total	451

FALL OF WICKETS. 1—35, 2—40, 3—55, 4—91, 5—183, 6—417, 7—419, 8—436, 9—440.

Bowling Analysis

M.C.C.

	First Innings					Second Innings			
	O.	M.	R.	W.		O.	M.	R.	W.
Bedser	14	2	41	2	Bedser	11	3	20	3
Loader	14	1	52	3	Loader	13	2	32	4
Wardle	16.5	5	36	3	Wardle	17	6	37	2
Appleyard	17	6	50	2	Appleyard	4	2	13	0

SOUTH AUSTRALIA

	O.	M.	R.	W.
Gregg	26.3	0	117	0
Horsnell	23	2	88	3
Wilson	30	7	78	3
Osborne	15	0	87	0
Dansie	7	0	35	0
Hole	7	1	36	0

M.C.C. WON BY AN INNINGS AND 143 RUNS

VICTORIA COUNTRY XI

Played at Yallourn, February 5th and 7th

VICTORIA COUNTRY XI

N. F. Chapman, c. Compton, b. Loader	1	c. and b. Wardle	18
R. R. Walker, c. Wilson, b. Loader	14	absent hurt	0
W. Young, b. Loader	56	b. Wardle	4
C. M. Miles, c. Evans, b. Wilson	13	st. Evans, b. Wardle	1
R. Milne, c. Edrich, b. Wardle	26	not out	25
J. G. Bath, not out	29	b. Bedser	10
G. B. Tozer, c. Evans, b. Loader	9	b. Wardle	0
R. T. Sager, l.b.w., b. Wardle	2	st. Evans, b. Wardle	3
R. H. Hollioake, c. Wilson, b. Wardle	1	c. and b. Wardle	18
L. Baker, st. Evans, b. Wardle	15	c. Wardle, b. Compton	3
K. H. Grant, b. Wardle	0	b. Wardle	6
Extras (b. 8, l.b. 4, n.b. 2, w. 2)	16	Extras (b. 8, l.b. 3)	11
Total	182	Total	99

M.C.C.

L. Hutton, c. Miles, b. Tozer	75
R. T. Simpson, c. and b. Tozer	59
T. W. Graveney, c. Miles, b. Hollioake	50
V. Wilson, b. Hollioake	17
D. C. S. Compton, c. Tozer, b. Bath	24
W. J. Edrich, c. Walker, b. Bath	36
T. G. Evans, c. Grant, b. Tozer	17
J. H. Wardle, run out	17
C. G. Howard, not out	0
A. V. Bedser, not out	2
Extras (b. 5, l.b. 3, w. 2)	10
Total (8 wkts. dec.)	307

Did not bat: P. Loader.

Bowling Analysis

M.C.C.

	First Innings					Second Innings			
	O.	M.	R.	W.		O.	M.	R.	W.
Bedser	13	1	63	0	Bedser	6	0	20	1
Loader	11	1	29	4	Loader	6	2	13	0
Wardle	16	5	46	5	Wardle	8.5	3	45	7
Wilson	2	0	18	1	Compton	3	0	10	1
Graveney	1	0	10	0					

VICTORIA COUNTRY XI

	O.	M.	R.	W.
Grant	12	0	78	0
Hollioake	11	0	69	2
Tozer	15	0	75	3
Baker	8	1	48	0
Bath	5	0	27	2

M.C.C. WON BY AN INNINGS AND 26 RUNS

VICTORIA

Played at Melbourne, February 11th, 12th, 13th, 14th, 15th

VICTORIA

C. McDonald, b. Statham	10
R. Harvey, c. Graveney, b. Statham	0
N. Harvey, c. Bailey, b. Statham	17
J. Shaw, l.b.w., b. Bailey	9
K. Kendall, c. Andrew, b. Bailey	1
S. Loxton, c. Statham, b. Appleyard	27
L. Maddocks, l.b.w., b. Bailey	0
A. Dick, c. Compton, b. Appleyard	41
J. Hill, c. Wardle, b. Appleyard	0
W. Johnston, c. Loader, b. Wardle	1
J. Power, not out	4
Extras (b. 1, l.b. 2)	3
Total	113

FALL OF WICKETS. 1—3, 2—26, 3—33, 4—34, 5—39, 6—39, 7—92, 8—92, 9—109.

M.C.C.

W. J. Edrich, l.b.w., b. Johnston	23
R. T. Simpson, not out	33
P. B. H. May, not out	33
Extras (n.b. 1)	1
Total (1 wkt.)	90

FALL OF WICKETS. 1—37. Did not bat: D. C. S. Compton, T. W. Graveney, T. E. Bailey, J. H. Wardle, K. Andrew, R. Appleyard, J. G. Statham and P. Loader.

Bowling Analysis

M.C.C.

	O.	M.	R.	W.
Statham	10	1	23	3
Loader	10	1	33	0
Bailey	10	4	22	3
Appleyard	6.1	2	14	3
Wardle	3	0	18	1

VICTORIA

	O.	M.	R.	W.
Power	5	0	22	0
Loxton	6	2	16	0
Johnston	5	1	9	1
Dick	6	0	22	0
Hill	3	0	20	0

MATCH DRAWN

NEW SOUTH WALES
Played at Sydney, February 18th, 19th, 21st, 22nd
NEW SOUTH WALES

R. Briggs, c. Evans, b. Bedser	..	0	b. Tyson	0
J. Burke, c. Cowdrey, b. Bedser	..	0	c. Graveney, b. Wardle ..	62
R. Simpson, c. Graveney, b. Tyson	..	6	st. Evans, b. Wardle ..	98
R. Benaud, c. Wardle, b. Bedser	..	1	st. Evans, b. Wardle ..	57
K. R. Miller, c. Graveney, b. Loader	..	11	c. May, b. Bedser	71
P. Philpott, st. Evans, b. Bedser	..	46	b. Wardle	11
B. Booth, not out	..	74	c. Evans, b. Bedser ..	0
A. K. Davidson, c. Graveney, b. Bedser		9	c. Cowdrey, b. Wardle ..	0
P. Crawford, c. Evans, b. Wilson	..	19	not out	0
O. Lambert, c. Cowdrey, b. Wardle	..	1		
J. Treanor, c. Graveney, b. Wilson	..	0		
Extras (b. 1, l.b. 3, n.b. 1)	..	5	Extras (l.b. 10, w. 2, n.b. 3)	15
Total	..	172	Total (8 wkts. dec.) ..	314

FALL OF WICKETS. First innings: 1—0, 2—1, 3—3, 4—16, 5—26, 6—109, 7—127, 8—167, 9—168. Second innings: 1—2, 2—161, 3—161, 4—196, 5—260, 6—263, 7—314, 8—314.

M.C.C.

R. T. Simpson, c. Briggs, b. Davidson..	6	c. Davidson, b. Benaud	..	24
V. Wilson, b. Miller	0	b. Davidson	..	4
P. B. H. May, c. Lambert, b. Crawford..	3	b. Miller	..	42
P. Loader, b. Davidson	0	c. Benaud, b. Treanor	..	8
T. W. Graveney, c. Lambert, b. Davidson	35	l.b.w., b. Benaud ..	..	28
M. C. Cowdrey, c. Lambert, b. Davidson	12	c. Simpson, b. Booth	..	33
L. Hutton, c. Simpson, b. Treanor ..	48	c. Simpson, b. Burke	..	59
T. G. Evans, b. Crawford	40	c. Miller, b. Davidson	..	39
J. H. Wardle, c. Crawford, b. Treanor..	16	c. Philpott, b. Treanor	..	12
F. Tyson, run out	3	c. Benaud, b. Treanor	..	0
A. V. Bedser, not out	2	not out	..	0
Extras (b. 1, l.b. 1, n.b. 5)	7	Extras (b. 13, l.b. 3, w. 1, n.b. 3)		20
Total	172	Total	..	269

FALL OF WICKETS. First innings: 1—1, 2—4, 3—10, 4—13, 5—35, 6—94, 7—135, 8—153, 9—157. Second innings: 1—36, 2—63, 3—68, 4—145, 5—189, 6—222, 7—250, 8—261, 9—261.

Bowling Analysis
M.C.C.

	First Innings					Second Innings			
	O.	M.	R.	W.		O.	M.	R.	W.
Bedser ..	19	3	57	5	Bedser ..	22.2	4	87	2
Tyson ..	16	4	27	1	Tyson ..	9	2	24	1
Loader ..	11	2	56	1	Loader ..	10	2	28	0
Wardle ..	8	2	26	1	Wardle ..	25	0	118	5
Wilson ..	1.1	0	1	2	Wilson ..	4	0	42	0

NEW SOUTH WALES

	First Innings					Second Innings			
	O.	M.	R.	W.		O.	M.	R.	W.
Crawford ..	15	3	47	2	Crawford ..	8	0	37	0
Miller ..	10	0	31	1	Miller ..	5	0	15	1
Davidson ..	12	3	25	4	Davidson ..	13	1	43	2
Treanor ..	11	4	44	2	Treanor ..	13.7	1	54	3
Benaud ..	3	0	10	0	Benaud ..	21	7	62	2
Philpott ..	1	0	8	0	Philpott ..	6	2	22	0
					Burke.. ..	3	1	6	1
					Booth.. ..	2	0	10	1

NEW SOUTH WALES WON BY 45 RUNS

Index

Adelaide, 47ff, 192ff
Aden, 13, 25
Aitchison, G. D., 176
Allen, G. O., 239
Andrew, K., 19, 79, 87, 99, 103, 232
Appleyard, R., 17, 18, 23, 39, 42, 49, 50-1, 75, 79, 89, 105, 106, 109, 127, 133, 135, 142, 144-5, 149, 160-4, 169-71, 178, 197-9, 201-2, 205, 224-6, 230, 233, 239-40
Archer, R., 15, 62, 86, 89, 95, 97, 100-1, 130-3, 135-7, 141-2, 158-60, 162-3, 165-6, 168-9, 171-3, 198-9, 202-3, 221, 237, 240
Avalon, 151

Baghdad, 188
Bailey, T. E., 15-18, 24, 38, 40, 61-2, 75, 85, 87-8, 92-6, 98-105, 130, 134-7, 144, 147-9, 156, 158-61, 164, 169, 178, 187, 198-9, 201, 204, 208, 211, 213, 221, 223-4, 228, 230, 237
Bannister, Alex, 66
Barnes, Sidney, 66, 158
Barranjoey, 151
Barton, 46, 188
Beames, Percy, 176
Bedser, A. V., 15, 17-19, 33, 42, 61-2, 71, 75, 87-8, 91-6, 99, 103, 127, 129, 148-9, 154, 162, 178, 180, 188, 192-3, 208-9, 221, 223, 227-8, 231, 236
Bell, Guildford, 111
Benaud, R., 62, 71, 89, 96, 98-9, 101, 103, 105, 132-3, 135, 137-9, 145, 157-9, 162-3, 166, 169-72, 175, 187, 197-202, 222, 224-7, 238, 240
Bentinck, Count and Countess, 188
Bilgola, 151

Black Island, 123
Bondi, 210, 213-15
Bookaloo, 46
Bowes, Bill, 21, 24, 66
Boyd, Robin, 182
Bradman, Sir Donald, 41, 94, 227, 239
Braund, 148
Bray, Charles, 21, 66
Bridgewater, 188
Briggs, R., 71
Brighton, 188
Brisbane, 83ff, 106-7, 125, 227, 230
Brown, F. R., 21-2, 27, 33, 107
Bunbury, 30ff
Burge, P., 221, 226
Buring, Leo, 213
Burke, J., 126, 133-4, 138, 144, 176, 193, 197, 202, 239
Buxtehude, 24

Campbell, Robert, 54
Campbelltown, 188
Canberra, 109
Cannonvale, 110, 124
Carmody, K., 39
Case, C. C., 176
Caserta, 24
Church, Commander W. J., D.S.O., D.S.C., 24
Clay, J. C., 19
Coff's Harbour, 84
Collaroy, 151
Colombo, 11, 13, 25-6
Compton, D. C. S., 16, 49, 51, 59, 61, 63, 74, 86-8, 91, 93, 100, 103-5, 107, 127, 154, 156-8, 163, 166-8, 178-9, 189, 192, 197, 200-1, 204, 211, 223-4, 226-7, 231, 236

267

Cowdrey, M. C., 16–17, 25, 31, 38–9, 49, 70–5, 79, 85, 87–8, 92, 95–8, 102–3, 105–6, 132–3, 135, 138–9, 156–60, 164, 166, 169, 178–80, 183, 189, 192, 194, 200–3, 208–9, 221–2, 225, 228–9, 233, 237
Cox, George, 73
Crawford, 71–2
Curl Curl, 151
Cutler, Ian, 112–13

Dalton, Harold, 236
Davidson, A., 15, 71, 126, 131–3, 136–8, 141–2, 145–6, 172, 175, 187, 193, 198, 200–1, 203, 205, 222, 224, 226, 237, 240
de Courcy, 62, 72
Dee Why, 151
de Saram, Derek, 25
Dobell, William, 54–5
Downer, Sidney, 194
Drennan, J., 50, 52, 62
Drysdale, Russell, 54–5
Duckworth, George, 19, 79, 107, 235
Duleepsinhji, K. S., 167
Duterreau, Benjamin, 186

Edrich, W. J., 16, 31, 39–40, 42, 51, 61, 71–3, 75, 88–9, 92, 94, 97, 99, 100–2, 105, 109, 132, 135, 139–41, 143, 156–7, 161–2, 165, 170, 172, 189, 193, 197, 199, 203, 220–1, 231–2, 234
Edwards, Arthur, 216
Epping, 188
Essendon, 153
Evans, T. G., 19, 40, 75, 88, 91, 104, 132, 136, 141, 145, 147, 156, 159, 161–2, 164, 168–70, 172–3, 178, 189, 197–9, 201–2, 204, 208–9, 224, 232, 234, 236

Farnes, K., 147
Favell, L., 49–51, 72, 88, 91, 100, 132–4, 138, 143, 160–1, 166–7, 169–70, 175, 187, 193, 196, 224–6, 237–9

Fingleton, Jack, 32–3, 66, 239
Forrest, Lord, 43
Fortune, Charles, 205
Fremantle, 13
Freshwater, 151
Friend, Donald, 54

Gibraltar, 11, 13
Gilligan, Arthur, 21–2, 27, 79, 194, 241
Glenelg, 59
Gocher, W. H., 216–18
Gover, A., 194
Graveney, T. W., 16–17, 27, 30–1, 39–40, 42, 49–50, 61, 74, 88, 100, 127, 131–2, 134–5, 137–9, 154, 189, 193, 209, 211, 220–2, 226–7, 230, 232, 234, 236–7
Great Barrier Reef, 114ff
Greenway, Francis, 76
Grounds, Roy, 182

Haig, 46
Hammond, 17
Hannan, Patrick, 44
Harris, D., 49
Harvey, R. N., 39–40, 42, 62, 88, 93–5, 101, 103–5, 135, 138, 144–8, 157–8, 160–2, 166–7, 169–72, 175, 187–8, 197–8, 202, 222, 225–7, 230, 237
Hassett, Lindsay, 19, 33, 41, 66, 79, 130
Hayman Island, 110ff
Hayward, U. and B., 27, 52, 194, 206
Herman, S., 54
Heron Island, 114
Hill, Clem, 94, 148
Hobart, 184–8
Hobbs, Sir Jack, 157, 176
Holden, P. and J., 27, 194
Hole, G. B., 39–40, 51, 88, 95, 98, 100, 104–5, 133, 135, 141, 144–5, 157–8, 161–2, 171–2, 175, 191, 193, 227, 237, 239
Howard, Geoffrey, 19, 79, 194, 235

INDEX

Hutton, Leonard, 14–16, 23–4, 27, 30–1, 38–9, 49–51, 59, 61–2, 70–5, 85, 88–9, 91–2, 95–7, 99–100. 104–7, 109, 127, 129–37, 147–9, 156–7, 160–6, 171–3, 175, 178–9, 188–9, 191, 196–200, 203, 205, 208–9, 220–1, 223, 226–35, 239
Hutton, Rear-Admiral F. E. P., 24

Jardine, D. R., 22, 227
Jericho, 188
Johnson, I. W., 19, 39–41, 62, 89, 96–7, 99–103, 105, 126, 154, 159–60, 163–8, 173, 193, 196–201, 203, 208, 220, 222, 224–7, 236–8, 240
Johnston, W. A., 62, 89, 97–103, 130–3, 136–42, 146–7, 159, 164–5, 167–8, 170, 173, 199–200, 204, 238
Jones, J. S., 217–18
Jose, Ivan, 194

Kalgoorlie, 29, 43–5
Karonie, 46
Kelly, Ned, 45
Kempson, Nicholas, 24
Kilburn, J. M., 66
Kingoonya, 46
King's Cross, 207–8, 212

Laker, J. C., 15, 18
Langley, G. R., 51, 89, 96–7, 133, 136–9, 142, 146, 154, 191–3
Larwood, H., 147, 179, 239
Launceston, 189–90
Lawrence, D. H., 20–1, 63–5
Lawson, Henry, 45
Leeds, 33
Light, Col., 49
Lindwall, R. R., 15, 75, 85–7, 89, 95–105, 130–1, 136–8, 140–2, 146, 156–8, 163, 165–8, 173, 175, 179, 193, 211, 220–1, 223–4, 226–7, 229, 237, 239–40
Loader, P., 18–19, 25, 31, 180, 189–90, 233, 238
Lock, G. A. R., 15, 18

McConnon, J., 18–19, 30–1, 38–9, 50, 75, 79, 88, 236
McDonald, C. C., 62, 176, 196–7, 199, 202, 224–6, 238
Mackay, 109, 125
McKay, 176
Mackenzie, Sir Compton, 32
MacLaren, A. C., 73
Macquarie, Governor, 76
Macquarie, Lake, 126
Maddocks, L., 154, 156, 163–4, 168, 173, 191, 193, 197–9, 202, 226
Mailey, Arthur, 176
Manly, 126, 210
Mascot, 126, 227
Mathers, J., 66
May, P. B. H., 16, 39–41, 61, 71–2, 74, 86–8, 94, 97, 99–102, 109, 130–1, 135, 138–40, 156–7, 163, 166–8, 178–9, 183, 192, 197–9, 203–4, 208–9, 220–1, 228–9, 234, 237
May, Thomas, 113
Melbourne, 60ff, 109, 153ff, 228
Melville, 167
Meuleman, K., 39
Miller, K. R., 41, 71–2, 75, 88, 92–3, 97, 99, 100, 103–5, 126–7, 154, 156–9, 161–2, 165–8, 170–2, 175, 183, 197–205, 208, 211, 221–2, 224–7, 236–9
Molnar, George, 210
Moorehead, Alan, 113
Morris, A. R., 19, 41, 71, 88–9, 92–5, 104–5, 126–7, 129–30, 133–4, 139, 141, 143, 149, 160–1, 167, 169, 175, 191, 193, 196, 202, 227, 238
Mosman, 126
Mountford, Charles, 55–8
Mount Gambier, 191
Mynn, Alfred, 21

Namatjira, Albert, 58
Naples, 13, 23
Newcastle, 154

New Norfolk, 190
Newport, 151
Nolan, S., 54
Northcott, Sir John, 112
Nullarbor Plain, 45–6

Oakman, A. S., 16
Oldman, Percy, 216
Oliphant, R. and B., 207
O'Reilly, W. J., 66

Palm Beach, 151–2
Panshanger, 190
Parks, J. M., 17
Peebles, Ian, 21–3, 33, 35, 40–1, 107, 153
Perth, 28ff, 229
Phipps, Diana, 210
Pimba, 46
Pittwater, The, 152
Pompeii, 23
Ponsford, W. H., 239
Port Arthur, 190
Port Augusta, 46
Port Said, 13, 24
Port Willunga, 53, 206
Preston, Norman, 66, 107, 194
Proserpine, 110, 124

Ramsey, Hugh, 190
Rawlinna, 45
Reid, 46
Rhodes, W., 73
Richardson, 148
Roberts, Ronald, 66, 107, 194
Roberts, T., 54
Robinson, Ray, 32
Rockhampton, 108ff, 125
Rosati, Dr F., 146
Rose Bay, 126
Rowbotham, Denys, 66
Russell Falls, 190
Ryder, Jack, 103

Sandham, A., 73
Sheppard, D. S., 14

Simpson, R. T., 16, 17, 30, 42, 49, 51, 61, 71–2, 75, 85–8, 97, 99–100, 127, 232
Spofforth, 148
Statham, J. B., 17, 38–40, 61–2, 75, 88, 91–6, 99, 103, 133–6, 142–6, 149, 160–4, 169, 171–3, 175, 178–80, 188, 196–9, 202, 205, 224, 226, 229–30, 237, 239
Stirling, Capt., 29
Stott, Sam, 109
Streeton, Sir Arthur, 54, 186
Swanton, E. W., 21–2, 25, 32–3, 66, 194
Sydney, 70ff, 128ff, 207ff, 228

Tarcoola, 46
Tasmania, 184ff
Thorpe, 21, 23
Townsville, 109
Treanor, 71–2
Trollope, D. H., 176
Trott, Albert, 148
Trumper, 148
Tyson, F., 18–19, 25, 31, 39–40, 50–1, 71–2, 75, 88, 92–6, 99, 103, 127, 132, 134–6, 141, 143–9, 160–4, 169–75, 178–81, 183, 188, 196–9, 201–2, 209, 224–5, 228–30, 237, 239–40

Ullyett, Roy, 51

Vaucluse, 126
Verity, H., 24
Voce, W., 179, 239

Wainewright, 186
Walker (Hampshire), 176
Walker, Sir Harold, 24
Wallis, Alfred, 186
Wardle, J. H., 18–19, 23, 25, 30, 38, 42, 75, 88, 106, 127, 133, 141, 144, 149, 154, 160, 162–3, 168–9, 178, 193, 197–9, 201, 203, 224–6, 230
Watkins, A., 16

Watson, W., 46, 71–2, 148, 221, 224–6
Watson's Bay, 126
Wellings, E. M., 21, 194
Whale, 151
Whinfield, Capt. N. A., 27
White, Crawford, 66
White, Percy, 43
Wilson, J. V., 16–17, 23, 30, 38, 40–2, 50, 71–2, 75, 87–8, 96, 109, 154, 163, 189–90, 232–3
Wirraminna, 46
Woodcock, John, 21, 23, 27, 32, 33, 66, 107, 194
Woodfull, W. M., 239
Woolloomooloo, 208

Zanthus, 46

The photographs used in the section entitled THE TESTS are reproduced by permission of Fox Photos Ltd, and Sport and General Press Agency Ltd.